CU00869394

ISBN: 9798662943971

Cover design by: Glenn Millar
Original Painting by: Robert Grattan
Printed in the United Kingdom

This book is dedicated to the memory of my 'Big Granda Stothers' a giant among men and my childhood hero and friend.

To my amazing family, Nicola, Caleb and Aramie, I hope this makes you as proud of me as I am of you.

I would also like to dedicate it to the thousands of band members across Northern Ireland and Scotland whose commitment continues to be an inspiration.

CONTENTS

MADE TO PARADE

Glenn Millar

INTRODUCTION

Made to Parade

I was just about to finish my friend Paul off at 'cribby' whenever we were rudely interrupted by Dee and Alan. Skidding past the cars parked a wee bit away from us, they came to a somewhat ungraceful stop and started to share the latest news "Lads, it's the bands, the bands are out, they're in the Avenue, c'mon or we'll miss them."

Confused I took my shot at the kerb anyway as my well beaten opponent abandoned the game and headed off in pursuit of Dee and Alan. "C'mon Glenn, it's the bands"

Not wanting to be left behind, my victory celebration turned into a rather dainty skip, thank god no one saw that, I'd be getting slagged for days. I threw the ball into my front garden and ran after my friends, running faster to try and catch up.

I had no real clue what the bands were or why we were running to see them, but my new friends seemed very excited, so I had no other choice but to follow them.

I think my ignorance requires a little explanation. I arrived here a few years after having been born in Canada, the city of St. Catharines to be precise. Most people have never heard of it. It's located not that far from Niagara Falls, and well, most people have heard of them. I have no memory of my time in Canada really, only what my Ma has told me.

My earliest memories revolve around my family moving a

1

lot, or at least it seems that way to me. We used to live in Euston Street, it holds the earliest memories I have. I can vividly recall jumping down the curling stairs into the hall and also losing my first ever pet, Buster, obviously not at the same time. Buster was a rough haired Jack Russell, and one day he just jumped out of the window of the car. I think we had been coming home from visiting my Big Granny or going to see her, I can't recall. It was hot in the car and the window was rolled down, I remember Buster like to put his head out the window, this day he obviously needed something more than the window down and jumped out the window to go looking for it. My Da said it was because I was wearing a Bay City Rollers T Shirt, I said it was probably because he reminded Buster of a smelly cat, I near followed Buster out the window. That's the only two things I remember about living there. We moved to somewhere called Craigavon next, and all I can recall about there is a shop called Crazy Prices! My Ma says they need to rename the place now as it's full of roundabouts, twelve of them apparently. Maybe some motorway maintenance Death Star had caused a disturbance in traffic flow that somehow required twelve roundabouts to sort it out. Anyway, we moved to Tower Street, which was just up the street from my Big Granny and Granda's house. They weren't giants or anything they just weren't my wee Granny and Granda, they lived up the Shankill.

Anyway, back to the moment in question, heading to the Avenue to watch the bands. We ran down my street towards Beechfield Street, turned right and continued on past Westbourne Street. I walked out onto the Avenue to be greeted by a wall of noise and a sea of colour. The sounds of flutes, drums and accordions filled the air, this sound seemed to stir the flags and banners held proudly aloft men in suits who walked in front of and behind the bands. It was like I had just stepped out into a whole new world. Templemore Avenue wasn't Templemore Avenue anymore it was completely transformed. I stood there in awe as each band passed by, the bands had their names emblazoned on big drums in the centre of their ranks, some of the names seemed to suggest something great about the band, names like the Pride of Down and Gertrude Star. They were loud and proud, walking with their shoulders pinned back and and heads held high. My mates transformed into different people, skipping and dancing alongside the bands, waving and shouting at people they knew. This was my introduction to the phenomenon of community celebrity. As I stood there trying to take it all in and make sense of all that was going on around me, a sound cut through all the rest, a different kind of sound, no less loud and no less proud, but different. They marched past in maroon, gold and blue uniforms and with an elegance that said these streets belonged to them and the tunes they played were like magic in my ears and the sound drew me in. Wherever they were going, I was going too. My feet seemed to have a mind of their own and they led me to walk alongside what would become an integral part of my life, being a member of Pride of the Raven Flute Band.

CHAPTER 1

Joining Up

I grew up in Tower street, East Belfast, in a two up two down terraced house, although I never understood why our house was called a two up two down, we had a third floor with an attic! And, we had an extension which meant there were three rooms on the second floor. Our street was split in two, the Madrid street end where I lived and the Newtownards Road end where my Big Granny and Granda lived. The end that my Big Granny and Granda lived in had been partly blown up during the Belfast blitz in 1941, the side of the street opposite to them and half of Westbourne street were missing and had now been replaced with the Rupert Stanley College of Further and Higher Education. I know, quite the mouthful, but to us locals, it was simply called the "Rupert".

My Big Granny had some cracking stories about the blitz, I used to think that she was making it up, but true enough, her neighbours told the exact same stories she did and my Granda never corrected her when she talked about the door being blown of the outside loo when the bombs hit the other side of the street! If there was one thing my big Granda loved more than my Granny, it was telling the truth. He always said 'If you tell the truth, it sets you free'.

My Ma and big Granny worked at the "Rupert" as cleaners, they used to work in the Rope Works and Gallagher's, I had no idea what that meant, but they kept saying that in conversations and everyone nodded as it they were accepting some kind of female Masonic code word. I later found out that the rope works made rope, I never saw that coming and Gallagher's was a feg factory. It turns out these places used to be two of the biggest employers in the area, outside of the shipyard, but loads had changed in Belfast since they were powerhouse employers though. Even the once mighty shipyard with its humongous cranes, Samson and Goliath, which you could see from my house, was on the decline, "You have to take what work you can find, beggars can't be choosers" my Big Granny would say.

Tower Street, was a Protestant area and, was just one street away from a Catholic area known as the Short Strand. So, basically you had two warring communities situated side by side, separated only by an imaginary line at the end of the last house on Thistle Street. There were two streets that led from our community into the other side, Madrid Street and Beechfield Street, both of these streets had their Catholic counterparts and for fun we used to dare each other to cross the imaginary border line, just so we could boast that we had been on a journey into enemy territory. I remember one night, not long after we had moved into Tower Street, there was some sort of commotion at the bottom of the street, there was a rising level of noise and there seemed to be a lot more people walking down our street than normal. Not that people didn't walk down our street, they just didn't walk down it in these numbers, something was definitely up. My parents recognised it too, they told me to stay where I was, yeah like that was going to happen! They went out to the front door and stood at the wooden gate that separated our house from the pavement, I had snuck up behind them and peered out the door looking to my right where the noise was coming from. At the bottom of our part of Tower Street where it joins Beechfield Street there was a crowd of around two hundred people and the noise was getting louder and louder, and it didn't sound friendly either. I thought I could see something on fire, I couldn't see flames directly, but there was definitely smoke rising between the end of my street and the Short Strand. My Da opened the gate and headed down towards the commotion.

"Be careful, Tommy, god knows what's going on down there" my Ma said.

"What's happening Ma and where's my Da going?"

"You were told to stay inside" came the decree from my mum, she didn't even look round, she kept her eyes on what was happening at the bottom of the street. But nevertheless, she did offer up the answer to my question.

"There's a riot going on son, your Da's away to see what's happening"

"A riot doesn't sound good" was my naive response.

"Welcome to east Belfast son, this won't be the last one of these you'll see" she said quietly.

Well at least it would be more interesting than Crazy Prices in Craigavon, even if it was a little more dangerous. My Mum turned to me and gave me a warning.

"Don't you get involved in this son, if I ever hear of you being involved in a riot, I'll put you over my knee and give you something to think about"

Well that turned pretty quickly I thought, "Right you are ma" I said in feigned obedience, the fact that she thought I would get involved in a riot was amazing. She was right though; it wasn't the last time I would see a riot.

Even though these two areas were so close together, they might as well have been a million miles away from each other for all we knew about the people who lived there. What we did know though was that they weren't like us and that we needed to throw stones at them anytime they dared venture across the imaginary line. After all that's exactly what they did to us.

Now, back to the Rupert, when it wasn't being a college of further education and the big blue steel gates were padlocked on a Friday evening, the car park magically turned into a football pitch! Every Sunday afternoon after Sunday dinner, there would be a match taking place, kids of all ages came to play. Sunday dinner took place at one o'clock, every other day of the week dinner time was five o'clock, but on a Sunday, that was teatime. I don't ever remember anyone telling me about football in the car park on a Sunday, it just seemed to be part of life in our area. Heading down to the Rupert on a Sunday and climbing over the blue steel gates, that rattled and shook as you made your way over them, was a permanent fixture in my weekly activities, just like going to school I guess, only a lot more fun. I would swing my right leg over and jump from the gate down to the ground, then, make my way round the mobile classroom towards the low wall that acted as a partition between the car park area and the actual school building, we called it the terracing, you know like the areas at football grounds that you stand in? Well that's where you waited to play if there happened to be enough people down to have more than two teams for the game that day. Andrew and Arty Storey, who lived up the street from my Granny were in charge of organising the teams, they always seemed to be able to get the five aside nets from the youth club that was also in the same grounds as the Rupert, it turns out their Ma was a key holder, and as long as the stuff didn't get damaged, the leaders in the youth club didn't mind them getting used. Although having nets never stopped us playing, two well positioned bricks or discarded jumpers were just as good. Andrew and Arty were good football players, always picked for their school team, but me? I was never amazing at football like some of my friends but, give me an opportunity in front of goal and I would put the ball in the back of the net. Although my talent in football turned out to be playing as goalkeeper, I was the youngest person to get picked for my school team as a goalkeeper, and that's the position I played the most on Sundays. The Rupert also served another purpose, it's where you went if you had a girlfriend, as there were plenty of wee spaces where you could hide out of the way and not get spotted kissing. That's what I was told anyway.

The Rupert was just down the street from my house and directly opposite my big Granny and Granda's house. In fact, everything seemed to be nearby. There were shops at either end of the street, although my end of Tower Street meant a trip across the Avenue to Bella's shop or on up a bit near the Templemore Hall church to go to Billy's. At the bottom of my Granny's street and to the left heading towards the city centre was Desanos ice cream shop, they did the best pokes and sliders in all the land, and the people who owned it were actually Italian. Anytime we went in we ordered our pokes with an Italian accent, they usually tried to throw us out of the shop. They thought we were taking the piss out of them, but that wasn't the case at all. We thought we sounded all sophisticated and like we could actually own a poke shop, the owners didn't see it that way though. Yes, everything was close by, all my friends lived a stone's throw away, literally. I had most of my family nearby too, well except for some of my cousins, they lived up the Shankill, it was always great going up to see them or when they visited my big Granny. You're never stuck for friends here either, there are loads of kids around my age in the area so even when I fall out with someone, over something amazingly important like Ian Rush being better than Kenny Dalglish, there is always somebody else that I can go out and have a laugh with.

Quite a few years had passed since my first encounter with the bands on that fateful Saturday afternoon when my world champion 'cribby' dreams were snuffed out and a new obsession was birthed. The bands! It was an encounter that had been repeated many a Saturday after. Sometimes we knew when they would be out, like Easter and July. But then, there were other times when you didn't expect them, there we'd be going about our usual business, playing football or getting up to some kind of mischief, playing a game of thunder and lightning, you know where you bang someone's front or back door as loud as thunder and then run like lightning to get away. It was usually best played at night, there was less chance of getting seen, but sometimes we didn't care and just went for it anyway, and then just as we are about to unleash thunder on a door, out of nowhere there would be the sound of drums in the air and suddenly we would be running towards the Avenue to see them in all their cacophonous glory. Over the years I never forgot that feeling I'd had during that first encounter, because I had it every time, I saw the bands, especially when I saw the Pride of the Raven.

Unfortunately, there was one other thing that was really close by, my school. Beechfield Primary School is at the Protestant end of Beechfield Street and sits right on the interface between the Short Strand. At break time there is only the thickness of the twisted steel railings, painted white, yet rusting and peeling, separating the two communities. School wouldn't be nearby for much longer, being in P7 means that I'll be heading off to secondary school after the summer holidays. Before any of that though I would have to pass the eleven plus!. The eleven plus is the exam you take to work out if you're smart enough to go to a grammar school. If I didn't pass, I would only have two choices of school, Orangefield or Ashfield Boys. In my head I was already thinking of Orangefield, mainly because I'd heard that most of the lads that went to Ashfield supported Glentoran Football Club and I wasn't a fan. I didn't care where I went to school though, it's not like I was going to need the education, anytime I was asked the question "What do you want to be when you grow up? I'd tell everyone "I'm joining the army when I'm old enough". That had been on my mind for ages. I was always going beyond the normal pretend army games and fake gun sounds of "dddbbbbrrro" a raspberry lip blow with the word 'ro' at the end, all the kids did it, but not me, I had all the gear and I even had a kids copy of a M1 carbine rifle used in the Second World War. My favourite films were war films, and I had an ever-growing collection of commando comics, my Granda had let me read one he had, and that was me hooked! Anytime we were in the newsagents and there was one I didn't have, I'd be hanging about reading it making subtle hints to my Ma, who would be picking up her daily copy of the Sun newspaper, to make sure she had the latest bingo card, she always said we would move away if she won the bingo, I'd have settled for the latest commando comic.

We had seen the bands at the weekend, and we'd had a great time as always, whistling the tunes we knew as we walked alongside our favourite bands. I had become more than just interested, I had started trying to replicate everything that I saw, grabbing anything that resembled drum sticks, beating the kerbs on the street I tried to copy the beats and rolls I had heard over and over again at the parades. My friends were the same and over time we have developed our skills, being able to whistle all the popular tunes and drum along to them, like we were already members of a band.

We went back to school on the Monday morning and at break time, after having just finished the obligatory game of twenty a side football in the playground, the bell went, and we were walking over to line up and go back inside. Alan was talking to wee Dee as I walked behind them.

"Here, did you see the Gert at the weekend?"

"See them? He exclaimed "You mean hear them! mate they were so loud I thought my Da's falsers were gonna fall out! Stitty was giving that bass drum such a beating"

He continued on excitedly and oblivious to everyone else who were now listening in "...and Jamie on the band pole, that cartwheel flick and catch behind the back is crazy, I was trying it all weekend. I lost my three best band poles in big Sadie's backyard, that aul bitch wouldn't give me any of them back, I rapped the door and she wouldn't even open it, she just shouted out the window and told me to "fuck off and play at my own door"

You see, band poles aren't expendable pieces of rejected tape covered brush shaft, oh no, they are lovingly created pieces of cylindrical timber-based art, so I could understand Alan's desire to retrieve his three best band poles. Most of us had at least five, two that were trial runs, band poles that we tried out different styles and designs on and while they weren't quite expendable, we just wouldn't take them out on the street to play with. The other three, they were a different story, they were the poles that we had spent a considerable amount of time and effort making. From choosing the right pole, everything needed to be considered from the right thickness and length to the design that you ended up going with. You didn't just create a band pole on some sort of whim, no way, creating the perfect band pole takes time and careful consideration. The tape we used came from the best supplier of band pole tape in the east, Glovers, famous as much for its variety of products as it was for their reasonable prices, but even more famous, because there wasn't a band pole that we knew of that wasn't decorated with Glovers tape. You have to buy it in packs of five to get your red white and blue tape so most of us ended up with a rather large collection of yellow and black rolls of tape, as you needed at least two packs per pole. No one with any gumption would include those colours in their design, although, there was one wee lad from school who'd the audacity to include some black on his band pole probably because he hadn't properly evaluated the amount of tape his design of choice would require, thus leaving him with a gap. Now instead of just waiting and getting tape or better still borrowing a little to use, oh no! he had to go and use a strip of black. I remember when we first saw it, we couldn't quite believe it, maybe the light was playing tricks on us, but as we observed him it became pretty obvious that he had broken the band pole design protocol and included a non-regulation colour! Needless to say, he won't be throwing that band pole up in the air any time soon, we took that thing off him, that insult to band pole design and did the only thing that abomination deserved, we threw it into big Sadie's back-yard.

As Alan continued with his story the laughter echoed down the line, we all had heard that line from big Sadie in our day.

"So, I got my ma round to her, such a fight in the street, every-one was out"

"Did you get your band poles back?" asked Dee.

"Too right I did, my Ma made sure of it"

The conversation drifted off to how we all had lost something in Big Sadie's back yard, but not wanting to be left out of the whole band conversation I chipped in with my tuppence worth.

"Pride of the Raven were playing well at the weekend, weren't they?"

Silence fell, petty much like a petrol bomb just before impact, then, mass laughter broke out.

"Pride of the Raven! playing well, bloody melody bands"

"Who listens to melody bands? Boring!!"

"Glenn loves the melody bands"

I stood there, momentarily a little lost for words, but I ended up retaliating pretty quickly "And just what the hell is wrong with the Pride of the Raven?"

"They aren't blood 'n' thunder like the Gertrude Star" said Alan rather matter of fact.

"And again, what's wrong with that?"

"Everybody knows, blood 'n' thunder is better than melody?"

There are two main types of flute band, blood and thunder and melody. Blood and Thunder bands are out to be as loud as they can, they beat the living daylights out of their drums and the flute players try to play as loud as possible, the skins of their bass drums are usually splattered with blood as each bass drummer tries to make sure every human being living and dead hears them playing! Because they were going for loudness the bass drummers usually end up busting their knuckles open and bleeding on the skins, hence the name blood and thunder. Whereas melody bands, well, they are a bit more refined, and play a different range of tunes and to me, well, they were far more interesting than them blood n thunder headers making noise for the sake of making noise!

"Well I think the Pride of the Raven just sound better!! And, you know what?"

"What?"

"The Gert sound like my class trying to play the recorder! In fact, I think I heard them playing three blind mice on Saturday!"

I didn't think that at all, but he was pissing me off slagging something I actually liked, luckily everyone laughed at my little quip, there's nothing worse than cracking a joke and nobody laughing. The moment was quite rudely interrupted by one of the teachers ringing a bell.

"Right everyone, settle down, quiet in the lines please" came the command and then the teachers gave their signals and we all headed back inside, class by class, line by line, starting with the P4's then working all the way up to the P7's. As we walked into the classroom, we were confronted by Mr Graham.

"Right everyone, hurry up, inside and take your seats" we made our way to our desks, all wondering what joys awaited us before the lunch time break. It wouldn't take long for us to find out "Millar, go to the music cupboard and get the recorders".

I busted out laughing "Sir can we walk down the Avenue with them, playing twinkle twinkle Gertrude Star?"

"Eh? What? What on earth are you blethering on about?"

"It doesn't matter sir, private joke."

"Right, well if you want to joke about, maybe you'll want to stay behind after school and joke about then?" That was that then, 'Grahamer' had taken back control of the room.

I left school that day still laughing about Grahamer's class and the recorders. I couldn't wait to tell Dee and Alan about it.

"He hadn't a baldy's notion what I was on about"

"He's probably never even stood and watched the bands"

"Well he couldn't anyway, sure he's always going on about that knee injury he has and then whips out the jar with his cartilage in it"

"Who does that, keeps part of their knee in a jar?"

"It's probably not his, more than likely belongs to some past pupil or something!"

"Mate, why would you even say that, how the hell am I getting that image out of my head now for god's sake"

We headed home to the wonderful joy that was homework but with the sound of flutes and drums playing on our minds.

None of us were actually members of a band, but that's all we seemed to be able to talk about and on Tuesday after school, we decided we were forming a band of our own. I have no idea why we hadn't thought of this before, but here we were standing in Beechfield Street doing more than just thinking about it. We were going to actually do it.

Someone had come up with the bright idea of creating drums from different types of boxes that were left outside Stewart's, the local Supermarket on the Newtownards Road. The only time I was in that place was when I was dragged in by my Ma to help her do the weekly shopping, now here we were heading down of our own bat, we'd all be out of excuses the next time we got the invite. We headed down to Stewarts after school and started to sift through the pile of cardboard near the front doors. We needed to find the right size of boxes for side drums and bass drums. We were so serious about picking them out, we were actually testing them for the right type of sound. God knows what anyone who heard us that day was thinking, we didn't care though, we were on a mission.

We picked out boxes we thought would sound more like snare drums and we found two bigger boxes that would get a really deep sound for a bass drum, we were the connoisseurs of card-board.

"It's a pity there aren't any round boxes" said Dee quite inno-cently "then they would really look like drums"

"Round boxes?? Are you listening to yourself mate?"

"Round boxes, you eejit, boxes are like their name suggests, boxy"

"Hat boxes are round, well my Ma said they are"

"And how many hats are Stewarts likely to sell, eh?"

"Aye but still doesn't mean all boxes are square"

"Right have we got everything we need here?"

"Looks like it"

"Right let's make a move then"

We left the front of Stewarts with our box selections and headed for home, when we arrived back, we got to work, coming up with designs for the drums. Before we could really do that, we had something more important to do, like coming up with a name for this new band.

Dee was the first to make a suggestion.

"What about Tower Street Star?"

"No"

"Madrid Street Star?"

"No!"

"Star of Westbourne"

"What about the Bethlehem Star"

"What about Star-Plan?"

"What about Star Wars Flute Band, you can pretend your band pole is a light saber! And our lodge can be the Jedi order!"

"Ha bloody ha, so nothing with star in it then?

"NO!" we shouted in unison.

"Although, Star of the East sounds good"

"Sounds like a Chinese takeaway mate"

"You'll be rewriting the sash next!"

"Sure this chow mein it is beautiful, and the soy sauce it is fine." Sang Colin, we all started rolling about laughing. We stopped laughing about five minutes later, and I said,

"What about Tower Street True Blues?"

We all looked at each other

"Yeah, I like that"

"Me too!"

"Settled then?"

We all nodded in agreement; we had officially formed the Tower Street True Blues. Now all we had to do was pester our folks for a pound or two cause we were going to need real drum sticks if we were going to be authentic and well, the Essey, or the band shop, was doing a wee deal on them, and this would make wee Dee happy, as they were the same type of drum sticks the Gert used! We would need more than just drumsticks though.

"You'll need to steal your sister's tennis balls so we can make a set of bass drum sticks Dee"

"No worries leave it me" said Dee.

"Glenn, try and get some of that tape your Da uses for marking things out"

"What for?"

"To dampen the bass drum and tighten the snares!! Said with an air of why isn't this obvious to you?

"Oh aye, right" I said none the wiser, I'd have to find a way to get my hands on it though, I could picture my Da's face when I asked him for some of the tape. Nevertheless, when I went home later, I mustered up the courage to ask him.

"Dad, can I have some of that tape you use to mark out stuff when you're working?

"You mean masking tape? What do you want that for son?"

"Ah just so we can put it on some cardboard boxes we stole from outside of Stewart's and are in the process of transforming said cardboard boxes into snare and bass drums for our pretend band, the Tower Street True Blues, now, the particular use of this tape will be to enable us to produce a tightened snare and bass drum sound"

"Howl on a wee minute, you want it for what?"

"Don't make me repeat all that Dad, I was trying to be smart"

"Take yourself off would ye, I'm not giving you tape for that, do you know how much that costs? Tape for drums and bass drums, I've never heard the like of it"

"So, that's a no then Da?"

"What do you think?" came the sarcastic reply.

"Ok" I said and walked off to go up to my room, "I'll just wait 'til you're out and then I'll just take a wee bit anyway" I said under my breath.

"And don't think about waiting until I go out and just taking it anyway!!"

How the hell did he hear that? It was like living with Russell Grant for god sake, you could get away with nothing!

The week progressed pretty normally, well as normal as forming flute bands without flutes and walking the streets with cardboard replica drums gets. For us, all of our spare time was now parade time and we took every opportunity we could. Kids from other streets had seen what we had done and started to copy us and before we knew it there were four more cardboard bands, including the Major Street Star led by John Keery and Stewarty. We walked everywhere and didn't care; we were living the dream. We were even stopping the traffic in the Avenue, cars were honking their horns at us, and angry drivers were telling us to get off the roads. We didn't take any notice of them until we were confronted by a rather stern looking Peeler.

"What the hell do you lot think you are doing? Get off the bloody road, you're causing an obstruction"

We immediately broke up and headed for home, we weren't about to mess with the Police.

If you'd seen the state of us, we thought we were the business, in makeshift uniforms, made up of our school trousers and the same colour of t-shirt. Wearing my school trousers came with a stern warning from my Ma, "If you get a rip in those trousers, I won't be replacing them, I'm tellin' ye now, you'll wear them 'til the end of the school year, do you hear me?"

After about twenty parades in three days we decided that Thursday would a day of rest.

The school bell went as normal at three o'clock, it was time to get out of school. All the bigger classes get out at the same time so the hustle and bustle of trying to get your coat and get out was something to be seen, hundreds of kids trying to make their way through the crowded cloak rooms in to the freedom that lies beyond the school gate, home time! I only lived a two-minute walk away from my school, but it always seemed to take me ages getting home. There was always some distraction, whether that be talking to my mates about what we were doing later, or a fight that had been arranged for after school.

"See you later on then?"

"Aye mate, are we gonna head to Avoneil and see if the nets are still up and get a wee game of continental going?"

"Sounds like a plan"

"No problem, I'll see if Darren and Colin are gonna go as well"

I was heading toward my house when I saw Darren at the top of the street.

"Alright mate, you heading to Avoneil later?" I shouted to him.

"No mate, I'm heading out tonight"

"Ah right, where ya of too then?"

"Band practice"

"Hold on, band practice!!" I ran up the street like two men and a wee lad, "You're in a band?"

"I joined a wee while back, but it's good fun"

"What band is it?"

"Pride of the Raven?

"Holy shit, WHAT??!!" The what sounded like my voice had broken and then decided it didn't like it and tried it's best to revert to its normal pitch.

"Did I just hear you right? Did you say Pride of the Raven?"

Darren cowered back a little as if he could sense a slaggin' was coming his way.

"Yeah, mate, Pride of the...." Before he could even finish, I interrupted.

"Can I go with you? They're my favourite band, Dee and Alan are always raking me for liking them"

I then rattled of question after question, my curiosity completely aroused and Darren did his best to assemble answers quick enough, I had to make sure he took me with him.

"Call for me when you're leaving, right, don't forget now"

"No worries get your homework done or your Ma won't let you go anywhere" Darren said.

"See you later on"

"Aye, see you then"

Well didn't I just skip home and head straight for the books. My Ma knew something was up, parents seem to be able to just sniff motivation out.

"What has you so cheerful then?"

"Em, what are you on about?"

"Getting your homework done usually I have to threaten you with your Da to get you to do it, what are you looking?"

"Nothing!"

"Yeah pull the other one son, come on, spit it out"

So, I told her the whole story about seeing the band for the first time and how I always looked out for them now and then asking Darren about going to football, and how this obviously couldn't just be coincidence. My Ma rolled her eyes more than once during my passionate monologue, obviously she didn't care about the background, she just wanted to know what I wanted from her. I eventually got to the point.

"So, the long and short of it is, Darren, well he's joined the Pride of the Raven Flute Band and, well, um... I want to join too" There was no response initially, she just looked at me like I had two heads and then my ma did her best impression of a machine gun spitting questions out at me, as if she was trying for the world record for how many questions can you ask your son about joining a flute band without taking a breath, she probably just broke it! They came thick and fast though.

"What night is practice on?" How long is it for? Where is the band hall? Is there anyone else your age in the band? Ending with the most important, "How much is this gonna cost me?"

I shrugged my shoulders as if to say "I don't know" but that was just a ploy, I knew the joining fee was three quid, you see you had to dance around my Ma, especially regarding money, we didn't have much, so she made it go as far as she could. She hated wasting money, so I would need to stick at the band if she was going to invest in it.

"Darren said something about the joining fee being three quid Ma..." I'd hoped I had said that quick enough for it to escape her attention, but I could already see her face starting to turn towards the "Its gonna cost me what?" expression, I needed to say something quick to sweeten the deal.

"But that gets you your flute and as I'm a junior I won't have to pay for my uniform when I'm ready to walk" I got this out just before she was sure to hit me with a negative response and the usual rant about how we needed heat and food and electricity and how unaware I was about how much it cost to put clothes on my back.

My rapid-fire response was a success, the "It's gonna cost me what?" expression turned quickly into the "at least I'm not going to get stroked every week for money as a result of this flute band caper" expression.

"Ok son, you can join, but I'm telling ya, you better stick at this and become the next James Galway or you're dead"

"Ok Ma" I said rolling my eyes, but that being said it was better to be breathing and alive if nothing more at this stage, I don't want to risk her changing her mind, in fact, I think I'll wait to tell her about the one pound weekly dues next week.

CHAPTER 2

First Band Practice

Ding-dong! the front doorbell rang, and even from three floors up I could hear my Ma going to open the hall door, then after a short but muffled conversation, using her best 'get down the stairs gulder' she beckoned me from my lofty attic perch.

"Glenn! Glenn! GLENN!

"Aye Ma, what do you want?

"What do you mean, what do I want?? I'll give you what do I want! Get down here now, Darren's at the door for you, c'mon hurry up"

I heard the hall and living room doors close, the ball is firmly in my court and no doubt I will be timed on how long it takes me to come down. I jumped down the five stairs directly outside my room and hurried down the two other flights of stairs to arrive down in the hallway and I could see Darren standing at the front door through the glass hall door, decked out in a royal blue t-shirt, and a bag in his hand, I open the hall door with a standard greeting, "Alright mate"

"Alright big son"

"Alright Darren, how's it going?"

"Not too bad at all, right, ready to go?

"I am indeed, here, is that the new Rangers top?"

"Aye nice isn't it?"

"It's a fucking cracker..."

Our conversation was interrupted by my Ma's super hearing "Glenn, I hope that's not you I hear swearing? Don't have me to come out there to you now, I won't care if Darren's there or not, you're not too old to go over my knee wee lad"

"Sorry Ma" Turning back to Darren, slightly embarrassed and in a slightly lower tone I say "Right mate let's get out of here, I don't want her annoying the Donald Duck out of me"

I closed the hall door behind me and zipped up my jacket as we headed out the gate. Suddenly a familiar gulder rang through the air "Lock the gate Glenn!" I headed back and put the latch on the gate and walked back towards Darren.

"I swear mate, she must have eyes on the back of her head!! Anyway, when did you get the new Rangers top?

"Sunday past there, my Da knew someone selling them up at Nutt's Corner Market"

"Nice, do you think he could get me one?"

"What do I look like to you? Lifestyle sports catalogue and delivery service?"

"I nearly didn't recognise you without your name badge on"

I knew fine rightly my Ma would never give me the money for a Rangers top. I'd get some long winded story about how other things were far more important than the latest Rangers top, little did she know how wrong she was, fitting in with your mates is way more important than electricity or light for that matter, but hey it was always worth the ask.

Darren was one of my best mates, even though he was a few years older than me. Actually, he would be going into third year at Orangefield Boys School, where I would be going into first year after the summer holidays. He was very popular with the ladies, plus, he could fight like fuck! That was always useful, because by default, if you knocked about with someone with the reputation of being able to fight like fuck, then you by association were deemed to be able to fight like fuck! The logic being why would someone hang around with someone who couldn't? Now, it wasn't that I couldn't handle myself, but I was just never in the same league.

Earlier today Darren had been telling me that he had joined Pride of the Raven Flute Band. And after my encounters with the band when I'd seen them in the Avenue, I didn't need an excuse, I was joining too and tonight was the night. Absolutely nothing was going to stand in my way. Little did I know that this would be the start of what would become a weekly ritual, heading up to the band hall on a Thursday night. Darren lived round the corner from me on Madrid street, his Dad, Geordie, was one of the local youth leaders and his nephew Colin, another friend of mine lived across the street from him, he was famous in the area because he was a junior boxer, he trained up at the Ledley Hall boxing club and had loads of trophies and medals. His Mum Sandra was always keen to show them off whenever he added to the collection. Darren said Colin's coaches had high hopes for him, they thought that when he was older that he would be good enough to think about going professional!

We started walking up my street, turning left onto Madrid Street, we headed towards Templemore Avenue and then turned right and made our way up towards the Albertbridge Road. The Avenue is split in two, affectionately known as the Avenue and the second Avenue, probably the only thing East Belfast has anything in common with New York City!!

"So, how far up are we heading?" I asked. Now, usually going anywhere that meant having to go past the second Avenue required a special license from the parental association of child suppression.

"Just up to the Beersbridge Road mate, wee bit down from the Woodstock"

"No worries, not too far then"

I was nervous, as meeting new people had never been my strong point, but this was offset by my mind racing with questions. What would it be like? Would I get a flute tonight? What if the guys in the band don't like me? What kind of secret location does a flute band practice in? I imagined some kind of James Bond espionage scenario, where secret knocks, code words and laser beams were the order of the day, well not really, although that would have been cool. I mean it isn't like you came across these places every day. We came to the end of the second avenue, and crossed the road at the Farmers Rest, a bar run by a famous ex-Linfield player, Warren Feeney. Even though the bar had an actual name most people just called it Feeney's. We walked the shortest part of the Avenue and turned right onto the Beersbridge Road; we hadn't walked more than a few minutes up the road when Darren drew to a halt just outside this bricked up place. It had a big bolted steel door and one of those spy hole things, maybe this was a bit James Bond after all? Although I have to say this place didn't look like very much at all, never mind a centre of musical excellence, it looked more like a hotel for rats and mice to be honest.

"Right, this is it" says Darren

"Are you sure? This is where the Pride of the Raven practice?" There was a hint of holy shit tinged surprise in my voice, "Mate, this looks like somewhere we'd collect wood for the boney from!"

"Aye, this is the place, what were you expecting anyway, the Europa Hotel?"

"This place looks like it's been bombed more times than the Europa Hotel!" Darren shook his head and laughed. He was right though, I had no idea what to expect, maybe I was thinking that it would be somewhere with decent seats and a hint of forest glade in the air? I definitely expected it to be bigger, a decent sized place, I mean, after all it had to house nearly forty odd people inside. How on earth where forty people going to fit in here? This was gonna be like those terrible house parties with family, bodies everywhere and I usually end up sitting on the stairs. Darren leaned forward and gave the big bolted door a blatter and we waited.

"Did yer Ma give you the joining fee?"

"Aye mate I'd some job getting it out of her like, she went off on a wee rant about how we needed it for the electric and that I'd be responsible if my brothers caught pneumonia, so I better, and I quote, "Become the next James Galway" Can you believe that?"

"Not expecting much, is she?"

"Aye mate no pressure at all like, I haven't even joined the band yet, and she's expecting me to turn into James Galway"

We were standing chatting away, almost forgetting that we had wrapped the door, then we heard the sound of a lock being opened and another and another. What the hell were they guarding in here that needs such tight security? After a lot of clunk clicking, eventually the door opened. A red headed man popped his head out of the doorway and had a quick look around, he spotted the two of us lurking at the door.

"Alright Darren, mon in, and who's this?

"This is my mate, Glenn, he's looking to join"

Peering at me with a hint of suspicion and potential he says, "Flute or drum?"

I responded with "What the hell is he on about? Darren you told me this was a pipe band?"

The red headed man, I later knew to be called Frankie laughed and said "You'll fit right in here kid, come on in"

We made our way in through the door into a very small hall-way with a set of stairs straight ahead and another door to the left that was the main practice area. Taking it in and looking at the hall for first time, I noticed that the walls were lined with trophies, I mean they were all over the place, crowded on a serious number of shelves. I started checking them out to see what they were actually for. There were loads for 1st Melody

Flute, others for 1st Style and Appearance, and best Melody Drum Corp and best Drum Major. Alongside this vast array of trophies were old pictures of the band from god knows how long ago. Looking at these black and white photos I could see smiles on the faces of everyone in the band, and pride as well, they all seemed to be proud of being in this band. There was one other strong characteristic, and that was the smell. The band hall had a very unique aroma, a mixture of smoke and spilled beer, and lightly infused with a dose of male sweat. Turns out this place used to be a shop front; it had now been converted into a band hall.

Over the course of the next fifteen minutes or so, there were quite a few bangs on the door and more people started to arrive. I noticed that most of them all shook each other's hands and a wee interaction took place that seemed to be repeated over and over again.

"Alright mate"

"Alright, how's it going?"

"Not too bad, yourself?"

"Can't complain, mate"

"No one listens anyway"

"You got that right; did you see the match at the weekend?"

The hall was filling up rightly now, there were pockets of people sitting grouped at tables, standing near the door and me in the midst of all this just sitting taking it all in. The door goes again, "Get the door Darren, stop sitting there looking pretty" said Frankie.

"And he's not even good at that" I said, that drew a laugh from the guys in the hall, but a glare from Darren. I gave him a look that said 'sorry about that', you see, older mates don't like being slagged by younger mates in front of even older mates, a weird piece of social decorum, but rules are rules after all.

Darren came back into the hall with this guy who to me looked a wee bit like Terry McDermott, one of my favourite Liverpool football players. They both walked over towards where I was sitting.

"Right Glenn, this is Terry, he looks after the learners"

"Alright Terry, aptly named"

"Eh?" Says Terry with a confused look on his face

"Sorry it's just you look a bit like Terry McDermott"

"Ah right, well lads it looks like we have another Liverpool supporter here"

"Ack for fuck sake not another one" said a rough looking black haired man standing at the makeshift bar area.

"Next thing he'll be telling us that he supports Linfield as well"

"Well actually" I stared to say when Darren tapped me on the leg, shaking his head, as if to say it might not be safe to say that in here, it was too late I just blurted it on out "I am"

"What did you say your name was again?" said Terry.

"Glenn, I'm actually named after the glens"

Glentoran and Linfield are the two biggest football teams in Belfast and a fierce rivalry exists between them and usually where you live decides who you support when it comes to those two teams. So, if you're from East Belfast you're supposed to be a glen man and if you're from South Belfast or the Shankill you're a Blue man. Those wonderful social rules obviously didn't apply to me. I became a 'Blueman' after a neighbour called Stanley who lived a few doors up from my Big Granny offered to take me to a match one Saturday about four years ago, obviously there was a need for my parents and Granny to be rid of me for a bit, so they said it was ok for me to go and off I went. They were playing the RUC football team that fateful day in the Irish Cup, and as I sat in the South Stand in Windsor Park, the home of Linfield FC, I became a Blue man! The whole atmosphere, the banter and craic from the fans was great and the songs!! Well they were something else and when the crowd got going it was something to behold. My decision was somewhat swayed by the fact that Linfield's colours were red white and blue, the stands were awash with scarfs and hats all pledging allegiance to the Blues. I was also kind of swayed by the fact that I ran into my cousins from the Shankill at the game, my Uncle Davy was a big blue man and now one of the family from the east had crossed the big divide.

Terry laughed, "A blue man named after the glens who lives in East Belfast, wanting to join a band made up of glen men"

Right, now I was absolutely shitting myself, the one question that never came to mind was football affiliation, what the hell have I got myself into? I had taken some stick in school for being a blue man, well a wee bit more than some stick, a few socially conscious glen men thought it might be a good idea to try and beat it out of me, their efforts failed miserably of course, it just wasn't the done thing in East Belfast.

"Don't worry son" Terry said, obviously seeing the colour

drain from my face, "We won't hold it against you for long! Right learners where are ya's?" Terry said and a group of four or five people made their way over to where Terry was sitting.

"I hope you all have been practicing lads?" There was some mumbling and incomprehensible chatter.

"I'll take that as a yes then, right then let's hear you playing your scales, then I want you all to play the Sash and the Lily alright? Ok, starting with the lower register on D, off ya go"

The lads sitting around me took their flutes out of their leather pouches, putting folders in front of them and begin to play a scale, going from the lowest note to the highest with Terry sitting there like a drill Sargent calling out what notes the learners were supposed to be playing. They stopped every so often as Terry corrected the wrong fingering of the notes for some who got them mixed up with another, like the difference between an F sharp and an F natural, I had absolutely no clue about what that meant, but I listened and watched intently just to see if there was anything I could pick up. I kept an eye on Darren, mainly just to see if he was any good or not. One thing I did notice though was that even though they were all playing the same instrument they all positioned their fingers and held the flute slightly differently from one another. That obviously didn't matter, as long as the right note was being played, but it did give me hope that I would be able to do this, everyone had their own way and that was ok. Once they were done with practising the scale, they started to play one of the most famous band tunes around "The Sash". We all knew the words to the Sash, well the first verse and chorus anyway. No one ever taught me the words to it, but I knew them just the same. The way it was being played didn't sound great, to be honest it sounded worse than my class trying to play three blind mice on the recorders, but hey they were playing a flute, and I couldn't, so I kept my mouth shut and waited 'til it was my turn for Terry to help me out. After helping the guys work on their techniques and giving them notes for some new tunes, Terry finally turned his attention to me.

"Ok Glenn, have you ever played the flute before?"

"No"

"Have you ever smoked?"

"No"

"Have you ever had to spit tobacco of the tip of your tongue?"

"No"

"Have you ever used a milk bottle to make a whistling sound?"

I was glad that the questions ended at this stage, if I had known that joining a flute band came with its own bloody multiple-choice exam called 'Things you've done that might help you play a flute' I'd have studied harder. Thank god I was able to say yes to Terry's last question, I was starting to feel like a right dick. Getting a sound from a milk bottle, I was over skilled at that, I mean that's something I did for fun, it annoyed my Ma something shocking. So, I'm thinking 'happy days this will be easy'.

Terry then reached into the bag he stored the notes for the other learners in and produced a flute and handed it to me,

"There you go, now let's see if we can't get you playing a note" Terry said somewhat hopefully.

There was a sense of excitement, this was my very own flute, well not really my own it belonged to the band, but this thing was about to become like my best friend.

"Right Glenn let's get you holding this right" Terry helped me hold the flute correctly and when he was happy, we were able to move on.

"Right the air hole is called the embouchure, we need to get it positioned correctly so that you can get the best sound from it, why don't you give it a go?"

"Ok here goes"

My first attempts were terrible, sorry make that worse than terrible, I somehow managed to make the flute sound like someone trying to blow their nose! I didn't care though, I was determined, so, I kept on trying. After a while and watching me start to get frustrated, and a few unhelpful sniggers from Darren and some of the other learners, Terry stepped in.

"Ok" said Terry, taking the flute from me and separating it into two pieces and handing me back the head of the flute only "Try this instead, roll the hole round towards your lips

"If this is a chat up line, it's not working" I said.

Terry laughed and said "Do you want to learn or not? Just do what I'm asking you'll understand why in a moment"

"Alright, alright" so I brought the embouchure round like Terry said.

"Now purse your lips and kiss the hole"

"Seriously!! What do you take me for??"

"Just do it" insisted Terry.

Reluctantly I did what I was asked, and Terry continued to coach me through it.

"Now roll the flute hole away from you until you feel it resting below your bottom lip"

"Done"

"Now try..."

Suddenly there was a note coming from the flute, not a squeaky one but a clean crisp note, Terry seemed impressed, and it certainly seemed to wipe the smile of Darren's bake and the other learners who'd been laughing at my previous attempts. After making sure I could make the note consistently Terry put the flute back together and got me to try again, and it wasn't just a fluke, after a few adjustments, there it was again a clear note coming out of the flute. Terry gave me a copy of the scale, a weird looking page that had all the notes that you could play on the flute written down on it with the finger positions required and what keys needed to be open or closed depending on what note you were trying to play. Terry went through it with me, explaining what way to look at the page and what keys were what on the page and on the flute. Then he showed me three or four notes that he wanted me to practice. I had to try them a few times there and then as well.

"Now remember Glenn, practice them every day I'm expecting you to come to practice next week knowing them and being ready to move on, ok?"

"Ok Terry, I will give it a go"

"Now don't worry if you don't get the note right all the time, believe me, you won't, you've done well tonight, just keep at it, even if you get frustrated, just remember what I've shown you"

"I will, I want to be able to play, I'll do whatever it takes"

"Good man"

And with that, my first ever flute lesson was over. I put my flute down on the table and positioned it in the same way that the flute was drawn on the sheet with the scale on it. I started to think about what keys were what and if I tried really hard that I could get even more notes learned for the next practice than Terry had asked me to learn.

"Right lads, main practice in fifteen minutes" said Terry, and at that more people seemed to arrive and take their seats around the hall, some of the learners left. They said their goodbyes and shook hands with some of the senior members.

"See you next week Terry?"

"Aye lads, you will indeed, now remember what I showed you, get stuck in and practice as much as you can".

I sat their thinking should I be leaving with them, but I was curious about what the main practice was like and besides Darren looked like he was staying, but I thought I'll ask Terry here anyway.

"Terry?"

"Yes mate"

"Do all the learners have to leave now?"

"Not if you don't need to, here, why don't you and Darren take a seat beside wee Alvin there and watch what he does, he's been coming along rightly over these past few weeks, and it'll do you good to hear the band playing anyway, and get some of the harder tunes into your head"

Darren and I made our way over to where 'wee' Alvin was sitting. "Alright mate, Terry was saying it would good for me to listen in and watch what you're doing, is that alright?"

 "Aye no bother mate, I'll help you follow the tunes the best I can"

"Great thanks mate"

"You got on ok with the flute earlier, I heard you starting to get a note out of it"

"Aye I did indeed, it will take me ages to pick it up properly I'm sure?"

"It will, but It's different for everyone, flip it took me three practices I think, before I got a note out of it, so you're doing alright"

"Really? That makes me feel a bit better, I was looking around and thinking everyone's probably laughing at me trying to get a note out of it, I mean at one point I actually thought I could blow down a house I was blowing that hard"

"No one was laughing at you believe me, we've all been there and felt like that, but once you start getting it and learning the scale and tunes, everyone just wants you to get better"

"That's cool, so, how long have you been in the band then?"

"I've been in the band for about four years now so I have. You see my Da and brothers are in the band too. At first I was kind of dragged along, but now I love it."

"Which one's your Da then?"

"Right, you see him up there at the front with the glasses?" Alvin was pointing to a reasonably tall man who kind of reminded me of Frank Carson, he continued "That's my Da there, Jim, he's a drummer, my two brothers are in the band to, that's Mark over there, he's a full blower and Colin he's learning to play the drum."

While Alvin had been talking to me, one thing he said really stood out for me. He had been in the band for four years already, what if it takes that long to learn to play the flute? I'll be older than my Da before I'm walking for fuck sake!

"Have you been learning the flute all that time?" I asked with a 'holy shit if it takes that long I won't bother coming back' tone of voice! My expression must have said that as well, Alvin started to laugh,

"No no, I started out playing the triangle when I first joined and then I moved on to the cymbals, I've been learning the flute for about six or seven months now and I'm hoping that I will be ready to walk by the last Saturday in August this year, I have a fair few tunes to get off the list first though"

That didn't sound too bad I could wait six or seven months, but the marching season would be over by then so it would probably be the following year that I would get walking. I was sitting there plotting out my career as a bandsman when I glanced at my watch and was hit squarely in the face with the fact that staying for the main practice meant I was going to be out way past the time I'd agreed to be back in the house with my Ma, but I didn't care! Who the hell was I kidding?

My Ma would be waiting for me and give me a right "skelpin' for being out late. But from the moment Terry called the first tune and the bass drummer got the practice up and running, I was lost! Lost in the sights and sounds that was the main band practice. For the next 90 minutes I sat there, glued to my seat, I'd never heard anything like it in my life. Hearing the band at practice was so different to hearing them march on the street. They played tune after tune, there were so many I didn't know, in fact I'd never heard of half of them! There were notes being played that were just magical to me. They played so many different tunes, I thought, how on earth am I going to learn all these? There was a moment while the band was playing a tune called Dinah's Delight, it just grabbed me, well one note did, and that one note became my motivation, I wanted to be able to play that tune. I had a lot of work to do to get there but get there I would.

I didn't want the practice to end, I was really enjoying listening to the band. After the last tune finished Terry just said two words "the Queen" and with that everyone stood, not really knowing what was going on I stood up with everyone else. The band then played the national anthem and that was that, the main practice was over, flutes and drums were put away. Darren and I made our way to the door to leave.

"Alright Glenn, see you on Sunday again then?" Alvin said.

"Sunday?? You mean this happens more than once a week!"

Alvin, started to laugh, I was like a kid in a sweet shop, imagine getting to end the weekend with band practice. It would make waking up for school a little easier!

"Oh, I'll be here on Sunday alright just try and keep me away!"

"Good luck with your scale"

"Thanks, see you on Sunday then" Darren and I left the hall and headed home.

"Well what did you think of that Glenn?" asked Darren.

"I thought it was brilliant they sounded even better than they do when they're marching on the street, the only thing I'm worried about now, is my Ma, she was expecting me home earlier than this"

"Just tell her you were waiting on me 'cause you didn't want to walk down home on your own"

"Brilliant! You know that might just do it, good call mate" I relaxed a little, as having a good excuse for an angry parent is an essential skill, you need to have confidence in it, it helps with the convincing.

"Here, wee Alvin is dead on, isn't he?"

"Aye he is, his Da and brothers are dead on to, all the other guys are as well, once you get to know them"

"Aye there's some banter out of them"

"Mate you haven't heard the half of it, when they get going, I'm telling ye, the craic is ninety"

We picked up the pace and walked pretty quickly towards the Avenue, we needed to, well, I needed to. Getting home as quickly as possible for me was now the priority, knowing you were late with a reasonable excuse is ok, but you need to make sure you aren't taking the absolute piss out of the situation, that could have far reaching future consequences, like being grounded and I didn't want to be grounded now that I had joined the band.

We came around the corner and back on to Madrid Street, walking past the now closed chemist on the corner and then crossing over the road and past the railings of the other Rupert Stanley building located on Templemore Avenue, the streetlights that led the way to our homes were glowing a misty orange colour, almost like they had halo's. The streets were empty bar Darren and myself, "there wasn't a sinner out n about" as my Granny would have said. The streets looked and felt strangely peaceful, you'd never have guessed that the space just a few hundred yards away between our area and the Short Strand could turn into a war zone at any time. We stopped at the top of my street, Darren and I said our goodbyes and I headed for my house.

"See you tomorrow mate?"

"Aye I'll call for you when I've got in from school and make sure you're still alive" said Darren laughing. All I could hope for now was that my Ma would buy my excuse and maybe she would even be interested in hearing me play a note on my flute. After all she's the one that wants me to be the next James Galway. As I opened the gate and closed it behind me I paused before I took the three steps that would lead me into the hallway, I thought about the first time I had seen the Pride of the Raven walking up the Avenue and now here at the tail end of one of the best Thursday nights in my life I realised that I had just taken my first steps in a journey that would hopefully lead to me walking the streets of Belfast with them. As I closed the front door behind me, I noticed that the living room door was open. And a familiar voice responded to my late return home.

"Glenn? Is that you?"

Uh oh, here we go.

CHAPTER 3

A Temporary Break In Proceedings

T hursday and Sunday nights had now become band night, and I absolutely loved it, I loved heading up to the hall, meeting up with the guys and having a laugh. But, the best thing about it and what I loved the most was playing my flute and doing everything I could to try and get better. I hung on every word and piece of wisdom Terry shared with me and I was relentless in my efforts to put it all into practice. I was having the time of my life. However, there was also a sense of frustration lurking away in the background like a sniper waiting on its target. You see, I wasn't going to be in Belfast for the summer. This summer, instead of being able to enjoy the pinnacle of the marching season, I was off to visit my estranged biological father in Canada. I'm told he had left my Ma when I was very young, I'd never really known anyone else apart from the man in my house who was my Dad. Finding out that wasn't the case was a bit of a shock but, it didn't change much for me. To me, Tommy was my Da, well, because he was there all the time, and he did all the Dad things. So now it turns out I have two! This whole trip to Canada had come about as a result of a few 'behavioural' problems in my last year at primary school and I'd had a few sessions with a 'special doctor' to see why that was the case. So, after doing a few drawings, answering some weird questions, and getting out of school early to go to these wonderful sessions, the doctor decided that it was necessary for me to go to Canada and spend time with 'bio Dad' and that this would magically fix whatever the issue seemed to be. No wonder they called this doctor a "special doctor", anyone who can prescribe eight weeks in Canada to spend time with a man I don't really know, definitely has something special going on alright! Bio Dad's name was Michael, but for me Bio-Dad would do just fine for now - it has a super hero ring to it I think and his special power? Well that was easy, it was running away. Anyway, as a result of this little adventure I now would now be away for the whole of July and August, just when the band was going to be at its busiest and I'd completely miss the majority of marching season. I was really looking forward to seeing the band out on the road now that I had an inside view of everything, and I would get to say hi and wave to people from the street like I was a professional spectator! But it would also mean two whole months without playing my flute. Whenever the 'special one' had written the prescription, and I was asked if I was ok with this? The first thing that came into my mind I have to say was, "As long as I can take my flute I don't mind" it wasn't a massive request but you'd have thought I'd asked for the moon as a birthday present! "Glenn there's no way you're travelling all the way to Canada just to play a flute you know" Mum had a way of always stating the obvious.

"But Ma, if I was James Galway though and I had a concert to play, then that would be travelling all the way to Canada just to play the flute?"

"Don't you get smart with me young man, you're not James Galway and you're not going to play a concert, you know full rightly what I mean! Tommy back me up here" she turned to my Dad with a look that said you better agree with me here or else.

"Listen, your Mum's said no and that's the end of it ok?" He dutifully responded.

"Ok then"

Well that was that sorted. No more debate, no more talk of what was in my best interests which apparently was the reason behind this whole trip being arranged and, I'm guessing the reason why I was shipped off to see the 'special one' in the first place. Nope, that 'best interests' stuff was all out the window and now more importantly was the task of making sure to I had all new clothes to take out to Canada with me.

"We can't have Mike thinking you were dragged up, no son of mine is going out there looking like a gypsy!"

I'm not sure if my Ma meant I looked like a gypsy now, I gave myself a wee glance and thought, "I look ok, thank you very much" but I couldn't escape the fact that a few trips to the shops and some endless fussing awaited me.

All this had transpired just as I was just starting to make good progress with the flute. I was playing the full scale with ease, low, middle and high register. And whenever Terry was calling out notes to play from the scale, I was able to with no hesitation. I'd started to learn some tunes as well. The National Anthem, the Sash and the Lily O', the Boys of Derry and a few others. I had even started working on a march called Children's Love. The great thing about all that was that I could actually play along with some tunes in the main band practice rather than just listen all the time. Now there was going to be a big gap. Two months. Eight weeks. Sixty-two days. What if I forgot everything while I was away? What if I came back and it was like having to start all over again? What if I really would be my Dads age before I walked with the band? Well, now that there are two of them, I reckon I should just pick whoever is the youngest! And besides all that I hadn't even said to Terry yet that I would be missing a whole two months of practice, heading away to Canada, this summer was going to be absolutely shit! After all I had been there and done all this before.

I'd spent eight weeks in Canada, on Mayne Island off the coast of Vancouver, on one of those cross community, why don't we all just get along, holidays back when I was eight years old. I'd spent the time living with the Fitzgerald's, an Irish family who had adopted a young native Indian named Wayne, you couldn't get much more cross community than that now!

This was going to be different though, I had no idea what to expect, what if I didn't get on with this bio-Dad character? What if he was an absolute dickhead? Can you imagine being related to a dickhead? Anyway, in my mind I had bigger things to be worrying about, I was due to fly out to Toronto on the first of July.

The lead up to that final practice was frantic to say the least, my Ma was running around fussing over me, and we were still waiting on my Canadian passport arriving, it should have been here weeks ago, but we were assured it would be here in time for me to go. It was quite the palaver getting it sorted or so my Ma said anyway, we had to go and get special photos done at a studio and then there were these forms to fill in as well having to send off my weird looking birth certificate to the Canadian embassy in London. My birth certificate was nothing more than a plastic square about the size of a bus ticket. My Ma and brothers' birth certificates were massive compared to mine. It was nice to be different though, something that made you stand out, something unique. being the same as everyone is definitely overrated. We were waiting on the birth certificate coming back with the passport, so that it could go back into the secret safe keeping place that was the wardrobe in my Ma's bedroom. The passport arrived ironically on the day of my last band practice before heading away. Mum seemed to be very excited about the passport arriving, she was running around with it like it was the FA Cup or something.

"It's here, it's here" she kept saying. I was wondering if she was just glad to be getting rid of me for eight weeks and this was the moment confirming it was definitely happening. Whatever it was, it reinforced the fact that there was no turning back, Canada awaited my arrival. My list of things that needed to be done for going away was slowly but surely getting sorted. I say my list, it was my Ma's list, in reality I was just an innocent bystander in this operation.

Passport - done
New clothes - not yet
Suitcase packed - not yet
Tell band you're away - no!

Telling the band that I was heading away was definitely on my list, probably the only thing on my list and Thursday seemed to crawl up on me and smack me up the face with the realisation that I had to break the news. I trudged up to practice, my heart just wasn't in it and Terry knew, he just took one look at my lovely smiling face whenever he got me to through the scale.

"What's wrong big son? You look like you're at your own funeral for god sake "

"It's worse than that Terry, I have to go away for a few months"

"Tell me you haven't killed someone? You doing a Michael Corleone?" he said laughing.

"I'm away for the whole summer, I'm off to Canada for eight weeks"

"Why are you sad about that? That's brilliant so it is"

"What's brilliant about it? I'm gonna miss loads of practices and not see the band over the summer?"

"I know where I'd rather be kid, eight weeks in Canada instead of here, I'd be away like a shot, I'm telling ye"

"Really? Wouldn't you miss the band and the 12th 'n all?"

"Off course I would, but opportunities like this don't come along all the time Glenn, you need to make the most of it, the band will still be here when you get back"

"I'm just worried I'm gonna forget it all and when I'm back I'll have to start all over again"

"You won't ok?" You will remember it no problem. It's like riding a bike you never forget, you might wobble at first, but it will all come back to you, I promise"

"Thanks that makes me feel better"

Terry turned to Frankie and Alvin's Da Jim, "Here you wouldn't half know this one loves the band"

"Why what's up Terry?"

"He's worried about going to Canada for eight weeks because he'll miss practices and the twelfth"

"Is your head cut? We'd all jump at the chance of being in Canada for the summer"

"Better believe it mate, are you anywhere near Niagara Falls?" asked Jim

"Aye it's not that far away from where I'll be staying"

"Then what the hell are you worrying about, Niagara Falls instead of Derry's walls, I know where I'd rather be"

I really hadn't expected this kind of reaction, these guys all loved the band as much as I did, and yet here they were actually telling me to go away and spend the summer in Canada. Well didn't I just feel wanted, first my Ma and now the band, seriously like!

"Nice to be wanted 'n' all" I said.

"It's not about being wanted kid, we love having you in the band, but there is more to life than the band! We all have things that will take first place over it, the important thing is that we remember that the reason we are in the band goes beyond the band, what we believe and what we stand for will always be there kid, always, even though the faces in the band change, it will always be the Pride of the Raven"

"Jim give it a rest will ya? It's not like we are seeing the kid head off to war or something! Listen to you getting on like Winston Churchill"

We all started to laugh and that was that, weeks of me worrying about it and actually, I had nothing to be worried about. I went and sat down at my usual main practice seat beside Alvin.

"So, you're really away for eight weeks then?" Alvin asked as the laughing died down. Alvin and I had become good friends from pretty much whenever Terry had asked me to sit beside him the night, I had joined the band. Alvin was about my age and well we just seemed to get on. It's funny how you just click with some people, he was good craic and because he was a bit further on than me, I got to learn stuff from him as well.

"Yeah mate I am, away for eight weeks, it won't be long running in though, I'll be back before you know it. You're getting to talk the twelfth, I'm gonna have to wait a whole year before I can even think about that"

"I know, I know, it will be good to see you back though"

Well at least someone was going to miss me, even if it was just a wee bit. Practice was great, and I was playing along to tunes I could follow from the notes and the odd one I had memorised and as usual after playing the Queen, it was time to head home.

Walking home from the hall wasn't half as bad as walking up, and with everyone having wished me well for the trip, now all I'd have to survive would be the shopping trips with my Ma for clothes and everything. I could tell by the way she had been getting on that she was going to fuss over me like a wasp at a rubbish bin!

I wasn't wrong, for the next few days I was dragged around shop after shop after shop, looking at shorts, t-shirts, socks and summer footwear. Of course, she would have to buy things that would match so that I didn't look like a tramp! This went well beyond the usual new summer clothes expeditions that I was used to. I ended up just having to stand there while she held up clothes against me to see whether they would fit or not, which when you think about it is a pretty amazing skill for her or anyone to have. I often wondered if she applied this to her own clothes. But sure enough, everything that was hung up against me actually fitted! This skill obviously drained my Ma of any strength and energy she still possessed as I had to carry all the bags home!

"You're a big boy now and seeing as you're going off halfway round the world on your own, it won't do you any harm carrying a few bags"

I expect this will now be an excuse I'll be hearing quite frequently!

With the shopping done and everything on the list checked of, all I had to do was wait for the day I was leaving, Sunday the first of July. My flight was leaving at ten in the morning so we would need to be at the airport for eight o'clock, I might as well have been getting up for school, bloody great start to the holiday!! That morning was all go, between breakfast and the endless checking my bags and asking if I had my passport, we made our way to the airport in good time.

My Ma took me over to the airline desk to check in my bags and then we headed for the departure lounge, we said our goodbyes and that was that. As I walked into the waiting area I was accompanied by a lady from the airline, she was looking after me as I was travelling by myself, her uniform was crisp and bright and she smelled like she had come straight out of a perfume shop, she was very pleasant and seemed to have a permanent smile. About an hour or so later there was an announcement that the flight for Canada was boarding and she led me to the gate. I was taken right up to the front ahead of the assembling queue. Wow, VIP treatment here or what! She escorted me down a drab looking corridor, that led to the plane, as we reached the door we were greeted by two similarly dressed women who asked to see my boarding pass, the kind lady showed them mine and then stood back.

"One of my colleagues will be looking after you on the flight and then they will take you to meet your family at Toronto airport, ok?"

"Ok, that's great, thank you" she turned and walked away, the smell of her perfume lingered as I boarded and took my seat on the plane. I settled into my seat, taking in my surroundings, checking out the magazine in the seat pocket, hoking through my bag to make sure I had some snacks, I couldn't help but think that I would be missing lots of stuff at home, the first of July parade, the bonfire at the top of the street and of course the Twelfth. I didn't have time for much thought though as the Captains voice come out of nowhere.

"Crew prepare for take off"

It took a bit of time for the plane to reach the runway, pausing before accelerating at immense speed, the world whizzing past then seeming to slow down as the plane lifted off the ground and Belfast began to fade away. I was now on my way to Toronto, then onward to St Catharines, my city of birth for the whole summer...

"Ladies and gentlemen, this is your captain speaking, we are making our final descent into Belfast, please return to your seats fasten your seatbelt and return your tray tables to the upright position. We expect to be landing in twenty minutes, the weather currently in Belfast is dry with a temperature of five degrees. On behalf of the flight deck and cabin crew today may I take this opportunity to thank you for flying with Air Canada and wish you all a pleasant journey onward."

In twenty minutes, two whole months away from my family and friends was about to come to an end. I'd had an interesting experience meeting Mike, I had met cousins I didn't know I had, I met my godparents and, I had even met my two sisters, Sherry and Miranda. I'd went on my first rollercoaster at MarineLand, and got soaked by a killer whale, I'd been to an amazing water park and to the world famous Crystal Beach and rode the Comet rollercoaster, forwards and backwards I might add, thank god no one had told me there had been accidents on that thing or I'd never have got on it! I'd rode the Great Canadian Minebuster at Canada's Wonderland, I had also been to see my very first baseball game, going to watch the Toronto Blue Jays was just awesome. I may have picked a little phrase or two up from the Canadian side of the family! I reminded myself that I'd need to knock that on the head though when I met up with my mates! There was so much more of me in Canada than I first thought, I mean I knew I was Canadian, but I didn't know just how much family I had living there. Suddenly there was a side of my life that wasn't as close as everything in Belfast was. I was excited to be coming home though, to see my Ma, my Da, my brothers and my friends. I was also coming home start a new school, and of course I was coming home to the band. I couldn't wait to get to practice and get caught up with everything.

"Crew prepare for landing" came the voice over the intercom and looking outside my window I could see the city passing beneath me so quickly and effortlessly, I mean I've lived in Belfast for ages and never seen it all, not like I was seeing it now from the vantage point of an aeroplane window. It actually looked like a city, well in comparison to Toronto it was tiny, but everything looks different with a new perspective. The plane landed and with a screech of the brakes and taxi to the terminal, my eight weeks away from home had come to an end. There was some robotic shuffling to retrieve hand luggage from the overhead storage. Everyone seemed to be in a hurry even though the exits hadn't even been opened yet. I waited for a space to open up in the aisle for me to join the queue and leave the plane then make my way to get my suitcase. My Ma had bought me a new leather case for going away and I pretty much lived out of it the whole time I was away. It was returning a little heavier than when it left, with presents and my new prize possession a Toronto Blue Jays replica jersey, it might not have been the latest Rangers top, but it was still red white and blue, well it was sky blue with some red and white, minor details and besides no one here in Belfast would have anything like it! Standing at the baggage reclaim area I watched the bags begin to go around, and there was no sign of mine, yet. I started to worry a little. I had checked four similar bags, and was told to leave them alone by other people obviously concerned as me about getting their luggage back. Then suddenly there it was just dropping onto the carousel, I ran up towards it and grab it just as someone else's hands were about to.

"I think you'll find that's mine" said the stranger.

"Really, that's funny because it has my name and address on it"

"Oh sorry, it looks very like mine"

"No worries, there's about four that look the same, I did the same thing a minute ago, hope you find yours" I lifted the bag made my way to arrivals and my awaiting family.

One thing I noticed since arriving back was the ever so slight change in temperature. I mean it was absolutely freezing, and the other thing that was significantly standing out for me was the harshness of the Belfast accent that just seemed to be coming from everywhere around me. I'd never noticed that before, it actually took me back a bit. Do I actually sound like that? But then my eyes were drawn to party of five standing a few hundred yards in front of me, Mum, Dad, my two brothers and my Big granny were standing there waiting on me. The first thing that came to my mind was, whose knee am I sitting on for the drive home?

I was happy to see everyone again and it took a whole five minutes to catch up with everyone about what had happened while I was away. The drive home from Belfast International airport, which incidentally isn't actually in Belfast, took us through the hills and past Nutt's Corner Market.

"I hear they are doing a good deal on Rangers tops up in the market, maybe we will go up this Sunday Glenn what do you think?" My Mum said.

"Aye we could do that, but it might be last year's top Ma, as they are bringing out a new one for this season"

"Seriously? Do they think people are made of money?"

"I don't know Ma, but we can go and have a look, sure you always find a wee bargain when you're up there anyway"

"Right enough you do, the wee run will be great, sure what else would you be doing on a Sunday?"

She turned to my Granny, "Do you want to come with us Mum for the run?"

"Aye sure why, not, maybe Tommy will wanna come as well"

This was great and everything, but when I arrived back to the house and went to my room the first thing I looked for was my flute! I had hidden it away amongst my treasured possessions to make sure that no one found it or tried to mess about with it, I'd even went to the trouble of placing a badge inside the leather pouch in such a way that I would know if someone had been snooping! To my relief everything was as I had left it and there it was my flute. I quickly put it together. Now for the moment of truth, I hesitated just for a moment, before raising the flute, what if my fears were realised? Had two months away really had caused degenerative flute disease? My hands just seemed to naturally slide into the G note position, my pinky on the right hand instinctively opening the D key, I brought the flute up to my mouth and as if no time had passed at all, that clean crisp note sound came out the flute and I was playing the national anthem. Amazing, not only had I remembered what to do, but I was playing the tune without my notes in front of me! What on earth was going on here?

Just then a familiar gulder came from the landing. "Glenn!! Put that flute away, you're only back for god's sake, c'mon your Granny is still here you know"

Not wanting to risk the wrath of my Ma, given that I was indeed only back, I decided that it was ok to comply, "Right Ma, I'm coming down now" I carefully took my flute apart and put it back in its pouch and placed it pride of place on the slightly battered chest of drawers beside my bed. I couldn't wait to get back to practice.

"Glenn, come on, we haven't got all day you know, your Granny wants to see you in your new school uniform"

"What new school uniform?" I said to myself, I hadn't been out with my Mum to get it yet. This could only mean one thing, my Granny had actually gone out and bought the new uniform for me and now I had to try it on. And that would mean a trip to Stanley Brooks' shop down near the Conn Club to get things changed, if it didn't fit. Stanley Brooks is a funny shop, how that man finds anything in that shop is beyond me, it's just clothes everywhere, even outside the shop he has clothes hanging off the window grills but ask him for a size twenty eight in maroon straight leg trousers with a wee pocket on the rear, and he'll find it them in about 30 seconds flat. I walked into the living room to find the school uniform discussion was still taking place.

"He'll need new shoes as well Isabel won't he? my Granny said.

"He will, he'll need something that's gonna last him, although his feet are still growing"

"I don't know who he takes that after, none of our side have big feet"

"I know his Da didn't have big feet either"

"Well we can take him down the road and see what we can find, and sure we always have the market on Sunday if we don't get anything"

"Right well that's that sorted, where is that wee lad anyway? GLENN!!"

"I'm standing right here Ma"

"Right, here's what's hap…."

Taking my life in my hands, I interrupt quickly "We are going down the road tomorrow to look for shoes and if we don't get anything, we can get something at the market on Sunday"

"Yes, but don't interrupt me when I'm talking to you"

"Aye son don't be doing that, that's not nice" said my Granny

"But I was standing right here when you said it"

"Still, you shouldn't interrupt"

"So, are we gonna try this uniform on?"

"Yes, where's them bags you brought up with his uniform in them"

"I left them over there by the dinner table, Glenn son bring them over and we can see what it's like on"

The next hour was spent trying on everything my Granny had bought, she'd went to the trouble of buying two of every-thing just in case, the whole thing started with Mum holding the clothes up against me, it wouldn't be getting new clothes without this ritual. So in between 'try this with these shirts' and 'go and get last year's school shoes just so we have an idea about what it will look like', I honestly felt like I was in a pantomime version of 'Are you being served' I resisted an "I'm free" for fear of the two women who were pulling and prying at this school uniform and preparing me for one of the big-gest days of my life, giving me a good slap. I hope they don't fuss over me in my band uniform like this I thought to myself. We didn't find suitable shoes on the road, but on the Sunday trip to the market, we found a nice pair of Dr Marten shoes complete with yellow line coloured stitching. Mum and my Granny were well pleased and that's all that mattered, if they liked them then all was right in the world, and we never even looked for Rangers tops!

We weren't long back home from the market, when Colin and Darren arrived at the door.

"You coming out mate?"

"Aye, where are we going?"

"Well Romeo here has got himself a girlfriend, she lives just of the Lisburn Road"

"Anywhere near Windsor Park"

"Not that far up but not too far away from there"

"That will mean getting two red buses won't it?"

"Aye, but we should be alright"

"Yeah there won't be anybody about the town most likely"

"I dunno, I always hear people saying that you need to careful in the town on Sundays, you could end up getting a beatin' or a chase from the taigs at the Markets"

"Have you got money for the bus?"

"Aye I have a few quid here that my Granny gave me for coming home from Canada"

"Good time then?"

"Aye mate it was great, so it was"

"Right away and tell your Ma, you're heading out with us, we'll wait for you down at the club gates"

I popped my head in through the door and shout, "I'm away out here Ma with Darren and Colin alright?"

"Alright don't be going too far away now"

"Alright" and with that I left the house, not closing the gate behind me and sprinted down the street to catch up with Colin and Darren.

We dandered past my Granny's house, I waved to my Granda who was standing just outside his front door. "Where you off to son?"

"Just heading out with Colin and Darren, Granda"

"You's two make sure you look after him now?"

"No problem Mr. Stothers we'll look after him"

"Don't be getting in any trouble now, don't give those peelers any excuse to have a go at ya"

"No bother Granda, right c'mon we don't wanna miss the bus here"

We ran up to the top of Tower Street, onto the Newtownards road, turned right and walked past the butchers and arrived at the bus stop just outside Walker's sweet shop.

"What number of bus do we need to get then?"

"Anyone that comes along here will get us into the town"

"I know that you eejit, but after that, what do we need to get?

"I think we need to get the 59 on the other side of the city hall"

"Really, we may hope there's one there when we arrive, 'cause I don't fancy standing around the town for any length of time"

"What's wrong?, scared of running into a few taigs are we?

"A few is alright if you're talking like three, any more than that and we are fucked, that's all I'm saying."

"The town'll be empty, stop worrying"

"I'm not worried, I'm just saying"

"Right have we all got money just in case"

"Just in case what?"

"In case my best double dinger doesn't work, that's what!"

"Ah right, and just what is a double dinger?"

"It's a used bus ticket that you just keep trying to use, you double ding it"

"And does that work?"

"Most of the time it does, you get the odd driver that will check"

"Right so let's see this famous ticket then"

Darren reached into his pocket and pulled out his wallet, "Fuck, I don't have any of my tickets with me!"

"Brilliant, so how are we gonna double ding now dickhead?

"You mean to say we have been here all this time and you hadn't even checked you'd your tickets with ye?"

"Well we have been standing here for a while and there's no sign of a bus, I'll run back and get them, just make sure you wait for me, alright?"

Darren sped off before Colin or me could say anything, "What's he like?" said Colin, "He'd forget his head if it wasn't screwed on"

I just shrugged my shoulders, there was no way I was getting dragged into this, these two were related and the last thing you want to do in this situation is even think about taking sides like.

Colin and I were standing there at the bus stop wondering if

Darren would make it back in time, Colin broke the silence - "I'm telling ye there'll be two buses coming along here in a minute and then we will be stuck waiting here another hour before we get one, I've gotta meet her in an hour or so."

"You never know mate he's a fast-enough runner"

"Aye, but he didn't need to go and get them, we have money"

Almost simultaneously Colin and I both looked to the right and sure enough there are two buses pulling up at the lights on the Templemore Avenue and Newtownards Road junction.

"See, I bloody told you this would happen! But oh no he has to be the big lad using his favourite double dinger, well I'm not waiting, I'm getting on this bus and that's it"

"What? I think we would be better waiting mate, three of us is better than two in the town"

"Well we can try and stall the driver for a minute, but I'm still going"

Colin stood at the bus stop as the lights turned green and the buses started making their way towards our stop, I walked the short distance to the top of Tower Street to see if I could see Darren coming.

"There's no sign of him Colin"

"Right c'mon then, we'll just have to go without him"

I knew this was a bad idea, but Colin was a champion boxer, if there was any fighting to be done it might as well be with him around. We bounced onto the bus and gave the driver our money and he gave us those lovely pink bus tickets and we looked around for some seats and we were immediately met with disappointment.

"Ah fuck! Spangle seats, I hate those seats"

There were two different type of bus seats, nice soft seats which were obviously comfortable and then there were spangle seats. Spangle seats looked like a sweet called spangles, funnily enough, these seats were hard plastic with an arse groove, you'd be better standing than sitting on these bloody things, they were horrible. We made our way up to the back of the bus and took up a two seat place each. The bus that had been behind this one had already went ahead seeing as this one had stopped. There was still no sign of Darren, the bus pulled away and was just going past Westbourne church when we looked behind us and saw Darren arriving like speedy Gonzales at the bus stop, the penny dropped pretty quickly that we had went on without him.

"There's Darren now!" I shouted.

Colin ran down the aisle to talk to the bus driver to see if there was any chance that he would stop at the next bus stop to let Darren get on, I started motioning to Darren out the window, like Lionel Blair on 'Give us a clue', to go to the next stop, I heard the bus driver saying.

"If there's no one at the stop, I'm not stopping"

Colin's protests fell on deaf ears and we ended up just waving and shrugging our shoulders as Darren faded into the distance and we crossed the imaginary line that separated us from the Short Strand and now made our way past the chapel and on into the town. Once the bus passed the chapel it would usually only stop in one more place before heading round to the side of the City Hall. Luckily with today being Sunday there were no more stops until the City Hall, as we were leaving Colin asked the driver where he would get a 59, the bus driver told him that we could get on the other side of the city hall. We made our way across to where the bus stop was, keeping an eye out all around us, we needed to be on our guard here. We arrived at the bus stop and thankfully there was nobody there.

"Told you, nothing to worry about" Colin stated as a matter of fact.

"Aye, but there's no buses here either mate"

We had been waiting at the stop for about five minutes when this bloke in a denim jacket arrived and stood beside us. Initially he didn't say anything, he was observing bus stop stranger protocol. He broke protocol a minute or so later "Been waiting long?" This took us a little by surprise, Colin and I just looked at each other, then Colin said. "Not long"

"Where ya' headed then?"

"Same direction as you if you're waiting on the same bus"

He laughed then said "Where ya from then?"

That was it for me, I didn't like this at all. We didn't answer but he followed up quickly with, "Nice top mate, interesting colours".

I had decided to wear my new Toronto Blue Jays top not thinking this would cause any issues. But essentially the colours were red white and blue, so with our wonderful small-minded communities this may not have been the wisest idea I'd ever had, but there was no time for regret now.

"I don't think there'll be a bus here for ages, maybe we should try and find another mate" I said to Colin, now getting a little fearful. Luckily Colin agreed.

"Aye that might be a good idea"

As we headed back towards the side of the City Hall we had got off the bus, the stranger at the bus stop shouted, "You're prods aren't ye?"

That was the invitation for Colin and me to start walking just a little but quicker, I took another glance over my shoulder, and behind us at the bus stop now stood a crowd of about twenty wee lads.

"Where the fuck did they come from?"

"I don't have a clue, but we need to get out of here"

They were now beginning to run towards us led by the bus stranger in the denim jacket

"Run Colin it's the taigs!" I shouted and we both broke into a frantic sprint.

"Get the orange bastards!" came the roaring cry from behind us. Colin and I bolted for the bus stops on the other side of the city hall, glancing over our shoulders making sure we weren't about to be swarmed and caught. We made it over to the bus stops and there was a number 21 just sitting there, thank God for that, this would get us home. The driver had obviously seen us running for the bus and then seen the crowd chasing behind us, so what does this wonderful human being decide to do? Well doesn't he just decide that it's time for him to leave and not take us with him! We skidded up to the side of the bus, banging on the folding doors and shouting for him to let us in, through the glass he told us to "fuck off!!" By this time our chasing horde had made their way right over to where we were, "If this bus driver doesn't help us, we are going to get a serious hammering!". Thinking quickly, I lifted up the round steel flap to the right of the folded doors and grabbed the emergency door handle, lifting it upwards, the bus ground to a stop and the doors swung open.

"Get off the bus, I don't want you on it" came the humanitarian cry from the bus driver.

"Ack mate come on" I shouted in desperation, "They're gonna kill us for fuck sake"

I stepped up onto the second step that lead to the bus cabin and the orange ticket machine, Colin had managed to make his way onto the first step. In complete desperation I just started throwing coins in the general direction of the driver as payment for the desperately required bus journey home, pleading with the driver "Come on mate, help us out here"

Just as I was saying this two of the chasing pack had now reached the bus and had grabbed Colin by the arm, Colin was trying his best to hold onto the chrome rails on the bus doors to keep himself from being dragged out. So, after sort of paying the driver, I turned around toward the open door trying to help Colin out. We both started throwing punches and kicks towards the people in front of us, and after a somewhat frantic exchange, we had hit them hard enough to make them let go and we made our way on to the bus. The driver wisely closed the doors and started to speed off while the rest of the horde began banging loudly on the side of the bus, spitting on the windows and calling Colin and I all the names of the day and politely stating what they would have done to us if we hadn't got away. Colin and I moved on up the bus aisle to find some seats. A few rows from the back there were some free seats, looking down at them, I was met with a sight causing major disappointment.

"Ack for fuck sake!"

"What? What's wrong?"

"Spangle seats again"

"Mate, right now I couldn't care less! I'm just glad to be on the bus we could have got emptied there"

"That was close" I said as both of us slumped down on to a spangle seat.

"Too close" replied Colin, "What were you thinking of wearing that top?"

"What are you talking about? It's a baseball team for crying out loud, the Blue Jays aren't exactly the UVF"

"It's still our colours though isn't it?"

"Ack c'mon you, it's sky blue, navy and white, the only red on it is a Canadian maple leaf, it's not like I'm wearing a union jack or a red hand of Ulster"

"That doesn't mean anything to them bastards"

Conceding to Colin's logic, I agreed, "Yeah, you're right, well at least we got away"

"Just about" he reiterated "If we had waited any longer, we'd be dead"

The bus continued its journey and we just sat on our spangle seats watching the world go by as we headed for home. Now, on our way back we would have to head past the Short Strand, and getting off at the stop near Pitt Park, so we wouldn't have to worry about an encounter with the other side. We saw the Pitt park stop appear in the distance and got up. Making our way towards the front of the bus, Colin pressed the button to alert the driver we were getting off. The driver said nothing to us as we went down the steps onto the street. The bus drove off, its engine sound growing quieter as it disappeared into the distance. We crossed the road towards Westbourne church and took a right on to the lower part of Tower Street. Saunter-ing back up towards my house, Colin and I had hardly spoken a word to each other since we had got off the bus. I know I was thinking about what could have happened if we hadn't got away, I'm pretty sure Colin was as well. I decided to break the silence as anything was better than replaying what happened over and over in my head, "Here, wait 'til Darren hears about this"

Colin seemed to appreciate the break in silence as he re-sponded sarcastically "Oh don't start, he'll tell us that we should have waited, and it wouldn't have happened if we had used his best double dinger!!"

"Aye like a bus ticket would have been much use against that lot, stand back or I'll double ding you!". We both laughed although not really sure if we should be. After five minutes or so, we arrived at my house. There were times when I have been out and I didn't want to go home, this wasn't one of those times. Right now, I would be glad of the familiarity it pro-vided, knowing that regardless of what happened to me else-where I'd always be safe here. Turning towards Colin as I took the latch of the brown painted wooden gate I said "Alright mate, I'll probably see you tomorrow"

Colin's tone was somewhat negative as he replied "I've got boxing training tomorrow"

Slightly confused by this I said, "Aye but I'll see you at school first surely?"

Realisation seemed to hit Colin straight away as his expression and tone changed immediately "Oh aye, you're a wee first year now aren't ya? Then I'll see you tomorrow, watch your back though, first years can get messed about rightly on their first day".

Now it was my turn for a negative tone "Really? After today I think I fancy my chances" I said laughing nervously.

Colin's response was far from encouraging "Well don't say I didn't warn ya, see ya tomorrow mate" and with that he headed on up towards Madrid Street and home.

"See you tomorrow" I said as I reached out towards the door handle, and walked through the hall door, I closed it behind me, happy for once to hear my Ma say "Is that you in Glenn?"

"Aye Ma, that's me in"

"Just in time for your tea, away and wash your hands"

"No problem Mum, I'll be straight down after"

I did exactly what I said I'd do, and Mum looked kind of confused, obviously not used to this level of compliance .

"Are you feeling alright?"

"Just happy to be home, Mum, just happy to be home"

CHAPTER 4

The List

With the incident on the bus well behind me, I drew comfort from the fact that band practice wasn't that far away, it would be great to get back to it, but until then, a new trauma awaited me, Orangefield Boys High School. Having been subjected to an impromptu uniform fitting on my return from Canada and the obligatory trip to Stanley Brooks for more trousers and a blazer. Not to mention how many pairs of shoes I tried on at McManus' shoe shop, Mum had decided I needed a second pair of shoes, just in case I wrecked the Dr Martens. I was almost kitted out for secondary school. I still needed a school badge for my blazer, I wondered why we didn't get one with the blazer. My Ma said something about waiting on a letter from the school, I didn't pay much attention, all I knew was at some point I'd get dragged down to Stanley Brooks again. There were quite a few people from my Primary 7 class who were going to Orangefield and I wondered if any of them would be in my class at secondary school or would I be walking into a room full of strangers? A few days after shopping for the school uniform, my Ma had got the letter she was waiting for with information about what else I needed for school and to let me know what class and house I was in, and where to go on my first day. As she read it out to me the whole thing seemed interesting, until it mentioned about getting the right badge for the uniform. There were four houses, each had a colour associated with them, everyone was sorted into a house and there were competitions and events throughout the school year for these coloured groupings of pupils. I had been assigned to Stewart house, so not only did it carry the shame of being named after a supermarket, to make matters even worse, my house colours were green! I was going to have a tricolour on my blazer, green white and gold on my school uniform, wasnt that just great? Mum said it would be too small to really stand out. I wouldn't be able to look at my blazer without it standing out, something would have to be done about this. I couldn't be knocking about my area with those colours.

All this preparation couldn't have been more different from primary school. Everything was different, I was used to leaving the house ten minutes before school started and still getting there on time. Now I'd have to take a bus and then walk. I had two options of bus having sussed this out from Darren and Colin who both went to Orangefield. The 76 Gilnahirk bus would take me through Clarawood Estate, where there was a gate to the school and a path down a hill passing sports grounds to the main school building. The 76 left from the Albertbridge Road, not that far away from my house, it was closer than the other option, to take a 32 up the Castlereagh Road. This would have meant a longer walk to get to school, and you would run into pupils from Grosvenor, the somewhat posher, snooty education establishment neighbours. I'd be leaving the house earlier now, to get the eight o'clock or twenty past eight bus to school, anything later than that and you'd be pushing it to get in on time. I was now the proud owner of my very own bus ticket, eight journey's on one ticket wasn't enough to get you through the week, so no doubt I would get my own favourite double dinger at some point, although from what Darren and Colin told me most people tend to walk home and only use the bus home if it's raining so you could almost get two weeks from a ticket.

The big day finally arrived, the first day of secondary school, I got up, got washed and put my uniform on, I needed a little help with the tie, but apart from that it actually looked ok. After the obligatory photo for Mum, I was on my way, not without my Ma checking and double checking I had everything.

"You know what bus stop to go to?"

"Yes Ma, and I know what number of bus to get"

"Have a good day"

"I will"

And with that me and my new school bag headed up towards Madrid Street and made the walk to the bus stop. "Have a good day she says, it's Monday and I'm off to school, what's so good about that?"

I rounded the corner of Templemore Avenue at the Albertbridge Road junction, and headed past Mountpottinger Methodist, the bus stop was only a few yards away, now. I was looking to see if there was anyone there that I knew, at first glance it didn't seem like there was. The only thing I had in common with crowd at the bus stop was the school uniform. No one was really talking, apart from a few clusters of lads, who obviously knew each other. I was trying to work out who they were, I hadn't seen any of them, and thought, where did these guys come from. I'm hanging around these streets all the time and have never clapped eyes on any of this lot before! Just then my mates Darren and Colin came round the corner, I was glad to see a few friendly faces, at first they didn't speak to me, probably some weird let's not talk to first years thing. But eventually they dandered up and said hello. We stood talking for a couple of minutes and then another familiar face came around the corner, Stirling, he had been in my P7 class at Beechfield and lived around the corner from me, on Templemore Avenue, which is funny, we said that about everyone, this is so and so, they live around the corner from me, far from true but everyone seemed to know what you meant.

"You want me to ding you on Glenn" Darren said.

"I'm alright mate," I replied "I've my ticket here"

"Why waste a journey on your first day, I'll ding you on, no probs"

"Aye why not, thanks"

I never really thought about it until, there was movement at the stop and everyone gravitated toward the silver pole with the red 'Citybus' bus stop sign at the top.

"Here's the bus now" Colin said as he made his way toward the pole like everyone else. Now without too much hassle a line formed pretty much in the order we had arrived at the bus stop. I doubt this happens all the time though. I stood with Darren and Stirling was just behind me.

"You must have plenty of journeys on your ticket if your dinging me on Darren"

"I've got my favourite..."

"Double dinger with you..." I finished Darren's sentence for him as the penny finally dropped, Darren was going to use the ticket that could have saved us from a beating in the town. My first day at school and I was being dragged into deception for free bus journeys.

"Right you go in front of me and just tell the driver I'm dinging you on, ok?"

"Ok" I said sheepishly, what if this didn't work? What if the driver checked the ticket? Imagine getting threw off the bus on your first day at school?

The bus pulled up, the doors opened, and the queue started making its way onboard. I went in front of Darren like he said, spoke to the driver and said, "My mate's dinging me on here," the bus driver looked thrilled to have been served that piece of information, he just nodded in the direction of the seats as if to say, "I don't care, just go and sit down"

Within seconds Darren walked up and took a seat behind me, he was obviously a dab hand at this.

"Stick with me kid and I'll have that bus ticket of yours lasting you months"

Laughing at this, the bus started filling up and Colin took the seat beside me, Stirling was sitting on the seats opposite and within minutes we were on our way. I'd never taken a bus in this direction before, I'd only ever taken the bus to go into the town. We headed down the Albert and stopped a few times on the way down and more lads got on the bus in Orangefield uniforms. It wasn't long before the bus was pretty much full and anyone getting on now was choosing to stand and hold onto what looked like boots straps hanging from the roof of the bus. Some older folks getting on the bus threw dirty looks at all of us, obviously raging that they couldn't get a seat with a load of schoolboys on the bus. There was a considerable level of noise on the bus, groups of friends talking, some new friends being made and the obligatory taking the piss out of other people on the bus. After a few more stops it seemed like the bus was only stopping to let people off now and we made our way up towards the Sandown Road, turning right and then after quite a long straight turned right again and we were heading for Clarawood estate.

"Won't be long now 'til we have to get off, two more stops now" said Darren as the bus chugged along slowly now as the hill was making it hard work for the engine.

Some people stood up to get off, I made a move to get up, Darren said "Just wait they're getting off early", and once we had moved off from that stop, we made our way forward. Well, most of us did, a few older lads seemed to be keeping a smaller lad in his seat, Darren and Colin were laughing, seeing me look back they said,

"It's a first year, the fun is just beginning"

What on earth was going on here. "I'm a first year" I said.

"Yeah we know, don't say it too loudly now"

"What's gonna happen to that wee lad?"

"He's gonna be late for school" they laughed

One of the older guys stood at his seat as the rest of us filed out the door, then at the last minute, he bolted and jumped of the bus, the first year had a look of shock on his face through the bus window as the driver closed the door and moved away from the stop.

Some of the older boys were waving and singing cheerio to him as the bus rounded the corner out of sight.

"Where's the next stop then?" I asked.

"Not that far away at all"

"It's just a wee rake, he won't be that late"

They dandered off laughing and I wondered what else would be in store for some unsuspecting first years today and would I be on the receiving end?

We walked down a path between two rows of houses and at the end was a gate, this led to a steep hill banked by grass and there were all weather football pitches on either side at the bottom of the path. The school buildings were in the distance, cars were coming into the car park and in the distance, there was the faint outline of Grosvenor Grammar school. This was where rich kids and smart Alec's who passed their eleven plus went, and they played rugby and hockey! Apparently the only thing it had going for it according to Darren was that it was a mixed school. There was Orangefield boys and Orangefield girl's schools, separate but right beside each other. Darren said if we wanted to see girls we would have to sneak across the pipeline, whatever that meant. I was sure I'd find out soon enough.

"Do you know what class you're in and where you have to go?"

"I'm in 1NJ"

"Ah big Janty's class, he's down in the science corridor, down the stairs from where my form room is, I'll show you how to get there"

"Great, appreciate that mate"

We walked past the bike sheds which were to the rear of two five a side football pitches and went right again and the car park came into view. To the left was the extension and on our right was the old school. My form class was in the old school, Stirling's was in the extension. I said I'd look out for him at lunch and the way home and with that he headed up the steps to the extension as I headed toward the main school entrance. We entered through the glass doors and we were met with a large open area, on the right was the school office and the Principals office. To the left where two sets of wooden doors that led to the assembly hall. Directly in front of us at the end of a tiled area of floor was a staircase with a water fountain to one side and a corridor of classrooms on the other. There was another corridor that ran along the other side of the assembly hall. This is where Darren left me as he pointed me in the direction of where I needed to go and where the classroom, I was looking for was. He went up the stairs toward his form room and now I was on my own again. I walked down the corridor, there was a strange hint of something in the air, I had no idea what it was, given this was the science corridor it could have been anything, as I walked towards what would be my form class room for the next ten months, it smelt like a mixture of gas and matches, in my head that wasn't a good mix! As I made my way further down the corridors my left hand side flanked by classrooms with glass that went from head height to the high ceiling and on my right by benched seating areas and what looked some sort of half grilled cage. There was already a group of boys hanging outside the classroom Darren had told me about. This was my class. I glanced around trying to find a familiar face, but there were absolutely none. Just then a man in a beige suit walked toward us, he seemed to appear out of nowhere and I guess we figured he was a teacher when he told us to "Think about forming a line boys and look like you're here to go to school" that was all the persuasion we needed to form a line at the classroom door. The man walked past us, his glasses on the bridge of what was a pretty big nose. There were some confused looks in the line, what the hell was that all about? We didn't dare move though, so we just waited patiently inline for whoever would open the classroom door and allow us to enter the class and begin our secondary education. It was then that I heard some familiar voices, I couldn't quite place where they were coming from, the sound of school shoes on the stairs gave their position away, and within moments Darren, Colin and two other lads came off the stairs towards our newly formed line, and they made a bee line for me.

"Alright lads" I said as they came can closer, feeling confident as my class now know, I've older friends at school. I should have known something was amiss whenever they didn't respond to anything I had said.

"Alright Glenn, welcome to your first day at Orangefield" said Darren mischievously and then proceeded to pull me out of the line, and Colin took pleasure in helping him. They dragged me into one of the cage-like seating areas at the side of the corridor and along with the two other older lads with them, they proceeded to kick and punch me until I was lying on the ground. This really took me by surprise, I hadn't expected to get a beating on my first day at school. As I lay on the floor, I instinctively brought my arms up to protect my face and my knees to protect my stomach, and they just kept laying into me. Then the bell sounded and as if it was signifying the end of a round of boxing, Darren and the rest of my welcoming committee stopped their introduction to secondary school life, Darren helped me up, and put me back in the line. Everyone in the line for my class were just looking at me and you could tell they were glad not to be on the receiving end of that, but there were a few who had a look of suspicion towards me. Who was this wee lad that had just got beaten up? What had he done to deserve that? As Darren politely helped me straighten my tie and blazer and dusted me down a bit, he ruffled my hair and said, "Make, sure you sit with us at dinner time alright? See ya later mate" and with that he ran off back in the direction of the stairs and out of sight. What an introduction to secondary school life. Now I was back in line, the man that had told us to think about forming the line reappeared from out of the classroom door. How the hell did he get in there after walking past us? And is this our form teacher? Look at how tall this fucker is, I thought to myself. Everyone else must have been thinking the same thing as we all strained our necks to look up at him. He just stood to the side and motioned with his arm for us to enter the class, we duly obliged. Now that we had entered the class, we had another big decision to make, where to sit. This could make or break the year, as we walked in there were six large tables with seats all round them, and the tables were adorned with very small taps, some of my new class mates started playing with them. The teacher made an announcement to not play with the taps unless we wanted gassed. I made my way across to the front table on the opposite side of the room to the door and I noticed a familiar face, someone who had went to my Sunday school, I sat down beside him, "Alright?"

"Aye, you"

"I'm alright too"

"I'm Stephen" that rang a bell now that he had said it. "But most people call me Moorsey"

"I'm Glenn, most people just call me, Glenn"

We both fake laughed at that, it wasn't funny, but I really didn't know what else to say.

"So what was the score with those guys that trailed you out of the line earlier" curiosity had obviously go the better of him, the gaze of others around the table turned to me as they were seemingly about to get the answer to what they had all been thinking.

"Ack they're mates of mine"

"Mates?"

"Aye Darren and I are in the same band"

Two other lads at the table seemed interested in that little tit-bit of information.

One of them asked me "So what band are you in then?"

I turned to see who was asking and said "Pride of the Raven"

"Flute?"

"Yeah"

"Me too, I play with the UVF band, I'm Junior by the way"

"Alright, Junior, how long you been with them then?"

"Few years now, didn't always play the flute though"

"Like my mate Alvin then, cymbals and then the flute?"

"Aye, same here"

Then another voice joined the conversation "I play flute as well, with the Pride of Down, I'm Fergie"

"Alright Fergie", I said. There was me thinking school was going to be shit and there's three people in my class who play the flute in bands.

The fact that these guys were in my class and at my table was great, I relaxed a bit, thinking this really might not be so bad after all. School became routine, the bus, the timetable, the walk home. Although sometimes I got the bus home, it was always a bit livelier that the journey to school in the morning. There was always a good crowd on the bus, and a mixture of year groups, the smokers always used to sit down the back of the bus, apparently it was easier to smoke down there, god knows why like. There was always some serious raking going on, and it got quite noisy on the bus and sometimes we got a grumpy bus driver who would tell us to shut up, no one ever listened. One time as we were getting the bus home, the raking was particularly bad, someone's hood on their coat had caught fire from a flicked feg butt and had started to go up in smoke. The person didn't even realise that their coat was on fire. Surprisingly nobody said anything until it was looking like it could get dangerous and then someone said to the lad.

"Here your coat's on fire" he near shit a brick, and I have to admit it was funny watching him try to get his coat off as fast as he could and put it out. The bus driver didn't see the funny side of it though. The bus started to speed up and everyone noticed.

"This guy must be on his last trip of the day; he's really motoring here" I thought.

We knew something was amiss when a few people got up and pressed the bell button to indicate they wanted off at the next stop, they went to the middle doors of the bus, but the bus driver just kept on going.

"Here bus driver, that was my stop!"

"Cry me a river kid, I've had enough of you lot raking about" came the bus drivers angry retort.

"What the hell! You can't do that, you have to let us off"

"I don't have to do anything of the sort, let's see how you all like getting left off at the Short Strand depot"

That really put the wind up us. Conversations sprang up everywhere across the bus.

"Is he serious?"

"We'll get hammered if he boots us of in the Short Strand"

"He won't, he's only trying to scare us"

That was what we were all hoping, but it became obvious after he sailed past the next three bus stops that he was deadly serious about booting us of in the Short Strand and that this was definitely no fear tactic. Talk turned from disbelief to tactics.

"We need to stay together when we get off the bus"

"If we stay in a large group, no one is likely to have a go at us, I mean there's fifty or so of us here"

"Aye that's alright, but we are gonna be right in the heart of the Short Strand, what way are we gonna try and leave?"

"I say the safest way is to head for the Newtownards Road, any other way and we will have no way out"

"So, we get off and move as fast as we can for the Newtown?"

"Right that's what we are doing, don't get left behind, because once we make our move no one is turning back, ok?"

Silence met this statement as the brutal reality that we were actually going to be in some danger once we got off the bus, sank in with everyone.

"Once we hit the Newton everyone head for St. Martins church, that means we will be on home ground as quickly as possible, we don't want a confrontation until we are safe, then, if we do meet any opposition, we can find bricks, stones and whatever else, we'll make sure we give them what for"

"We need to be giving this bus driver what for, the bastard"

"Let's just concentrate on getting out of the Short Strand first, ok? Never mind the driver"

The bus swung around the corner coming off the New-townards Road and into the Short Strand, there were some people hanging about and a few more near the shops we passed as the bus flew into the bus depot. The bus driver seemed to really want make things difficult for us. He parked as far away from the exit as possible. He was really putting us up against it.

The bus came to a grinding halt and both sets of doors opened.

"Right you lot, get off the bus now and fuck right off" he left the bus and headed across to the staff entrance taking the money box with him.

This was it, we had to get off the bus and get out of here without anyone having a go at us, we would be hard to miss, a group of prods this size, right in the middle of the Short Strand, our orange tinged uniforms would be a dead giveaway.

"All those in Stewart house should be grand with your tricol-ours on your uniforms"

A nervous laugh broke out, but this was far from a funny situation. We disembarked and spotted that there were a few buses we could go behind to disguise our trek to the exit and from there it would be anyone's guess as to how this would all turn out. We approached the exit with caution, this was it, we were going to have to go for it.

"Right, I'll go and give it a quick scout, see if there's anyone about, then we make a run for it" said one of the older lads.

He crept forward and had a look out, moved forward like a sniper seeking a nest, trying his best to keep his cover and not get seen.

Almost as soon as he had gone forward, he came back

"Right, we need to go now, the coast looks like it is clear"

With that we all bolted from behind the bus, out the exit and turned left to head towards the Newtown. We streamed out like a line of ants, and a few heads turned as people who were going about their daily business observed this line of school kids running like they were escaping a fire or an earthquake. I was running with one thing on my mind, don't stop, and get in front of as many people as you can. Being a skinny lanky shape, sprinting was a natural thing. We passed the shop not that far from the depot, this must have drawn the attention of some people in the shop who wanted to see what the commotion was, the penny must have dropped as I heard a loud shout of "Prods" behind us. I didn't need any more encouragement to move faster, that shout meant that our cover had been blown and we could expect bricks, stones and other missiles to be making their way in our direction any moment now. The last thing you wanted in this situation was to be running with your back to stuff flying in your general direction. We had no choice though, there was only one way out for us, and we were running for all we were worth. As we rounded Seaford Street it looked like we were about to get out of here without a full on confrontation, how wrong that thought was, out of a side street came about ten lads, when they saw us running they just knew instinctively we weren't local and they tried to get in our way, we skidded and jolted, turning with skill, evading their attempts to get a hold of us, they managed to get themselves in front of the next group behind us, and were holding them up, some of the lads smashed through them, they turned round to see what if anything they could do to help out,

"Lads come on back we need to help them out, come on"

Against our previously agreed plan, we headed back into the Short Strand and saw these guys blocking the way forward with their back to us, fortunately for us they hadn't realised that we had come back. We just rushed at them, pushing them out of the way, creating the space that was needed to get the rest of the stranded bus passengers through and on our way round to St Martin's church and safety. As the last of the group arrived there were sighs of relief, for all the bravado, there had been genuine fear among us, it could have all been very different. I thought about the Sunday trip into the town and how Colin and I had been lucky enough to get away that day, and here I was again in another situation that I was lucky to walk away from safely. Maybe another time I wouldn't be so lucky but for now, I was able to walk home safely. Home for me wasn't that far away, the same couldn't be said for everyone else though, some of them lived near the Holywood Arches and Sydenham, they had some walk ahead of them, something told me they didn't care bout that given we had just escaped from the Short Strand in one piece.

Now my mind was turned to a new routine, homework and lots of it, there's nothing like homework to bring you back down to earth and get on with somewhat normal things. Wait 'til I tell the guys in the band about this one I thought, no one is going to believe it.

With homework becoming a new routine after school I was keen to get back to another routine, band practice.

Everything else was organised around this bi-weekly event, I had to be there, absolutely nothing could get in its way. My family will probably tell you different though, they will tell you that every day is practice day for me and they will definitely tell you that me and my flute go everywhere together, well around the house anyway. Mum says that I can practice as much as I want to, as long as my homework gets done without any hassle. Now to arrive at that compromise this early in life is a small price to pay. Now I was on a mission, one I definitely chose to accept, to be the first in my learner's class to beat the list.

As the weeks progressed and I practiced more and more, the better I got, everyone could tell too, my family and all the guys at the band. Terry was giving me more and more tunes to learn. He was meticulous in his approach, nothing he ever asked you to do was pointless. Every week he made me play the scale, every note, name every note, call out a note and ask me to play it, play the scale in one big long note, double notes triples, quadruples fives and sixes. I never queried why, but I always got why with the next tune he gave me, the techniques he made me work on always seemed to be in the next tune, funny that eh? He was an amazing tutor, he had to be, the learners class was full of all ages and abilities, so for Terry to be able to work in a way that helped us all learn in a way we understood, took skill, and it was no accident that Terry was one of the most popular guys in the band. He was one of the busiest members in the band, when he wasn't teaching us learners, he was putting the main band through their paces.

He was a walking encyclopaedia of tunes; he knew every piece the band played inside out and a million more beside. And, if anyone forgot their notes for a tune or if he had run out of copies to hand out, all Terry needed was a blank piece of paper and a pen. Like take last weeks practice for instance, Frankie was asking for the notes to a tune called National Emblem.

"I don't seem to have a copy with me Frankie"

"That's alright Terry, bring one to the next practice sure?"

"No, it's alright mate, I'll do one up for you now, do have you a blank page and a pen?"

"I don't Terry, sorry, never worry sure"

I had this big navy blue hard back book that I carried to practice with me, all the tunes I could play and all the tunes I was trying to learn were written down in it. I ripped a blank page out and handed it over to Terry "Here, you can use this sure" I said. "Thanks Glenn" Terry then proceeded to just write out the tune note for note, with rests and held out notes and repeats etc, he was like the Jedi Master of flute tunes using the force to make the pen do his bidding. Terry was like a flute savant, name a tune and off he went writing it down. Off he went into his own wee world, everyone else just sat there smiling and pointing at him.

"Here Adrian, check this out" said Frankie motioning towards Terry "Just writing that tune out of his head, no need for a flute"

"I don't know how he does it"

Frankie just continued smiling, there was a sense of pride or something on his face, I felt it too, this guy was my teacher, it was amazing just watching him do his thing. Now there was no way that I could do what Terry did but, that didn't stop me trying to do what he did, I wrote all the tunes out myself in my navy book, it felt more personal, like I would learn the tune quicker, like it would already be in my brain, and all I needed to do was to get my brain to transfer that information to my fingers. I needed the notes to play most of the tunes, but I desperately wanted to learn them all off by heart, because that's how you got out on parade with the band you had to beat the list and know every tune without the notes.

So, I've mentioned this list twice now, I guess I need to fill you in on what it actually is. The list was Terry's way of keeping a track of who was able to play what tunes off by heart. It had all the tunes the band played in a column on the left hand side of the page, well actually there were two pages one for kick or traditional tunes and the other for military marches. Along the top of these two pages were all the learner's names, we all had our own column with an empty space at each tune for a tick. The only way you could get a tick at a tune was whenever you played a tune the whole way through, without the notes and without a mistake. Now, this sounds reasonably easy right? Oh no no no, this wasn't easy at all, you had to perform and complete the tune in front of the whole band! Terry's had good reason for this, his thinking was, if you could play the tune in front of them then you could do it anywhere. And to be honest you didn't want to mess up in front of the band, these were the guys who walked on the road, they were the Pride of the Raven, you had to be ready, you had to be able to play. We all wanted to impress them, well because we wanted to be them. After a few frustrating weeks I had started to hit a wee streak of success, every week I was getting tunes ticked off. I was making my way through the list rightly, I was catching up on some of the guys who had joined before me, even my mate Darren. Although Darren has missed quite a few practices recently, which I thought was a little strange, I mean he loves the band as much as I do. I must make a point of catching up with him and see what's happening. I hadn't really seen him around much at all either, I'll call for him tomorrow and see what the craic is, I thought to myself. Anyway, as I walked home from another practice, I thought 'You know what, I'll just call by Darren's house and see if he is in. It was late enough like, but I was dead sure he would be up, although his Da might not appreciate me ringing the doorbell at this time of night. Biting the bullet, I opened his front gate, and I could hear him playing the flute, well at least he is still practicing even if he isn't coming to practice, I thought. His Dad opened the door.

"Alright, Glenn, a bit late isn't it?"

"I know, sorry Mr Boyd, I just wanted to see if Darren was in, missed him at band practice tonight so just wanted to see if everything was alright"

"Darren" his Da called , "It's Glenn at the door for you" A few moments later he appeared at the top of the stairs and made his way down the stairs and had a wee juke to see who was there, even though his Da had just said it was me.

"Alright Glenn, what's happening?"

"Alright Darren, missed you at practice tonight"

Darren was slow to reply, "Yeah? good turnout?

"Yeah good turnout, few new members as well"

"That's always good"

"Definitely, Terry was asking about you tonight, so I said I would call by and see what the craic was"

"Was just busy tonight mate, had a few things on, but I will be there next week alright?"

"No worries mate, sure I'll see you over the weekend"

"Aye no bother, I'm sure I'll see you in school tomorrow"

"Aye right enough." And with that I headed on round home. By the time Thursday had rolled around again, I still hadn't seen much of Darren at all, which was really strange, we always hung out and did things, not every day, but a lot of the time anyway. I left my house to go the hall I thought 'I'll just call for Darren, and we can head up together we haven't done that in a while'. I made the short trip round to Madrid Street, checking out the border with the Short Strand, to see if there was any activity there, all was quiet, so I called at Darren's door, after a second ring of the bell, his Da answered.

"Alright Glenn, if you're looking for Darren he's not in son, he said that he was heading on up to band practice"

"Ah right, happy days Mr Boyd. I'll see him up there then?"

"I'm sure you will son, he seemed eager to get there early"

"Thanks Mr Boyd, catch ya later" and with that he closed the door. I skipped away picking up the pace so I could get to the hall quicker because I knew what was happening now, he was making a go at the list! That sneaky fucker was trying to complete the list! I mean what other explanation could there be.

I arrived at the hall and gave the big steel door a rattle, Terry opened the door.

"Ack Glenn, good to see you, what are you playing for me tonight then?"

"Been working on a few Terry, hopefully I remember them all, so has Darren got many of the list tonight?"

"Darren? He's not here mate"

"What? I called at his house before I came up and his Da said he was away to band practice"

"Well he hasn't turned up here yet, do you know what's going on with him? He hasn't been here for a good few weeks now"

I was so sure that he was making a play for the list I hadn't considered any other option. What the hell was going on here? Why would his Da tell me he was at band practice when he wasn't?

"I've no idea Terry, he definitely told me when I spoke to him last that he was coming tonight, I'll see him tomorrow in school and see what the craic is"

"No bother, let us know what you find out, if he's not gonna come back we could be doing with his flute, there's two learners sharing a flute at the minute"

"I'll definitely find out tomorrow then"

"Good lad, thanks"

I ended up knocking five tunes of the list that night, well Terry gave me a bit of grace with two of them as I only made a mistake with one note in a few of them, and he sat beside me during the main practice to listen to me play them with the band, and seeing as I played them without the notes and didn't make a mistake he decided to put ticks in the boxes for me. He was good like that, it's not that he gave you the benefit of the doubt, if he knew you had it, he'd make sure he got it out of you, and he knew you wouldn't be attempting a tune if you hadn't got it right before you'd came to practice. You couldn't pull the wool over his eyes; he was way too smart for that.

I made my way home as usual walking down Mountpottinger Street, across to Paxton Street and down the second Avenue, there would be no diversions tonight. I was playing the tunes I now had got ticked off the list and as I arrived at the crossroads between the Avenue and the Albertbridge Road, who did I spy coming up the Albert from the Avoneil direction? Darren. I stopped playing, this obviously grabbed his attention, as he looked up in the direction I was walking from. He waved and shouted "Alright mate" I crossed the road and we both met up outside a shop that used to be called Nabney's, now it was being renovated into a furniture shop or something.

"Hey were did you end up tonight? Your Da said you were away to practice and well you weren't there like"

"Yeah, I know, I had things to do"

"Like what?"

"Ack just things"

I was just about to ask him if he was coming back to the Raven when I recognised something silver in Darren's hand.

"What's with the silver flute?"

Darren tried to put the silver flute behind his back, but it was too late, and I already knew what it meant.

"You haven't done what I think you've done?" I queried.

"I guess that depends on what you think it is I've done?"

"You've joined another band?"

"I have"

"So, when your Dad said you were at practice, he wasn't lying. Did you let Terry know?"

"No, I figured I'd run into you soon enough and you could take my flute back, aren't you going to ask me who I've joined?"

I was a little shocked at this revelation given that he was the reason I was able to join Pride of the Raven and now he was abandoning me.

"I don't need to ask who you've joined, there's only one band that plays those flutes, you've joined the Defenders haven't you? Ack mate, anyone but them!!"

The Ballymacarrett Defenders were the other melody flute band in East Belfast and the Pride of the Ravens biggest rivals. Even though we were all technically on the same side politically, there was a healthy competition and respect between the two bands to try and outdo each other. Always trying to learn harder tunes and doing something to stand out from the crowd. This rivalry went as far as not playing certain tunes because they were a Raven tune or a Defenders tune, it didn't matter if it was a great tune or not, you just didn't copy another band. This was like a Liverpool player joining Manchester Utd, it's not meant to happen, one of my best friends has not only joined another band, but joined a band that were our biggest rivals, I was completely taken aback.

"But why mate?, I don't get it?"

"I just like their style more, and I think I have a better chance of walking with them quicker"

"Ah so it's the list then? Can't get through the list so you're going for an easier option just to get walking on the street?"

"No, no, it's not like that at all"

"Sounds like it to me"

"I bet I'll be in a uniform before you"

"Is that right? We'll see mate, we'll see"

Unknown to him, Darren had just given me even more inspiration. I was on a mission to complete the list and get a uniform on before him and the Defenders.

"Well I'm heading to the chippy, you coming?" asked Darren, oblivious to my inner scheming.

"Aye, what are ya buying me?"

"You're a geg!"

"So, where have you been the last week or so? I haven't seen hide nor hair of ya"

"Aye, I know, got myself a girlfriend!"

"Oh right! Well you can tell me all about her over the pastie supper you're buying me".

We headed in the direction of Eddie Spence's, one of the best chippies in east Belfast. It was ironic that we went there as it wasn't far from my band hall, after all it was my band hall now, not Darren's. We dandered off together as if nothing had happened. We would have some banter over the next few months about each other's bands, but I walked towards that chippy knowing he wouldn't get one over on me.

To say that I was determined is an understatement, I was practising harder than ever, every opportunity I had to learn another tune off by heart I took it. I would come home from school as fast as I could to get some practice in before I actually sat down to do my homework, I had to keep that deal with my Mum, it was a win-win for me, the quicker the homework got done, the quicker I got back to practice. When my friends called for me to go out and play football, they got polite "no's", football could wait. I was preoccupied.

Not everyone took this focussed determination so well, my Mums head was turned with my practice regime. I had turned learning a tune into a very rigid repetitive process, playing a tune over and over again. Once I made a mistake, I reviewed the notes to go over in my head what I had messed up on, and then I started from the top again. There were more than a few times my Ma popped her head through my door.

"Can you not play something else?"

"What?" I said barely taking a breath and trying to keep playing the tune.

"You've been playing the same thing for over an hour now, play something else or take yourself off outside"

"But I need to learn this one Ma, I need to get it ticked off the list"

"I don't care about the bloody list. You're sending me and your Da round the twist"

"I'll play it in a lower register then so you can hear it, like this"

I gave her a quick demonstration of what I meant, it basic-ally meant playing the notes without fully producing a sound from the flute, I could still work on getting the tune right though.

"That's better, now, your dinner will be ready in ten minutes"

"No probs, I should have this one done by then"

"Great" she said, with the slightest hint of sarcasm.

There was another reason she hated my practice regime though. We had a pet bird, a cockatiel called Hooker, named after the TV show character TJ Hooker, which happened to be my younger brothers favourite tv show, you know the one where Captain Kirk from Star Trek pretends to be a police offi-cer? Hooker had one skill, apart from scaring the bejeezus out of my Granny when he was out of his cage, He could mimic sounds. One of his best was the phone ringing! I remember my Mum being at the front door talking to one of the neigh-bours about god knows what, and Hooker starts mimicking the phone, and my Ma rushed in to answer the phone, as soon as she walked in through the door the bird stopped making the sound.

"Ack Glenn did you not think of answering that?"

"You tell me never to answer the phone in case it's someone looking money!"

"Don't get smart with me wee lad! If it rings again answer it, ok?"

"Aye no bother" so she left and went back to the front door, the bird must have sensed this because it started making the phone noise again. I decided to go into the kitchen to boil the kettle, just so I had an excuse not to have answered the phone. This is going to be funny to watch. I heard my Ma shouting in for me to answer the phone, but I didn't respond. She came in again and the bird stopped as she opens the door. "What did I say not two minutes ago Glenn?"

"What Ma?"

"The phone Glenn, the phone was ringing again that's twice now it could be something important you know, someone could be dead or something"

"Do you think so? I wonder who it is?"

"Less of your cheek son"

Just then the bird started making the phone noise again and I couldn't help but bust out laughing. The penny dropped with my Ma, "That bloody bird", she stormed into the kitchen and opened the bottom drawer and lifted a tea towel, heading back into the living room towards the cage.

"I'll shut you up bird" and threw the tea towel over the cage, "There, how do you like that?" She said as if she half expected the bird to answer her back. Did this stop the bird? Not a chance, it came down to the bottom of the cage and peaked under the tea towel and started making the phone noise again, it was like it just knew how to wind her up, it was priceless. It had the same routine for my practice regime, Hooker had listened to me playing so much and whatever the tune of the week was the bird made the same mistakes I did, and stopped and started from the top again just like I did, so I can understand how this was annoying to my Ma and Da. They were listening to me practicing even when I wasn't in the house!

Every spare moment was practice time. I even got into the habit of practising when I was walking to and from the band hall on Thursday nights, come rain or shine I would be playing my flute. I was obsessed. I was very careful not to be playing any of our new tunes. You see, they were supposed to be a closely guarded secret. It's not like they were on the same level as the coca cola recipe or Colonel Sanders' secret spices, but there was something great about playing a tune that no one else was playing, healthy competition Terry called it, and the Defenders had spies everywhere! Well, not exactly, the only person I had to make sure that didn't hear them was Darren, I couldn't risk him hearing our best new pieces. The last thing we would need is some other band learning one of these tunes and playing it on the road before us. All bands did this, it seemed to be just part of the way they operated. Now, navigating my way home from practice was a skill, especially now that I had taken to providing the good people of East Belfast with a solo public performance every Thursday and Sunday night. I formed the best route to make sure as many people as possible heard. I stuck to the main streets going home for that reason and also because you never know who'd be hanging about in the side streets and the last thing, I'd need was someone wanting to steal my flute. Although, playing while walking through an entry was great, the sound was amplified and there was a natural reverb that made the flute sound brilliant. But it did have its downsides mainly having to contend with the smell of the old bins and busted black bags left lying to fester days before the bin men were due to arrive. Plus, there was always the chance of walking past someone getting bucked, who needs that type of distraction?

There was something liberating about playing on my own walking home. There were times when it seemed like the world just drifted away and the only sound coming from anywhere was from my flute and at that moment all was right with the world. I was lost in the music, it helped me keep things in my head, especially if I had learned a difficult tune I wanted to make sure I didn't forget it. I had found something I was actually really good at, like I was meant to be doing this. Some of our neighbours commented about my playing, it was mostly complimentary, although I did get the odd request to "Shut up" and "Don't you know what time it is?"

One of the more appreciative neighbours was Brian, he lived in Westbourne Street which was right next to my street. He was a Christian, and played the piano in a local church, one of those hallelujah places where they lifted their hands and sang a lot, but he was dead on. He'd always stop me every time he saw me, just to talk to me about hearing me playing on the way home, or to ask if something was wrong if there was a night he didn't hear me play. He was always so encouraging, and he even listened out for me when I practiced at home as sometimes I left the sky light in my room open when I was practicing.

That world wasn't always peaceful and quiet, there had been plenty of times after navigating my way from the band hall to home that I encountered signs that other things still happened regardless of whether I was around or not. Glass strewn all over the street, scorch marks on the road, half broken bricks, pieces of breeze block often welcomed me on the final walk from Madrid Street to my house. A reminder that the animosity between the two communities hadn't gone away, for every day that nothing happened there were three that something did. My Mum said that even though she gurns about me playing the flute a lot, she's glad that I have an interest that keeps me out of the way of this 'rioting shit' as she called it. It was hard to completely ignore what was happening, but being in the band though stopped me from wanting to get involved, compared to playing the flute, rioting seemed like a waste of time.

I had joined the band almost nine months ago and it was now nearly December although I'd only been practising solidly since I returned from Canada and got stuck back into things in September. However, the spaces in my column on the list were starting to get fewer and fewer as the weeks went on. Terry seemed to reckon that if I kept going the way I was, then I could be walking with the band in time for Easter Monday. I couldn't believe it. I was actually close to getting a uniform and parading.

My big Granda was very proud of the fact that I had joined a band, he was a member of a lodge and a member of the Black, I didn't understand what that was really, it was called the Royal Black Perceptory, they were like a lodge only a bit different, it was really hard to get into the black apparently, whatever that meant? I'd heard something about getting a black ball meant you couldn't join. I'd asked my Big Granda about that, but he told me it was something I didn't need to worry about until I was older and that I'd have no reason to worry about getting in if I wanted to join. My Big Granda always asked to hear what I could play when he visited the house or to came up and take our pet dog Mitzi out for a walk, he would sit down on the big chair at the front window and ask me how I was getting on.

"Well what have you learned this week son"

"A tune called 'Blaze Away' Granda"

"Right will"

"Right will what?

"Let's hear it then"

"Really, you want to hear it?"

"Of course, I do son"

"Right hold on, I'll just go and grab my flute" I'd fly up the stairs two at a time, put my flute together and run back down stairs to perform.

"Ok, ready?"

"Ready"

I would start to play and in no time my Granda would be tapping his feet along with the tune, sometimes Mitzi would try to sing along, which sounded so funny and my Granda and I would busted out laughing.

"Mitzi you want to join the band girl? You'll need a uniform if you want to walk with the band?"

Well at the mention of the word walk, Mitzi was down on the floor again nudging my Granda with her nose as if to say "Right you come on, we've been listening to this guy screeching on a black stick for long enough, let's go for that walk" My Granda stood up and walked towards the kitchen to get the dogs lead.

I had told my Granda that there was a possibility I would be able to walk with the band at Easter, he had said that if I did, he would see about getting tickets to go and watch Liverpool play at Anfield, he would even bring my cousin Alan as well.

So now with the potential of a trip to Anfield to watch Liverpool play, I doubled my efforts and set myself a target. I promised myself that by the time the band practices started up again after Christmas, I would be ready. I would go back and conquer the list. I would officially become what is known in band circles as a full blower. I told myself that before I went to bed that Christmas Eve, I would know every tune the Pride of the Raven played off by heart, and the dream of being told that I would be able to parade with them would be the best Christmas present I'd get this year.

CHAPTER 5

Farewell and the Future

"**R**ight, Glenn, you've got this"

"I know I do; I've just got to relax and play the tunes, you know them, just do it like we practiced"

"I know, I know... I hope I can nail that phrasing right at the end of Dinah's Delight"

"Nail it? You've been hitting it solid every day without a mistake"

I turned away from the mirror and sat on the end of my bed. I'd been having these conversations with myself almost every day, imagining exactly what Terry might say to me when I walk in and lay down my plan to beat the list in one night! My imagination had been running wild, my room wasn't my room anymore, it was the band hall and when I played, well, I could hear the band playing with along with me, somehow that made the tunes stick in my head more. There were days when I pretended that I was walking with the band, calling the tunes and imagining those two five beat drum rolls inviting me to raise my flute and play my heart out, waving and nodding to people in the avenue as we marched by. My Mum had to tell me off a few times though.

"Glenn!!!! What the hell are you doing up there? You sound like your about to come through the ceiling"

"I'm just practicing marching and marking time"

"Well if you don't stop, I'm gonna send your Da up to mark time on you with his belt, for god sake we can hardly hear the TV down here with you!"

"Sorry Mum"

"Aye, you'll be even sorrier if you don't stop! Do you hear me?"

It would be hard not to hear you I thought to myself, half the street could probably hear her!

The past four months or so had been a journey. A journey into myself, I had never been as motivated to do anything as I had been since joining the band. I knew I had the capacity to learn, albeit something my schoolteachers had no knowledge of, but learning still the same. But it wasn't just that, other things were happening too. I was discovering more and more about music, melodies and counter melodies and the beauty of a well-placed note or a well phrased segment, I was experiencing something new all the time.

I always remember the first time I heard the band play Dinah's Delight, and when it got to the trio, there was this magical note, even now hearing it, makes the hairs on my neck stand up. I was discovering the beauty of music, the language of music, how it can take you through a series of emotions and back again in a split second. I was discovering style and technique all at the same time, because to be make those sounds have that impact you had to be good, you had to make that flute reach out and draw attention. I was learning to perform and understand what it meant to be able to play under pressure. I was learning to be a team player, when to hold back and use dynamics and when not to play at all. I was developing new relationships, friendships, that went beyond the usual stuff with my mates, I was learning that sometimes to be good at something you have to sacrifice other things.

That's something my mates didn't understand, I'd overheard them one day going home from school, walking behind them listening as they queried whether they should call for me or not.

"Should we say to G, about football later?"

"I dunno? He'll prob just get his Ma to say he's busy playing the flute"

"That's all he seems to do now is practice"

"And even when he does come out, he's always whistling some new tune or talking about the band"

"I know, I love the bands too, but he's obsessed"

They were right, I was obsessed, I wanted to achieve something, and only practice would make that happen, and if they couldn't see that, then, what kind of friends were they? And besides, I did do things other than practice. Every Saturday I was away with my Uncle Davy and my cousin Alan to watch Linfield play, that took me on a whirlwind tour of some of the saddest places on earth, like Larne! The only things Larne had going for it was the ferry to Scotland and the road to Belfast. The football ground, Inver Park, was pitiful to say the least, whoever thought that planks attached to oil drums constituted stadium seating obviously was a few sandwiches short of a picnic and their team wasn't much better either. The matches were great craic, the banter was brilliant and even better when Linfield won. But when they lost, that was a different story. The stick that was dished out to referees and the manager was something else, you'd be thinking these guys supported another team, they were so passionate about Linfield, it was like how dare you lose and let us down! I knew that I would have a big decision on my hands once I started walking with the band, there would be a lot of parades on Saturdays, well competitions, but when the band wasn't out, I knew where I would be, cheering on the Blues.

There were two other guys in my class that played the flute in bands as well, Fergie who played with a band called the Pride of Down and Junior, he played with a band called Ulster Volunteer Flute. It was great having these guys to talk to about bands and tunes, you still had to be careful though, none of us shared any notes with each other! The other great thing about them was that they were Linfield supporters too. Fergie had given me my first copy of the Blackskull tape, a band from Scotland, before I got my own up at the Nutts Corner market. The Blackskull and another Scottish band, the Pride of the Myle were having a real influence on Belfast bands, especially ones with younger members who wanted to do something different from the traditional set up. What these bands were doing gave them the inspiration they needed, changing tunes, adding parts in and leaving parts out, putting different drum settings to them. This change in style wouldn't impact the Pride of the Raven though, we had a style all of our own.

In the run up to the Christmas holidays in school our form teacher had asked if there was anyone with hidden talents that would perform at the First Year Christmas party, before anyone had a chance to say anything, Junior automatically volunteered the three flute players services. Mr Johnston was all biz at the thought of this, and we were happy to get the chance to show off a little in front of the whole year group. The whole year group, suddenly I was a little nervous, what on earth would we play? And what if we messed up or made mistakes? We would look like right dicks in from of the whole year group. I wasn't that keen on making a fool of myself in front of a hundred or so peers.

"What were you thinking mate? We are gonna have to play in from of the whole of first form!"

"And?" was Junior's blunt reply, "Unless you're lying about the band and tunes you can play, what are you worried about?"

"Just making a mistake or something"

"Well then don't make a mistake" Fergie piped up, "So, what are we gonna play?"

"Yeah, it can't be anything our bands play",

"Aye we should do something different"

Junior had it covered though "I've already had an idea of what we can play, do you know the theme to the lone ranger?"

"The William Tell overture?" I said.

"Aye, is that what it actually called?"

"Now how the hell do you know that?"

"I dunno, I just do"

"Well I was thinking that we could play that and maybe run it in to the theme tune from Dallas"

"That stupid American soap opera?"

"Yeah, don't act like you don't watch it. You've had a few thoughts about Sue Ellen, I know you!"

"Shut up, you arsehole"

"Right that's settled then? We will play those two tunes?"

"Yeah I don't see why not"

"We will need to practice though and make sure we are playing the same thing"

"No worries, I will write the notes out and we can take it from there"

"Ok"

So just like that we had arranged to play at the end of year party and sorted out what we were playing. We got to practice a couple of times together and we finally got to hear each other play, they were both good players, I have to say I held back a bit, better to make sure the final performance was the best. By the time the party actually rolled around, I was ready for it, and after the customary silly games and quizzes and prizes etc, our form teacher went to the front of the assembly hall and began introducing us to the rest of the year group.

"I want you to welcome three talented lads from my class with a flute rendition of the William Tell overture and the theme tune from Dallas I give you, Glenn, Junior and Paul"

After a reasonable round of applause, we took our places and had a quick look at each other, "Ready?" 1,2,3,4 and we were off, the time just seemed to fly by, we played perfectly in unison together and there was a better round of applause once we had finished and lowered our flutes. We got a few comments from our classmates as we took our seats, "well done lads, that was great", it was definitely nice to be appreciated. There were a few other performances from other first years, guitar players mainly and they were actually pretty decent. And that was it, after a final word from the headmaster wishing us a merry Christmas, the party was over and the two-week Christmas holiday had officially started.

I saw more of my mates over the Christmas holidays, but only because the band had called a halt to practices. They would start up again in the second week of January and I couldn't wait. It was torture. I was marking the days on my calendar like a convict waiting for their release date. I was confident thought that all remaining blank spaces in my column on the list were about to become extinct.

It wasn't my only excitement; all of my mates were excited about this Christmas as we were all getting new BMX bikes. Christmas morning was a complete buzz, as I came downstairs to see my bike, a red and silver spitfire with a 'Haro' number plate on the handlebars, mushroom handlebar grips, and a seriously shiny red helmet with mouthguard! It was probably one of the coolest presents I'd ever received. We all met up at the top of tower street at around half ten in the morning, we were like a convoy of cool heading away on our first BMX adventure with the almost identical words ringing out from all our parents, "Be careful and make sure you're back in time for Christmas Dinner!!"

We went everywhere on our bikes, and we even ventured as far away as Ormeau and Vicky park, as they had BMX tracks up there, we even ventured to other areas of the Newtownards

Road as we had heard that the Lunn brothers had built a quarter pipe and were teaching people how to do aerials.

We were always trying to do tricks and replicate what we had saw in magazines and programmes on TV. My Granny had obviously missed all that. I remember she was at her mate Sadie's house, and me, wee Dee and Alan were riding through Thistle Court on our bikes. It was a good place for BMX as there were short walls that acted a bit like ramps and there were loads of obstacles so work your way around. I was trying to do an 'endo' just opposite Sadie's house, which basically involved riding up slowly to a brick wall or any perpendicular obstacle, getting the front wheel to touch the wall, pull the front break hard so that the back wheel came off the ground and you had to try and get up over your seat and sit on the back wheel and get back on to your seat before the back wheel hit the ground again. It wasn't always easy to do, but Granny had obviously saw me and she came out and gave me a clip round the ear.

"What's that for Granny?"

"What the hell do you think you're playing at, have you got no respect for your parents? Crashing your bike into a brick wall over and over, your Mum saved up all that money to get you that bike" It was just as well I didn't believe in Santa anymore, big Granny the myth slayer!

"But Granny that's what…" I never got to finish the sentence

"Don't you give me all that, I saw you from Sadie's front window, now get you on home, and I'll be telling your ma when I'm finished here"

"But Granny" I tried to protest again.

"Go, away on of that with ye, what do I keep telling ye, children should be seen and not heard"

My mates were killing themselves laughing at me getting a telling off in the street. It's as well she only saw the 'endo' attempt. If she saw the size of the ramp we had built in Susan Street, and the time that I had fallen off about eight feet in the air as my bike went gracefully through the air and me its twin albeit a foot behind it, the bike landing in a heap and me landing on the tail of my arse! She'd have been chasing me with her poker!! It wouldn't have stopped me though that ramp was so good I couldn't wait to do it again and again.

My Ma was happy that I was spending more time outside the house, obviously because it meant she didn't have to listen to me playing for hours and hours in the house and probably even more so because Hooker wasn't trying to mimic me! But these BMX adventures aside, I still took the time to practice and make sure that come that first practice after the Christmas break, I'd be ready for Terry asking who wants to get some tunes off their list? I'd be straight in there.

"Well tonight Terry I want to clear what's left on my list" that felt good, every time I had played that through in my mind, a massive smile appeared on my face, I was going to make it happen, I was going to become a full blower, I was going to get a uniform and walk with the band at Easter, and more importantly I was going to walk with the band before Darren even got a sniff of a parade with the Defenders! My confidence was increased by the fact that I'd heard him practicing one night, trying to play Blaze away, and not to brag or anything, it wasn't great. I already had that one down, so I made a point of playing that one night coming home from practice and once when I knew he was calling for me, nothing like rubbing it in!

With the Christmas holidays coming to an end, it was coming up to New Year's Eve or Old Years Night as it was called in my house. I always thought calling it that was like we were trying to hold on to the past for just a little longer. There was going to be a party at my house, this meant that all the family would show up. All my Aunts, Uncles and cousins as well and more than likely a few friends from around the area too. Everyone would share their stories about previous New Years and talk about ridiculous New Years resolutions. There'd be lots of food and a pile of drink as well. Everyone started arriving about half seven and they had all brought something with them, the kitchen table was just bunged with crisps and chocolate, and given that we never really had loads growing up, this was a rare treat. My big Granda was always the life and soul of the party, he had the best stories and the best jokes. The party was in full swing and about ten o'clock my Granda said his goodbyes, he said he was feeling tired and wished everyone a happy new year, and invited us all to his house in the morning for one of his famous fry's.

This was something he did nearly every Saturday, I loved heading down to his house, my Granny would be sitting in the living room polishing the brass and there was this smell coming from the kitchen, my Granda cooking up a seriously good Ulster fry. We used to stand at the breakfast bar and watch this giant of a man cook for his family, he'd talk to us about Liverpool football club, he loved Liverpool and we all did as a result. He would share stories from his time in the merchant navy, we never grew tired hearing them, even though we could probably recite them word for word. My Granny would always get her tuppence worth in though.

"Tommy, stop boring the kids with the same old stories, they'll die of starvation with your 'jackanory' going on!"

We would all be mimicking Granny when she said stuff like this, but my Granda wouldn't let us get away with it. He taught us to respect our elders and our Granny especially, after all she was very skilled with the poker she'd been polishing!!!

We thought nothing of him leaving and we all wished him a happy new year, he smiled as he left and even waved in through the window as he passed by, a signature move. We all partied on, eating our cheese and pickle on a cocktail stick and whacking the beetroot into us like there was no tomorrow, always careful to stay away from the corned beef sandwiches, although there was only one thing worse than corn beef sandwiches, and that was egg and onion sandwiches, they are absolutely stinking. I could never understand anyone liking them, but they were a constant presence at any party, or any other social gathering, no matter the occasion, these vile things turned up. Before long there was a sing song going, everyone singing their tune and being encouraged to go for it and then the big moment was almost upon us, and the count-down was on, 1 minute to go people, then it's the new year!

"5,4,3,2,1 HAPPY NEW YEAR!!!" Everyone was hugging and singing, and everything was just right in the world. Not long after that however people started saying their goodbyes for the evening, the main reason for gathering had come and gone and taxis started showing up outside the door and honking their horns, by 1am everyone was away apart from my Granny and the house looked like a bomb had hit it.

"I'll call up in the morning and give you a hand tidying up" she said to my Mum "And then you can all call down to my house and get your fry"

"Sounds good Mum"

"See ya later Granny"

"Right you need to go to bed" my Ma said turning to me.

"Night, see you in the morning"

And with that we were in a new year, what it had in store for us nobody knew. I had some of what it had in store though, Easter wouldn't be that long rolling in and hopefully I'd be walking with the band.

A few weeks into the new year, something happened that would change everything. My Granda had taken the dog out for a walk as usual, he had called into our house to see every-one and had stayed for dinner before heading home. I went to bed as usual, it was unusually warm in my room, and I had opened the skylight to let a bit of air in and drifted off to sleep. I awoke at the sound of the phone ringing, I looked at the time, it was after midnight, who would be calling at this time of the night? I heard footsteps pounding like thunder going down the stairs and followed by a scream and sobbing, then more footsteps going down the stairs, Dad was up. I didn't know whether to venture down or not, I opened the bedroom door and heard loud crying and my Mum, saying over and over, "No no, not my Daddy" my Dad popped his head out of the living room door and looked up the stairs, he wasn't surprised to see me.

"Son you better come down. I've got something to tell you"

I made my way down the stairs and into the living room, my Mum was sobbing and shaking on the chair nearest the phone.

"What's going on Da? Why's mum crying so much? What's hap-pening?"

"It's your Granda son, he's gone"

"Gone where, when's he coming back?"

"I mean he's passed away son, he's died"

"What do you mean he's died, he was perfectly fine a few hours ago when he left here, he wasn't sick or anything, he can't be, he was alright, he was...." the emotion of the moment kicked in and tears fell in floods from my eyes, and a cry came from the pit of my stomach, so sore that I fell to my knees. Everything after was a blur, and the house grew strangely quiet, like it was aware that someone had left and would never enter again. There was lots of activity that night, I remember bits and pieces. I woke up in my own bed though, apparently I just passed out and Dad had lifted me up to bed, I awoke thinking I'd had the strangest dream, when I went down stairs I was reminded that this wasn't a dream, far from it and the tears fell again and again.

It was as if nothing else mattered and it couldn't have, I had no way of dealing with this, what prepares you for this?

The next few days were pretty much spent at my Granny's house, waves of people ebbed and flowed in and out the door to enjoy what seemed like an endless supply of tea and sympathy as well as trays of egg and onion sandwiches! My Granda had been brought home, from where I don't know, there was obviously somewhere he had been taken after he died. He was now in the living room, at the front window where he had always sat, but he wasn't sitting on his favourite chair, now he was lying in a coffin. Mum had told me that some of the people who had come to pay their respects went in and spoke to my Granda just like he was still there. As for me, I couldn't bring myself to go in. My Mum and my Aunt Lillian tried to encourage me to go into the living room and say goodbye to my Granda. I told them I didn't want to, I told them that I would rather wait until I was able to say hello again. My Mum and my Aunt broke down at this, I just went out and sat on the front step. It was too much for my mind to take in, he was here only a few days ago, alive and well. And now, he was gone, no more stories, no more Saturday morning fry, no more calling up to the house with Mitzi after taking her for a walk.

After two days of the constant gathering at my Granny's house, things changed, or should I say, finalised. Funerals are like that; they unashamedly bring things to a solid end. The tea drinking and the endless supply of sandwiches and people calling to my Big Granny's house, would all end. There would be no more recollections and stories and laughs because the serious side of all this, the main event so to speak, the knockout blow was about to happen. We all had to say goodbye. The small terraced house my Granda had called his home for many a year was now packed with family and friends all wanting to say their final goodbyes to a man they loved. As I stood there in the hallway of my Granny's house, I still couldn't bring myself to go into the living room where he lay. I couldn't remember a time where I didn't want to see my Granda and yet here I was, unable to take the few short steps that would have brought us together again one last time, I didn't want to see him lying there lifeless, I didn't want that to be the last memory I had of seeing him. I preferred to remember seeing him walk past the window of my house, smiling as he waved in at us all. An unfamiliar voice came from the living room and I found myself listening to the minister from Westbourne Presbyterian church talk about my Granda. Through the doorway into the living room I could see my Granny, her heart breaking with each mention of the name that no doubt had once had the complete opposite effect, it was surreal, almost like I was watching it on TV or at the cinema. As I lost myself in the few memories I could recall I was jolted back to reality with the whispering of an "Amen" and a tap on the shoulder as the funeral men needed to get past me to go into the packed living room, to make preparations for the coffin to be brought out into the street. The room emptied and I found myself standing at the door looking out at the mass of people who had turned up to pay their respects.

My eye caught a familiar face near the railings of the Rupert just opposite the house, was that Terry? It was! How did he know about this? I hadn't been able to get word to the band? I walked over Terry placed his hand on my shoulder.

"Sorry for your loss, Glenn"

My loss? I had never thought of it like that, and all that I had been holding in broke. I started to cry.

"So sorry to hear about your Granda"

"How did you know?"

"Darren told us mate"

"Darren?"

"Yeah we ran into him near Eddie Spence's, he filled us in on what had happened, I felt I had to come kid"

"Thanks, I really appreciate it"

"Think nothing of it, you're Pride of the Raven son and we support each other, no matter what, you may get back over to your family, it looks like they are ready to go, we'll fall in at the back and we will see you at practice soon, take your time though, no need to rush back ok?"

"Ok" and I headed back for my Granda's final journey.

Walking behind the cortège my mind wandered again to memories of happy times spent with him and then to things ahead of me he would never see or do together. He would never get to see me walking with the band or take me to An-field to watch Liverpool. Trivial? Perhaps, but in that moment between farewell and the future they were massive contemplations. The procession only lasted so long and the coffin was put into the back of the hearse for the journey to Roselawn Cemetery. There was a short service at the graveside and the coffin was then lowered by ropes into the ground "ashes to ashes, dust to dust" said the minister as some of the freshly dug earth was shovelled back on top of the coffin to seal my Granda's final resting place.

We headed back in the cars to my Granny's house, where the mood was sombre, but not as heavy as before, the tear stained hankies now firmly imprisoned again in the pockets they had escaped from only hours earlier. The men were heading to the bar for a drink, while those who didn't drink and the majority of the women stayed behind and tucked into even more sand-wiches and cups of tea. I eventually went into the living room, staring out the window I half expected him to walk past like he had countless times before, now that hope was more of a dream than a realistic expectation. One by one everyone left and soon the house felt eerily empty. I was comforted by the fact that my Granny wouldn't be alone tonight, my Mum and Aunt Lillian would be there with her, but I also knew that my Granny would have to face the fact that she would now have to share her house with memories rather than with the man she loved so much.

That would be the same for all of us though, all we had now were the memories that had been made, no more could be made together. There were other things that would live on though, things that he would have wanted us to do, his hopes for us all, they lived in us and to some degree they would push us forward into each new day.

One thing that pushed its way forward was time, and the days passed as normal and soon it was Thursday again, and the first practice I had thought about attending after my Granda's funeral. I hadn't missed practices for so long, I never wanted to, I always had the inspiration and desire to go, and this Thursday was no different. This walk up was no different. I saw no need to change it from any other walk up, I took the same route as I usually did, and yet it was completely different in one sense, because never before had I walked to practice this determined, never before had I so many tunes in my head, and because now I wouldn't get the chance to let my Granda hear how much I had progressed and for me to tell him that I was finally a full blower with the band. All these thoughts and more were racing through my mind as I banged on the door, I looked up towards the sky and whispered "This is for you Granda" I had to hold back tears which caught me by surprise and my chest, heavy with emotion, made me step back and take a deep breath. I got myself together just as the door to the band hall opened and I was greeted by Terry at the door who seemed surprised to see me.

"Alright Glenn, I didn't think we would see you this week"

"I know, and I very nearly didn't come, but those blank spaces on the list won't get filled if I'm not here"

"You gonna knock a few more of it then?"

"No Terry, I'm gonna finish it off" I said with the kind of determination I imagined climbers had when heading to conquer Everest. Hearing this in my voice Terry said.

"Well, you better come in then"

I walked into the hall with both purpose and burden, I said hello to the guys in the hall and then took up my usual seat and got my flute out of its pouch, as I put it together and aligned the embouchure, I could feel butterflies in my stomach. Had I been too confident? What if I didn't finish my list off? What if I made a dick of myself here?

"So, where do you want to start?" said Terry

"True and Trusty"

Tilting his head to one side and with a look that said fair enough, he spoke "Right, off you go then"

I raised my flute, breathed in and started, note after note flowed from somewhere within me, I didn't hesitate or even think, I just closed my eyes and played. I opened my eyes at the end of the tune to see Terry putting a tick in what was a previously empty space.

"What's next?"

Melrose, Waveney, Merry Bandit, Royal Union, Bronze Star, Controversy, Grenadiers, were all soon marked off the list, a few other learners and members heads turned as they seemed to take notice as I played tune after tune, watching Terry as he ticked each of them off the list and after I finished playing the march, Gladiators Farewell, I asked.

"Ok, what's left?"

Terry closed the book with my list in front of him and looked up at me.

"Nothing Glenn, that's you done!"

"Really?"

"Yup, you did it, well done"

I took a moment, then the biggest smile broke on my face, as it sank in. I had completed the list. All that practice, the repeating and driving my Ma crazy, and giving our pet cockatiel "Hooker" a whole new repertoire of sounds, had paid off, to say I felt proud of myself was an understatement.

"So that means..." I started to say but Terry finished my sentence for me,

"That means you are a full blower, you get to walk with the band now, I'll bring it up after practice tonight"

I said nothing, I just put my flute away, and headed up to the bar area, bought myself a Coke and headed upstairs to the pool table. As I walked up the stairs, past the photos and trophies on the walls, I was now part of all this. I couldn't wait to tell my Ma, and all my mates, I was a full blower. Not a pretend band member in a pretend band with cardboard drums. I reached the top of the stairs and walked into the pool room and put a fifty pence piece down on the pool table, "I'll play the winner" I said.

"You not down in the learner's class, mate?" said Mark as he lifted his head up before taking his shot.

"No mate, not tonight"

"Oh, what's wrong with you, the list too much for you?"

"Not at all, there's nothing left on it for me to learn"

"Seriously?" he said looking at me like I had just appeared with no head.

"Yup"

"Well done, that's another full blower in the ranks"

There were more 'well done's' and 'good on ya's' from the rest of the guys there.

"No more listening at full band practice for you then"

"Nope, I'm afraid I'll be playing every tune now"

After we had finished playing pool it was time for main band practice to begin, we headed downstairs and took up our seats and got ready for the first tune to be called. Terry started to speak "I was going to wait until later to bring this up, but I might as well do it now, we have another full blower in the ranks, young Glenn has polished off the list and is now ready for the road"

There was a wee round of applause and 'well done' from members of the band and a few pats on the back from those nearby, I was sitting there with a red face both embarrassed and proud to be mentioned in front of the whole band.

"Right hurry up and call the first tune then" I said trying to get the focus of me, there were a few laughs. Terry called the first tune and my first band practice as a full blower kicked off, it was great playing along and not having to have my book open to play along for any of the tunes. I surprised myself in that I made a few mistakes, maybe I was thinking about it too much but nonetheless it was a great practice and now I had the privilege of looking forward to walking with the band. I would have to attend the meetings now and take in details of parades as I would need to be turning up. It wasn't really that long until Easter, and there would be a uniform to sort out.

CHAPTER 6

The Meeting

Having just completed the list and Terry announcing before the practice that I was now eligible to walk with the band. It was now time for the customary meeting at the end of practice. Alvin had filled me in on how the meetings worked, they were usually always a good laugh, but they also had a serious side as well. They formed part of the practice ritual and it was where any business or news related to the band, fundraising activities or big decisions were dealt with. It was also where invites from other band to take part in their competitions were read out and decided on.

Alvin also told me that they were all very well organised. There were officers in the band who looked after the business of the band, and the people who filled those positions were decided every year at the annual general meeting. I hadn't been to one of them yet, in fact I hadn't been to a band meeting either, as a learner you weren't allowed to attend band meetings, they were for full members only. So, tonight would be my very first one. Usually after the main practice ends there is a lot of milling about, idle chit chat and joking about, people get ready to leave, instruments being put away upstairs or set to the side to be taken home with their owners. The end of practice was almost as loud as the practice itself. Alvin and I were sitting at a table just down from the bar area, he pointed out the officers, and who played what role. As he was pointing them out, all three men took up a position near the door to the main hall, where the drummers usually stood during practice. Billy, the chairman, was getting set up for the meeting and you could tell that he was starting to get a little agitated, the room wasn't coming to order as quickly as he would have liked. While the meetings were a necessity, the fact that they happened at the end of the night meant time was definitely of the essence. He'd obviously had enough of the idle chatter and noise, and in a firm voice he called the meeting to order.

"Right lads, come on, settle down, there's a lot to get through tonight so let's try to get it all sorted as quickly as possible, I don't want be sitting here all night, we all have homes to go to after all"

"If you've met my wife, you'll know I'm not too keen to go home" said George, but Billy was well prepared for him in his reply.

"And I'm sure she's hoping some night you won't"

This was met with laughter and also a dying down of general noise as the room recognised the chairman meant business and it was now time to listen.

"Ok lads, we are ready to go here, get it together ok? We really need to get through the correspondence sent through to the secretary and also make a start on the arrangements for Easter Monday"

"That's not a kick in the teeth away now" Alvin said turning to me, his response was overhead and affirmed by the chairman.

"Exactly Alvin, so we best get a move on"

The chairman, was an older member of the band, looking at him I'd have said he had been a member from the year the band was formed. He was well respected by everyone, so, when he spoke, everybody else just shut up, and if a meeting was descending into stupidity as I'd heard they are were prone to do, he had this look he gave and everyone knew it was time to shut up and get back to the business at hand. As chairman he called the shots and had the final say on anything the band couldn't agree on. He was joined by Eddie the band secretary, he was the one who brought all the correspondence to the attention of the band and Adrian, he was the treasurer, he looked after anything to do with the band's finances. There were three members that formed a band committee as well, Terry, Jim and Rigby, his first name was Billy, but seeing as there were a few of them in the band he had a nickname.

"Everybody ready to go then?" continued Billy, "Good, right Eddie, will you read the minutes from the last meeting and let's get this kicked off there's lots to get through tonight"

"No problem Mr Chairman, alright lads these are the minutes of the last meeting" Eddie then gave a brief overview of what had been spoken about and agreed upon at the last meeting. Whenever he had finished, the chairman gave the band the opportunity to bring anything up from that meeting.

"Any matters arising from the minutes? He asked looking intently around the room, sensing no queries he said "No? ok then we are good to proceed, over to you Mr Secretary, what delights have you got for us this evening?"

"Thanks Mr Chairman" said the secretary as he shuffled what looked like letters in his hand, "Well lads there are just the three competition invites for us to consider tonight, then we can get to sorting out the arrangements for Easter Monday, the first letter comes from the Ballymacarrett Defenders"

There were pantomime boos and hisses coming from the rest of the members sitting at the meeting.

"What do they want now? They going to apologise for stealing our latest march?" said Parky and laughter broke out across the hall.

Eddie raised his eyebrows and then continued on reading the letter "The officers and members of Ballymacarrett Defenders Flute Band, formally invite Pride of the Raven Flute Band to attend our annual competition, taking place on April 24th. The parade will commence at Ormeau Park following the agreed parade route. Prizes will be awarded in all the usual categories. We would appreciate it if you could confirm your attendance, many thanks…" the secretary tailed off, knowing that the majority in the room could fill in the blanks. At the end of the silent acknowledgment that all was understood, Smokey kicked the meeting off by standing up and sharing his very strong opinion on this invite.

"I don't know why we go to their competition every year, it's not like we have a chance of winning at it" he found an ally in Alvin's brother Mark.

"Aye, that's why they invite that band from Kilkeel, the Pride of Ballinran, up every year, they give all the first-place melody trophies to them"

Sensing the negativity rising, the chairman brought the meeting back to order, only slightly raising his voice so as to draw everyone's attention away from the impromptu discussion of the matter at hand.

"Ok lads I didn't ask for a debate on this, the secretary is merely making us aware that we have been invited. So, with that in mind do have we any proposals for taking or not taking the competition?"

"I propose we take it" said Stevie, "It's a local parade and it's a rule in the band that we take all local parades, so it's not really up for debate regardless of whether we win or not"

Any seconders for Stevie's proposal?

"Aye I'll second it" said Frankie

"Any amendments?"

Smokey piped up "I'll amend it, I propose we don't take it"

"And seconders for the amendment"

"Yes, me" said Mark

"Ok lads we have a proposal and an amendment, so that means we need to take a vote. All full members of the band are expected to vote, so no sitting on the side lines please. Ok, we will start with the amendment first, all those in favour of not going to the Defender's competition raise their hand" He scoured the room and began counting the hands in favour of not going, 1,2,3,4,5, he spotted Alvin being indecisive, so instead of waiting, he prompted him to seek clarification "Alvin is your hand up or down?"

"It's down"

"Down, ok"

I was so taken with watching everything going on, I didn't

even notice that the chairman was staring right at me, My non participation in this hadn't escaped his notice, he quickly brought me into the meeting, "Glenn are you not voting?" At first, I was looking round the hall to see if somebody else called Glenn would respond.

I totally forgot that now I was no longer a learner and a full member of the band, I could vote in meetings, so I raised my hand.

"You're in favour of not going to this Glenn?" He was just checking that I understood what was going on, "Oh no sorry, we should go" this seemed to please the chairman as he finished the count and could now continue.

"Ok, that makes five in total for the amendment" the Chairman continued with the voting process.

"And now, all those in favour of the proposal that we take the competition"

He hadn't even finished his sentence when a sea of hands went up around the room, again he counted them of making sure he had got exact numbers, standing up and peering around the room to make sure he hadn't missed any one or anyone had opted out.

"I count twenty in favour of the proposal, that's that sorted then we are going to the Defenders competition"

He took his seat again.

"Mr Secretary will you confirm our attendance with the Defenders, and we will make arrangements closer to the day to sort out meeting times etc"

We went through the same process for the other two letters the secretary had with him. I started to wonder how on earth the secretary got these letters, that were addressed to the band, on headed paper and everything. I mean it's not like the band hall was somewhere the postman would stop by, in fact we didn't like people knowing we were there at all, but it was a bit hard to keep the sound of twenty flutes, a bass drum and five drums a secret!!

"Is that everything Mr Secretary?"

"There is one more thing, I'm not sure whether we should look at it now or wait."

"What is it?"

"Our lodge from Scotland have sent their invite for their twelfth of July celebrations in Motherwell this year"

I turned to Alvin and said.

"Why on earth do we walk in Scotland on the twelfth?"

"Oh no, we don't mate, they have their twelfth parade earlier than ours, because most of the bands in Scotland come here to walk the twelfth"

"Oh right, so do we go to Scotland every year?"

"Yeah pretty much, it's great, the lodge there love us and the crowds at the parade love seeing the Belfast bands over"

I had no idea this was even a thing, suddenly in my mind we were international artists about to go on tour across Scotland and Northern Ireland, this was amazing. My thoughts came back to earth with a bump, Mum! How on earth would I be able to convince her that going to Scotland with the band was a good idea? Well she had allowed me to go to Canada to meet bio-dad so, Scotland shouldn't be a problem.

"I think we need to discuss this now" said the chairman, "If we leave it any later, we might not have time to get things organised, is that ok with everyone?"

No one objected so we were going to decide on this now.

"What terms are they offering then?" asked Rigby.

"I'll read the letter out then, it's all in there for us"

"Ok, let's hear it"

The secretary read the letter out and what I could gather from it was that we would all be put up in lodge members houses in the area, we would be there for the weekend and home before the twelfth in Belfast. We would be getting a bus from the hall to the ferry and the lodge would have one waiting for us when we got off.

There was the customary question regarding a proposer and a second, unsurprisingly there was no amendment raised for this one, and just like that we were going to Scotland for a parade!

The chairman refocused the guys, reiterating that there was still a lot to be discussed.

"Now, Mr Treasurer have you anything to bring to the band?"

"No, nothing of any urgency Mr Chairman, we can wait until after the Easter parades to work on some fundraising, especially now that we have agreed to go to Scotland"

"Ok then, arrangements for Easter Monday, can we make sure that we pass on whatever we decide to those who haven't been able to make it tonight? Good, ok Mr Secretary can you go through the arrangements?

"No problem, Mr Chairman"

It amazed me how the members addressed each other in the meeting, it's like they forgot the whole lads banter thing and had a level of decorum and respect that was hard to find elsewhere in life, except maybe a courtroom. A group of grown men, listening intently to what each other had to say, apologising for interrupting and acting according to a set of rules that were partly written and partly tradition. Tradition plays a big part in being a member of a band and not just in regard to the parades and the tunes, but in how things are supposed to get done, this wasn't some hap hazard group of Neanderthals, it was a team.

The Secretary went through the arrangements for Easter Monday, we would be meeting at the hall at seven in the morning. I didn't even get up that early for school! What if I slept in? What if I missed it all? That would be a disaster, I could feel myself starting to get distracted and missed what was being said. I checked in with Alvin. Apparently, we would then go to the worthy president's house, have breakfast there and then walk to the Avenue where the parade would leave at 9:30am. The destination for this year's parade was Londonderry, always a controversial location due to the nature of the troubles and a lot of things that happened with parades there over the years.

There was some debate as to whether we would actually get there or not, it seems there was an issue with the parade within the local council and there may be some trouble should the Apprentice Boys from Belfast attempt to join their brethren in Londonderry. I didn't care, I was just happy to be walking with the band, I couldn't wait, and then I heard my name being mentioned and suddenly my attention was drawn from my thoughts to what was happening in the meeting as I heard Terry stating " We are going to need a uniform for young Glenn here, this will be his first parade after all".

There were some murmurs and then the chairman asked a question "What spare gear do we have? Does anyone have any idea?" There was a moment of silence and then Frankie responded.

"We do have some spare uniforms, but I don't think there is anything that will fit the wee lad, I mean look at the size of him, he turns side-ways and disappears" There was some laughter at this.

"So, what you're saying is that everything we have is too big"

"Yeah that is exactly what I am saying"

"Ok, what other options do we have? We don't want to be in a position where he isn't walking"

"I think we still have some jumpers with the bands badge on them, and there are a few ties as well" said Terry.

"Ok Glenn do you have a white shirt you can wear" asked the chairman.

"Aye I have a few from school I can use"

"So, all we need is a pair of trousers then?"

"I do have a pair of maroon trousers at home I could wear"

"Right that works, and we can see about getting some of the gear that we do have tailored to fit you later"

"Why can't we just go to Alexander's and get him a uniform made?" asked Mark.

"Well we could, but I don't think that would be the wisest decision seeing as we have been talking about the possibility of a new uniform for next year, there's no point, given the amount of money we will spend on the new one"

A new uniform! My ears pricked up at this, when was this decided? What colour would it be? When would we have it for? A million questions were racing around my head, realising that I had missed so much from not being at the meetings. This had obviously been a closely guarded secret, even Alvin, my best mate in the band, hadn't breathed a word of this to me.

"Mate, how come you didn't say anything about the new uniform?"

"I couldn't, it's something that was for discussion in meetings only, but sure you know now"

"Right enough, I can't wait to hear more about it"

Meanwhile the discussion about what I was going to wear as a uniform continued with another band member trying to make a case for making sure I got a proper uniform to parade in.

"Well he can't wear his own trousers and a jumper all year round"

"We said we would look at getting something altered so that

it fits him, that's the best we can do at the minute, are you ok with that Glenn?"

"Oh god aye, I'm just happy to be walking with the band"

"Good man, we will have to get you a hat and plume as well, that thankfully won't be as difficult as getting you a jacket, we will bring a few down for you to try out on Sunday and you can take one home with you then"

"That's great, thanks"

"Right I think that's all we can do about that at the minute, we might as well look quickly at Easter Tuesday too"

We went on to discuss the arrangements for Easter Tuesday, another of the annual parades with the Junior Orange Lodges, their destination was Bangor this year. Once this had been sorted, I could sense that the meeting was drawing to a close.

Even though I had a sense of apprehension, I couldn't wait to get home and tell my Ma about the arrangements. I'm sure she'll be glad to have me out of her hair for a couple of days. She always talked like she needed a break from me and my brothers, there were literally times when I thought she couldn't stand us. It turns out she's tired from working and cleaning up after us all around the house. I was brought back to the meeting hearing the chairman ask if there was any other business, there were no responses.

"Ok then, I propose the meeting closed, goodnight folks and see you all next week"

I said my goodbyes and made the usual walk home following my traditional route. My mind was buzzing, Easter parades, and the trip to Scotland, that was going to be a cracker. Three days away with the band, walking in the big Scottish parade and god knows where else we would end up. Alvin had told me that the lodge in Scotland like us to play at some of the clubs around the area and have what they call a sash bash! I couldn't wait, the craic was going to be mental, and I think more than a few memories are going to be made! I bounced into the house and just verbally vomited all over my Ma recounting all the details of the meeting and the arrangements for Easter and Scotland. And just when I am about to break the world record for words in a minute, I was rudely interrupted.

"Right son, slow down, there are other things to consider ok?

"What do you mean other things?"

"Well for a start Easter Monday isn't a problem Glenn, the Tuesday isn't as straight forward. We have arranged to go out on Easter Tuesday, the whole family, your Uncle Davy, Aunt Lillian, all your cousins and your Uncle Billy and Aunt Anne as well, and you have your Easter clothes to wear, I didn't spend all that money for you not to wear the stuff"

"Ack Ma, come on! I don't want to go to Portrush, I want to walk with the band, these are my first two parades, I've already said I'm going to them, I can't back out now!"

"Well you'll just have to tell them you're not going son, it's all arranged, and it has been for a while"

"Well how come I'm only hearing about it now?"

"Need I remind you young man, we make the decisions around here not you, ok! And besides, your cousin Alan is looking forward to seeing you, you both get on well sure"

My Ma's ability to switch from strict disciplinarian to rational mother was almost as fluid as water, which made it difficult to argue with her at times, but this time her slippery ways were not going to deter me.

"I know we do Ma and I'm always happy to see him, but I've been practicing for this for ages and I don't want to let the lads down"

How could I get her to realise how seriously disappointed I was, this was like losing the World Cup! It wasn't right. But no matter how much I protested, I just got shot down.

"Don't be so daft, I'm sure the band will survive one day without you, they've done alright up to now, it's over and done with Glenn, so stop going on about it ok? You're going to Portrush and that's final"

She left me standing there like a lost cause looking for a hand-out and muttered something along the lines of, "Ungrateful wee shite, most kids would be biting your hand off to go to Portrush for the day, but no, he wants to traipse around Bangor with a band". And that was that, the discussion such as it was, was over, deal done, end off! Well to my Ma anyway, to me this was only round one!

As I climbed the stairs up to my bedroom, the only thing on my mind was how on earth do I tell the guys in the band that I won't be there on Easter Tuesday? They always talked about getting a full band out, they understood when people had to work, but me I was going for day out with my family to Portrush, they'd never understand that, and let's face it, it sounds like a shit excuse, doesn't it? I've come up with better to convince my teachers why I haven't done my homework and here I am trying to convince grown men that I can't parade with the band because my parents want me to go and make sandcastles! Even though that was the truth, I was going to look like a right dickhead! I didn't want to miss the Easter Tuesday parade. There was still time though, maybe I could do some stuff around the house and sweeten my Ma up a bit and she would let me go anyway?

It was worth a shot, and so mission 'charm your way to getting what you want' was on. For the next week or so, I turned into the most helpful person in the world, 'Mum can I help you with this?' 'Do you need a hand putting the shopping away?', 'Can I help with the washing up?' I mean I was the epitome of youthful virtue, but my Mum was the Sherlock Holmes of bullshit detection, she knew fine well that everything I was doing, had one ulterior motive. It was the most un-covert covert operation in the history of espionage, I might as well have went around wearing one of those Marx brothers glasses and fake moustache sets you can get from Elliott's fancy dress shop. I needed to raise my game, after all I was dealing with a master in their field, an expert in foiling their offspring's personal ambition and their 'parents know best' super power was at its peak level of suppression. It was clear what I had to do, I had to go rogue! I would need to be tough to pull this off, I needed to be two steps ahead all the way, "She doesn't stand a chance" I thought to myself. Operation ABC (Absolute Bastard Child) was now in effect. If killing her with kindness wouldn't work, then the opposite probably would. I would be as bad as possible, I'd end up getting grounded which would mean no trip to Portrush. You can't go on family trips if you're grounded! Someone would have to stay with me or better still I'd be told "We don't want you on this trip, so you might as well go and walk with the band".

This new offensive initially brought about positive results, it got me out of eating those awful tongue sandwiches as I chewed them up and just spat them out and pretended to boke. I was sent to my room for this and to me that was all the confirmation I needed that this new offensive strategy would ultimately bring me victory. There was a downside to this plan and I had to be prepared for, I would probably get the arse beat of me more than once as a result, but I needed to stay strong in the face of adversity, this was my siege of Derry and there would be No Surrender! Mum wasn't about to surrender either, she was well prepared for this type of warfare. Instead of throwing the food out as had happened with the tongue sandwiches, now food that I refused to eat just seemed to keep reappearing. If I didn't eat it, then just like magic it would be waiting for me at the next available mealtime. When I woke up one morning to find the cold bowl of stew I had refused to eat for dinner the night before was my breakfast instead of some nice heart-warming 'Ready Brek' or even a nice bit of slightly burnt toast, I started to realise that maybe I was in over my head. The only way to end this siege of stew, unfortunately was to eat it, cold! I had to concede, no matter what I tried to do to get out of this Easter Tuesday family day out, was just not going to work. The sooner I gave in, the sooner I would eat somewhat normal food again. And besides, there were other things to be getting on with, like fundraising for the band.

In my desire to overcome the Easter Tuesday disappointment, I had forgotten that Alvin and I had organised to run a ballot to bring funds into the band. We had pooled some of our pocket money to buy prizes. We were able to get, a screwdriver set, a vase, a three pack of playing cards, a washing up pack from Glovers, and a box of chocolates, that's all we were able to afford. We thought it was brilliant, we had got a few books of ballots from Glovers as well and every week we were selling ballots to guys in the band and to our family members and friends, we must have tortured everyone about this ballot. We treated it like it was biggest thing to happen since sliced bread, everywhere we went, a book of ballots came with us, we excitedly shared the prizes they could win, as if their lives depended on winning a screwdriver set, I mean you would never want to be caught short and not have the screwdriver you needed! We were relentless and everyone humoured us, it was all for a good cause after all. We decided that we would draw the ballot at the meeting before the parade on Easter Monday and hand the prizes out accordingly. We sold the ballots at fifty pence each and wrote the name of the person buying the ticket on the back of the copy left in our book. These would then go into a hat or a box or something and we would draw them out. We decided that we wouldn't actually draw them out ourselves, we would get someone else to do that, we didn't want anyone thinking we had fixed the ballot. Imagine if Alvin or I drew out a ballot with our name on it! We were doing our bit to help out, at the end of the day, it takes money to run a band, with uniforms, instruments and a band hall to maintain. Yes, we all paid dues in every week, but that would never be enough to pay for everything needed to make the band function.

The night of the big draw arrived, Alvin and I needed to be prepared for the night's proceedings. During the practice while the learners were going through their paces with Terry, we spent a bit of time working out how we were going to do things, who would say what and who we would ask to draw the ballots for us. We had managed to find a big lunch box to put them in, it was clear so everyone could see there was no shenanigans going on with the draw, it was the best thing we could find, but it would do the job rightly. We also had counted the money up and we were surprised to find that we had raised seventy-five pounds for the band. We were absolutely ecstatic at this amount, when we had come up with the idea, we thought if we raised about thirty quid or so we would have been doing really well, this was more than double that amount. We were all biz! Once we were settled and knew what we were doing. We got our prizes together, we sealed the lunchbox and put the money in some cash bags we had got from the treasurer and headed downstairs to the main practice area. We sat together and made sure we didn't let the lunchbox or prizes out of our sight.

Practice proceeded normally and the band was sounding well, it passed in a blur as each tune ending brought us closer to the meeting and the ballot. With the playing of the national anthem, practice was over and now it was on to the meeting. There was the reading of the minutes from the last meeting and a run through of the arrangements of Easter Monday and Tuesday. There were a few invites to parades and competitions and even a letter from the lodge we would walk with on the twelfth of July. After they had been dealt with, the secretary went on to the next piece of business.

"Well lads, I'm sure you're all aware that over the past few weeks, Alvin and Glenn have been selling ballot tickets to raise some money for the band. And tonight, is the big draw, so, without any further ado, I'm gonna hand it over to them and good luck to everyone who has bought a ballot, So, Alvin and Glenn, over to you"

Alvin spoke first "Thanks very much Mr Secretary, well as you know we have been selling ballots for the past few weeks"

"Aye the Secretary just told us that" said Rigby

"For god's sake Billy, let them get on with it"

"Ok Ok, they should know they are gonna get raked at some point like"

"I know, but let them at least finish the thing before getting stuck into them"

Alvin continued on, "As I was saying, we have been torturing everyone we know about buying ballots, we just wanted to do our bit for the band, I will hand you over to Glenn, who will tell you what the prizes are and how we are going to run the draw"

There was a wee round of applause as Alvin sat down and I stood up to speak.

"You really didn't have to clap lads. I would have got up and spoke anyway"

"Listen to Paisley Junior here, he'll be encouraging us all to get out and vote" there were some laughs at this and I was a little red faced, but I got on with the job at hand.

"Ok, so we have five prizes and we are going to draw five names out of the hat, we'll if we had a hat, we would do that, we have a lunch box instead"

"A lunchbox, I hope your school dinner isn't one of the prizes"

I ignored the comment and continued explaining the prizes.

"So first prize is this wonderful screwdriver set, it comes with all manner of screwdrivers in it and I'm sure will come in handy at some point for whoever wins it, our second prize is this wonderful floral vase, our third prize is a blessing in disguise for someone, a wonderful collection of cleaning materials from the cleaning experts at Glovers, and for the gambler or magician in training our fourth prize is this wonderful pack of three decks of playing cards, and fifth prize is a box of chocolates"

There were some collective 'oohs' and 'aahs' as I announced the prizes, like the audience in an episode of 'The Price is Right' or 'Bullseye'.

"We are going to need some help with this as we don't want to be drawing the ballot's out ourselves, so we thought that we would call on some trusted members of the band to help us out. For the first prize we are going to ask Terry to draw the ticket from the lunch box, Terry if you would"

Terry left his seat and walked over to the lunch box and ruffled his hand around before grabbing a ticket and handing it over to me to read out the winner.

"So here we go, for our first prize, the winner is, Alvin Nelson"

There was a stunned silence in the room which was then met with cries of "Fix, fix, it's a bloody fix"

I was killing myself laughing the very thing we didn't want to happen had happened.

"We were prepared for this happening, and we decided that we wouldn't take any of the prizes should any of our names be drawn out, so Terry if you could draw another ticket out for us that would be great"

Terry had another go and this time he drew out Billy Rigby's name.

"Congratulations Billy, you are now the proud owner of this wonderful screwdriver set"

Billy accepted his prize graciously and took his seat again.

"And now we will draw the ticket for our second prize, and to help us we would like to ask Alvin's Dad to help us out here, Mr Nelson, come on down" I said dramatically.

"He really does think he's presenting 'The Price is Right'

doesn't he? I heard someone say.

"Well he's not doing a bad job of it I'll tell ya that"

Alvin's dad came up to the front of the hall, put his hand in the lunchbox and drew out the next winning ticket, it was a name I didn't recognise.

"That's one of my Mums friends" Alvin said, "I'll make sure she gets it"

"I'm sure you're a bit young for her mate"

"Right lads knock that off"

Alvin and I looked at each other and just sniggered, we knew what he meant, it was pretty funny.

"Well that's the floral vase gone now, so we have the cleaning pack, the cards and the chocolates, left to go.

The cleaning pack was won by a member's wife and the pack of cards was won by another friend of Alvin's mum and the chocolates went to Frankie.

"Well that concludes the draw for the ballot" I said "We would like to thank everyone who supported us and put up with us pestering them over the past few weeks, and we hope the prize winners enjoy their prizes. Thanks, and maybe we will do it again soon"

Alvin nudged me as I sat down, "Tell them how much we raised and then we can hand it over"

I had completely forgot about that part. I stood back up again.

"Oh, did you have another prize to hand out"

"No, I just forgot to tell you how much we raised"

"And hand it over too" there was laughs at this.

"We raised the grand total of seventy five pounds for the band, we know it's not loads, but we think it's a great effort given the short period of time"

There was a round of applause as Alvin and I handed over the money to the treasurer and took our seats again, a few members ruffled our hair and told us 'well done' and then the secretary spoke again.

"I just want to speak on behalf of the committee and the members of the band, and express our thanks to Alvin and Glenn for taking the time to run the ballot and doing such a great job with the prizes, and standing up and doing the draw in front of you lot, that's no easy thing"

There was some more clapping and "Hear Hear" from the members gathered.

The secretary continued "It's kids like this that are the future of this band, wanting to do something that goes beyond just turning up every week paying their dues and being a member, so I just want to say again that we appreciate the hard work you have put into this and that we are privileged to have such dedicated members like yourselves, you are a credit to the band lads, and you have done us all proud"

There was another round of applause after this and a few more pats on the back as well.

"Now get the drinks in with the money you didn't hand over"

There were quite a few laughs after this, Alvin and I just sat there red faced and said nothing. We had done our bit for the band. We were proud of ourselves and it was great to hear that from the secretary and other members of the band as well. It was nights like this, that made you feel you were part of something special, worthwhile even, and realise that you weren't just turning up every week just for the sake of it, there was more to it than that, it was like an extended family, and I loved it.

CHAPTER 7

Easter Monday – The First Parade

6 am Easter Monday, I awoke with my Ma's words from the night before ringing in my ears.

"Set your alarm and try to be quiet getting ready. I don't want you clunking about the house making all sorts of noise, if you wake your brothers up, I'll go through you for a shortcut!"

This had been followed by the altogether more helpful,

"I'll leave your shirt and trousers ironed and sitting out for you on the table, and I'll leave some money for you on the mantlepiece ok?"

As if there wasn't enough pressure on the day, I'm was now trying to navigate from my room to the bathroom without making a noise, the stairs down from my room creaked more than my Granny's knees. This was going to be bloody impossible. I opened my bedroom door and stood at the top of the stairs, pausing to think about the best way to tackle the minefield of creakiness before me. I could just go for it, just walk down the stairs like a normal human being, my chances of pulling that off on a day like this were zero! There was only one way available to me, I would need to climb down the bannisters. I imagined the bloke from those wildlife programmes narrating my decent. "The young bandsman finds himself atop of the formidable and legendary bannister range. With three in total to negotiate, the one closest in proximity presents him with the steepest descent. If he is successful in navigating his way through, the transition to the secondary landing banister will be difficult to say the least, requiring his footing to be sure and true. The next stage would be the shortest, requiring him to land in such a way as to ensure that only minimal steps are needed to cross the short mezzanine landing and arrive safely at the entrance to the bathroom".

Psyching myself up I headed over the first banister, so far so good. I struggled to find the right footing for the next one and happen to kick the bannister, I held my breath at the noise, as if that was going to stop anyone hearing it. No reaction, it looks like I may have just got away with it. Just the next section to go through and I would be there, it was at this point I realised that I would need to get back to my room as well, and this method just wouldn't work, so, just as I was about to put my feet down and claim the triumphant conquest of Mount Banister, I lifted my head up in the direction of my Mums room, and there she was standing in the door way shaking her head with the 'I'm going to go through you for a shortcut' look on her face, I shrugged my shoulders as if to say it's not my fault.

Having been rumbled I took the traditional route into the bathroom to get washed and ready for the day ahead, I looked at myself in the mirror, winked and acknowledged that today would be an aftershave day, not that I shaved yet, but today required the utmost in my grooming skills, and smelling good was high on the agenda. I had a choice, Brut or Hai Karate, to me that choice was simple. Brut, because nothing beats the great smell of Brut, that's what the adverts say anyway. I put enough on for the whole band, my face stinging with every splash on my skin.

After finally making it downstairs I had the immense privilege of making my own breakfast, Which I have to say I did quite easily. Making toast on the gas grill is something that has to be experienced, one sided toast that's crisp on one side, slightly soft and moist on the other, and butter melting away on top, pure beaut!

"I've no idea why you gurn so much about making me toast Ma" I said to myself, "It's not like it's hard or anything!" If she had heard me talking like that, I'm sure she would have given me something to gurn about! That was one of her phrases, she had loads of them, but there was always something sinister about this one, if I was crying about something or other and she didn't want to listen, she would roll out a "I'll give you something to cry about" that always seemed to make you stop immediately, I guess the threat of getting smacked with something was way worse than whatever I was crying about in the first place.

With breakfast out of the way it was now on to the more important stuff, getting my uniform on. It wasn't the full uniform yet, but what I did have was close enough for me. The sight of those maroon trousers and my maroon V-neck jumper emblazoned with the bands crest proudly embroidered on the left hand side just above the heart, a fitting location I thought, made my chest puff out with pride. I'd never liked wearing my school uniform, but suddenly my school shirt was transformed into a band uniform and for once I was actually happy to be wearing a tie! Although this one was so much easier to sort than my school tie, clip on ties were the way forward, and I wouldn't mind letting the Principal know when I got back from Easter holidays. The bands crest was on the tie, and I was pleased that when I put the jumper on that the V-neck didn't cover that up. My hat and blue plume were all ready to go, one of the guys in the band hand spent a fair bit of time joining two coat hangers together to give my hat the right shape, which I was completely grateful for, if I'd been left to sort that out, I'd have gone out looking like that game Frustration, you know the one with the wire and you have to guide a wire loop around it without it buzzing? The only other thing I needed was of course my flute, I couldn't forget that. I went back into the kitchen to get my shoes, they were absolutely gleaming, my Uncle had been in the TA and he had polished them for me, he knew how to bull a shoe up until they were like mirrors. I carried them into the living room and sat down to pull them on. I stood up and took a look at myself in the mirror, "Looking good Glenn, looking good" I thought to myself, here I was in uniform about to walk with Pride of the Raven on Easter Monday, I'm not sure I'd ever felt as proud in my life.

I was jolted back to reality with a quick glance at the clock, "Shit! I'm late" remembering there was money on the mantlepiece, I threw it in my pocket and then I started to make my way out to the front door, when I heard the familiar tones of my Ma's voice.

"Glenn..."

"Sorry for making too much noise Mum"

"It's ok, you didn't son, I just wanted to get a picture of you in your uniform before you left"

Well didn't that take me by surprise, I really thought I was going to get told off for the bannister antics. She made a fuss of me as I stood at the front door and took picture after picture with one of those wee disposable cameras. No doubt I would get the job of taking them round to the chemist to be developed, but at least I would want to see these pictures. Usually when we got pictures developed they had a picture of the back of someone's head or there would be some other weird thing going on and I wondered if some of them would overlap like the ones she took at the caravan or of the dogs, where one picture was made up of two pictures, I never understood how that happened though.

"I really need to go here Ma or I'm gonna be late"

"Right ya better get a move on then. We will see you in the Avenue, I'll bring the camera"

"Ok Ma, I will see ya later"

"See ya later son, have a good day" she went back inside closing the hall door and I could hear her carefully cajoling the rest of the house to get up or they would be late for the parade. I started making my way to the band hall. I was tempted to ring Darren's doorbell just to rub it in that I was walking with the band. I knew I'd see him one way or the other though, he'd either be standing where I'd stood so many months ago, watching and waving, or he'd be standing there in uniform as well. I hoped for the former and satisfied my mind that he wouldn't be walking. I can't wait to see his face when he catches sight of me in my uniform I thought, and it was that thought that propelled me to the band hall. There was hardly a sinner on the streets as my Ma would say, and why would there be? Not even the sun was up at this time of day! I walked with a sense of pride, catching a glimpse of myself in every car window I passed. I rounded the corner from Frank Street and headed towards the familiarity of the band hall and it was a hub of activity, guys standing outside smoking and drinking. One group caught my eye they were laughing like crazy. I wondered what they were laughing at, so I made a beeline for them and the guys were happy to see me or at least it seemed that way.

"Morning Glenn, you ready for your first parade?"

"Too right I am! I can't wait to form up, what were you lot laughing at there? I thought Tommy was gonna have a heart attack"

"Ah you have to hear this one, we were all round at big Adrians last night, having a few drinks, we're well into our second bottle of vodka and Adrian is completely gone, he starts telling us about how amazing he is at his job, when he loses his balance and falls over and hits his head of the fridge, a full on smack, hits the deck."

"Shit was he alright?".

"Aye he was grand, we put him up on the seat the table and his head down to sleep it off"

"So, what's funny about that?"

"Well when he finally comes around after like an hour or so and he wakes up and says 'What happened to me lads? I've woken up with a really sore thumb!" He bangs his head off the fridge, and he has a sore thumb! That set everyone off again, I have to admit it was pretty funny. Breaking away from the merriment, I asked "Is Terry here yet?"

"Aye mate he's inside"

"Alright I'll see you in a bit then"

I headed for the door of the band hall and those last few steps didn't just change my location, they changed my life. I was part of something, a member of a band, a brotherhood. There was something different about meeting up at the hall for a parade rather than a practice, a different kind of atmosphere, not that it was tense or anything, not in the slightest, there was a buzz in the air, a sense of excitement, expectation drenched in anticipation of the day ahead. I looked around the room and there was Terry in his usual seat with an array of flutes in front of him and a few of the smallest screwdrivers I have ever seen, he nodded as I caught his gaze.

"There he is!! First parade big son, you ready for this?"

A big smile broke on my face

"Oh aye Terry, raring to go"

"Now remember what I told you about breathing?"

"Yeah, stop and you die?"

"Very funny, be careful with your breathing, it's a completely different kettle of fish playing the flute in the hall and walking on the road"

"I'll be grand Terry; I've been marching around my bedroom for days!"

"Ok don't say I didn't warn you!"

"I know, I know, Terry?"

"Yes mate"

"I just wanted to say thanks"

"What for?"

"Well, all your help, I wouldn't be here today if you hadn't taken the time..." Terry interrupted me.

"Listen Glenn, you did all the work, you put the effort in, I just gave you a steer in the right direction, but you're here because you got yourself here,"

I didn't know how to respond to that, that wasn't the kind of thing I usually heard about myself, let's just say it very rarely happened, and even more so in the hall, usually it was all raking and joking so when it did happen, you knew it was meant.

"Thanks Terry, I don't know what to ..."

"Right do me a favour. Go and gather the flutes up, I want us to get tuned up before we hit the road"

"No probs"

I gave a shout up the stairs, "Right lads, finish your game of pool, Terry wants the flutes down to get tuned up before we get on the road" I had the same approach for everyone outside.

"Listen to band captain junior there, first parade and he thinks he runs the show"

"Yeah, whatever you say, Terry wants to tune up, so come on let's go"

"Yes sir"

The majority of the flute players made their way into the hall, took their seats, got their flutes out of their pouches and started to warm up. For some this meant covering all the holes on the flute and just blowing through, making no sound, but making sure air was passing through the whole of the flute, others had a little rag and produced a small bottle of olive oil, dipped the rag in the oil and pulled it through the flute, and all most everyone rubbed some cork grease on the joint between the head and the body of the flute before joining it together.

"Alright lads, everyone ready?" asked Terry, there were nods of approval a silent go ahead, Terry had a look around the room, taking a mental roll call of who was there.

"Right where's Adrian?"

"He's probably getting his thumb bandaged up" said Billy, everybody busted out laughing, the story of the night before had obviously made its way around the whole band.

"Can someone go and get him for crying out loud"

"Will do" said Billy, he headed for the door and then we heard a loud gulder. "Adrian!! Hurry up will ye, Terry's trying to get us tuned up here"

Billy re-entered the hall "He's on his way now"

"What the hell is he up to?"

"No idea, standing talking shite as usual more than likely"

Adrian entered the hall to some jeers and cheers

"Here, Adrian, what's your kids favourite bedtime story?" he looked perplexed, and yet ready to take a raking!

"Here we go" he said.

"Jack and the beanstalk?" Said Billy, "Aye he's the Giant, Fee Fi Fo Thumb, my head hit the fridge now my thumb is numb" in his best 'Jackanory' voice. The room was bubbling with laughter, a well-rehearsed line I thought, far too good to be just off the cuff.

Terry ran us through some exercises that helped us tune up, listening carefully for any flute that might need an adjustment. After about ten minutes we were good to go, then out of nowhere, a whistle brings the room to silence. The band captain, who calls the shots on the road, was now in charge.

"Right lads, time to form up, the club is waiting for us and then we have to get to the Avenue, so drink up and let's go"

This was it, the moment that I had been working towards was right outside the door. After checking ties and trouser hems and a whole host of other little things, we all made our way outside to the street. The Drum Major who walks at the front of the band took up his position, mace pole in hand, he reminded me of one of those American drill sergeants, with his moustache all wispy and his barked-out orders. "Right lads let's get formed up" This was something I hadn't seen before, as far as I knew the band captain was in charge when the band on the road, I guess I still had a lot to learn. The drummers with their chrome drums glistening in the morning sunlight, took up the space directly behind the Drum Major. Then behind the drums the bass drum took up the centre of the band flanked by the two cymbal players then it was the flutes, five rows and five flute players per row, I was left of centre in the front row and the other rows were ordered according to size and seniority, with pride of place being the back row of flutes.

"Band! Stand at ease!" Shouted the Drum Major and we all stood with our feet shoulder width apart, I was well versed with this from doing drill routines in the Boys Brigade. And there was me thinking that wearing that pillbox hat and silly white pocket haversack thing was a waste of time!

"Band, Attention!" and with this we duly complied. The Drum Major then turned and faced the front.

"Tandragee!" shouted the band captain, that's how we knew what tune to play, he'd call one of the tunes on the list, I would need to make sure I listened, so I didn't play the wrong thing.

The Drum Major shouted again, "Band, on the rolls, by the centre, quick march!" the drummers kicked in with two five beat rolls and we were on our way, we almost immediately had to wheel right and head towards the Woodstock Road. We hadn't walked too far when I heard "Glenn, hang back and get in step", I had strayed forward in my rank and was out of step, a quick adjustment and a skip had me back in line with everyone else, although this wouldn't be the only time I heard that phrase throughout the day. I guess marching in my bedroom and doing drill with the BB is nowhere near the same as marching on the street with a band. We marched for about 10 minutes and I'd already drifted out of line and step about five or six times,

"Glenn, sharpen up here, you're all over the place" I heard Rigby say, I looked round and tried to get back in line, I hunched my shoulders as if that was going to help me, but luckily for me we came to a halt not long after that. Today's parade was with the Apprentice Boys of Derry, and they don't have lodges like the Orange order does, they have clubs. These clubs are named after men who were involved in the siege of Derry, and their sashes and regalia are maroon in colour which I thought was very fitting seeing as our uniform was maroon. Not far from where we had stopped, they stood waiting with their banners and flags, all ready to be unfurled and released into the crisp Easter morning air. The Drum Major barked out his orders, "Band at ease", "Band fall out". After a quick right turn, we broke ranks, hats off and jackets were opened. There were some refreshments available for us, and even though it wasn't that long since I'd had my breakfast, I was feeling a little peckish.

About fifteen minutes later, the band captains whistle rang out again and that meant it was time to form up again. We followed the Drum Major's instructions again and we were off. We headed for the Avenue to meet up with the rest of the parade and head off for the day. We started marching on the tap, that's when the lead drummer taps a single beat to keep us in step and no sooner had we taken about ten steps I heard the dulcet tones of Rigby again

"For God's sake Glenn come on, get in step!"

I had strayed again. Now Terry was taking the brunt of the stick from Rigby.

"What kind of learners are you training up Terry? We might as well get this guy a pram and push him around"

"I taught him how to play the flute I didn't teach him how to walk"

"Maybe you should have, if he'd two left feet he'd still be out of step"

The guys were laughing away at this, I was kind of embarrassed, I was making a mess of this, I told myself to concentrate more and that would keep them off my case. We approached the top of the second avenue, and I could see the place was hiving with activity.

Walking into the Avenue was such a buzz, it's where I'd had my first encounter with the band, and here I was walking not watching, would I be inspiring someone to join as I walked past? I was jolted back to reality with another, "Get in step

Glenn"

There were bandsmen and Apprentice Boys everywhere. You could hear the sound of drums being tuned and the odd flute playing a new tune or someone trying to show off. Spectators were starting to line the streets, and the parade hadn't even started yet! The buzz was almost like a football match prior to kick off, everyone was primed and ready, the anticipation was thick in the air. We crossed the intersection at the top of the Beersbridge road, the band captain called Blaze Away. I absolutely loved this tune, more so because I had heard my mate Darren who had joined the Defenders, struggle to play it. As we passed Paxton Street I could see the blue uniform that belonged to the Defenders. I wondered would I see Darren, what if he was in uniform as well? I needn't have worried as we passed the Defenders, Darren was there, not in uniform but in his new Easter clothes. I smiled as I played and got closer to him seeing me, I looked across and saw his face as he saw me walking in the ranks. He obviously took it bad, he pointed at me and said "Look at the dummy fluter" I was absolutely raging! Dummy fluter is a derogatory term for someone who walks with a band and pretends to play the flute for the most part, they might well have been learning but they certainly couldn't play every tune their band played and they were usually there to just 'fill a rank'. How bloody dare he, calling me that! I played all the louder, not that that would make much difference to him, but to me I was proving a point! We wheeled right and marched into the other half of Paxton Street and finished the tune. No sooner had the drum major called 'fall out', and I was off on a mission to find Darren and give him a bit of what for. "I'll give him dummy fluter" I thought to myself, 'Has he heard himself playing?' When we broke ranks, I ran like a mad man towards where I had seen Darren standing just moments earlier

"Hey Glenn where you off to? Don't be going too far we will be forming up again soon" I heard Alvin say.

"I'm just going into the avenue to talk to Darren" I shouted back.

I rounded the corner and began weaving my way through the crowd of men, women and children, saying hello to a few people I knew but determined to get to Darren and give off! I finally made my way to where he was standing, he was now at the edge of the pavement watching another band arrive, I shoved him where he stood and one of his feet slipped of the painted kerb stones, he turned with a start.

"What the..." he turned and saw me standing in front of him, before he could finish his sentence I shouted, "Who the hell are you calling a dummy fluter?" Darren's facial expression changed from one of I'm about to tear someone's head off to, oh it's you.

"I was only raking mate, don't take it to heart"

"Only raking? Not funny at all mate, just cause you're not walking, what's wrong, could the tailor not make a uniform in time for you?" I was raging and not listening at all to what he was saying.

"No, actually I have left the band" this stopped me in my tracks as I was about to go off on my practiced speech that I'd made up on my way round to him, about how much I had practiced and earned this.

"What? Why did you leave?"

"Well I started going with our Colin to the Ledley"

"Boxing? You gave up the flute for boxing?"

"Yeah, Colin's the star, but the trainers are saying I'm pretty good"

Well this kind of changed everything, what do I say now?

"So, training takes place on practice night I take it?

"Aye it does, can't be in two places at once"

"You never know mate; you might get back to it someday"

"Maybe, the flute isn't really my thing, but by the sounds of you some nights I can tell you've come on leaps and bounds"

Nobody really gave you compliments growing up in East Belfast, it's something I've never been sure of why, so you knew it was genuine when someone actually did it. You couldn't acknowledge it or anything like.

"Well, let me know when your first fight comes up, I'll be there"

"Will do mate, thanks, and be careful today, I hear there's talk that the peelers aren't gonna let the parade get anywhere near the train to Derry".

"Aye the guys were saying in our meeting the other week, where did you hear about this?"

"My Da. He's in Belfast Browning Club and they were saying at their last meeting the cops had been in touch to say that they would be making sure the parade doesn't go anywhere near Derry, something about parity of esteem, whatever the hell that means!" This wasn't really news to me, but he was looking out for me and that meant a lot to me. "Thanks for the heads up, I'm sure the guys in the band will have something planned if we don't get there" I said glancing at my watch, "Right well I may get back round to the band here, I am sure we will be heading off soon"

"Have a good one and I'll see you later sure"

"Alright mate, catch you later"

I sauntered back to where the band had stopped, what if my first parade actually doesn't last that long? And with not being able to go to the parade tomorrow, when would I be out again?

I walked on up the street and stood with Alvin who was with his Dad and brothers, "Everything all right?"

"Aye all good, Darren was saying he'd heard the same thing as us that the cops won't let us get on the train today that the parade is being banned from going to Derry"

"Well we knew that was a possibility. Only one way to find out kid, we will march to where we are supposed to and see what happens"

"Sure, we are out tomorrow as well, don't forget"

"Aye, I won't be though, my Ma has arranged some family day out to Portrush, so I won't be there"

"What? ack c'mon Glenn, you've gotta be there, these are the first parades of the season and your first parades ever!"

"I know and I said all that to my Ma, but she just went on about how we need to meet up as a family and how I was a bit of a weirdo for wanting to walk with the band and not go to Portrush"

"Well I can see her point"

"Really? because I can't!"

"Ack she's probably just trying to do right by everyone, sure you'll have a good day up there on the dodgems and the Big Dipper at Barry's"

"Aye sounds like great craic" I said with just the slightest hint of sarcasm "I'd rather be walking with the band though"

"I know, I know, but we will be out lots over the next four or five months, so you have plenty of parades ahead of you"

"Yeah, I guess you're right"

"Right come on, don't let that spoil your day, we'll be off soon"

The now familiar sound of the captain's whistle blast rang out through the air again "Right lads, form up let's get it together now" and like metal drawn to a magnet we all took up our places and stood ready to be on our way again. The street we were in meant we would be near the end of the parade today, and as we stood there waiting on our cue to go, the sounds of the first bands in the parade told us things were underway. One thing I hadn't noticed as a spectator was the roar of noise that came from the bands, it was different standing here in the ranks than on the footpath. Here in the ranks we were surrounded by noise all around us, from the front and back and every direction there was the sound of drums, flutes, accordions, whistles, booming drum majors, you could hardly hear yourself think, I had to try hard not to get caught up in everything that was going on around me and focus on what we were playing. As we started to march, we were playing Shangai Lil', we wheeled right out of the street and then headed straight onto the Avenue, to our left I could see the Orange Hall, with flags flying proudly, there was even a Canadian flag as well! As we walked down the Avenue and neared Madrid Street, I heard familiar voices calling out my name, "Glenn, Glenn" I turned to where the voices where coming from and there were my family decked out in their Easter clothes. Waving like they were trying to stop a bus, big smiles, my Granny especially seemed particularly happy and I couldn't look at her and not think about the one person who wasn't there, my Big Granda, I put my flute down momentarily and waved to them all, I tapped the badge on my chest and pointed to the sky in tribute to my Granda, and with that I raised my flute and played with all the emotion I could muster. My shoulders pushed back with pride and I stood as tall as I possibly could with my chest puffed out, I would find myself waving quite a few times as we walked down the Avenue. More neighbours spotted me and waved, all with big smiles, the only one that came close to my family was that of Big Brian from Westbourne Street, one of their own was walking the streets, I was no longer wee skinny G from Tower Street, I was a fluter, I was a bandsman!

The parade made its way along the Newtownards Road and through the town and arrived at Central Station only to be met by a convoy of meat wagons, otherwise known as Police land rovers, grey like storm clouds about to quite literally rain on our parade. The biggest game of Chinese whispers took place as the news filtered down from the start of the parade right down to the very last band at the rear.

"They're not letting us get on the trains, they have the entrance blocked and the platforms sealed off, they say we are going to City hall" said Stevie.

"What are we going to City Hall for?"

"No idea kid, probably just somewhere for us to go so they can work out what we do next"

So, we were off to the City Hall, this wasn't quite what I had in mind for my first parade, it really didn't matter where we were going, just as long as we were going somewhere. It never crossed my mind that we just decided to go to city hall, what about all the traffic? What about everyone in town? Didn't we need to let anybody know we were coming or something? I was thinking all this when I got a nudge in the back, "Glenn, come on, get back in step" momentary lapses of concentration definitely impacted my ability to march, so with a quick sorry and a skip, I was back in step again. It didn't seem to take us long going from central station to the City Hall, we were met with a line of police there as well, this was turning into a disaster. What on earth was so wrong with our parade that the peelers had to keep interfering? As we stood for what seemed like ages at the city hall, I noticed that some bands and lodges broke rank and started to disperse, others marched away on their own, back to wherever they had left from early this morning I guessed. The band captain appeared where we were gathered and told us that the parade wasn't going anywhere, and they had failed to agree on an alternative location to assemble for the return parade. "So that's it then?" said Alvin's Dad, "We just head for home?"

"Pretty much - but on the upside, we get to parade back - they're gonna get Ian, you know the motorbike cop from Mountpottinger barracks? Well he's going to accompany us back"

"Ooh a police escort home, aren't we privileged"

"Aye aren't we just!"

Then a familiar voice guldered from behind me.

"Right let's get formed up and be on our way lads" the band captain was taking charge and getting us gathered together.

We formed ranks again, the lead drummer started the tap and we were now making our way back to east Belfast. The cop on the motor bike stayed a short distance in front of us, looking back occasionally probably just to check we were still there. And then as we approached a junction, he would speed up to it and check for traffic and make sure it was ok for us to keep going. As we approached the bridge heading over the Lagan, the band captain broke ranks and ran up to the drum major and started having a chat with him. I turned to Stephen "Here, what's that wee conversation all about then?

"No idea mate, I'm sure we will find out soon enough though"

We came off the bridge and started to walk under the over-pass, and the noise from the band grew crazily loud as the bridge over head provided us with a lot of echo. Just up ahead of us the motor bike cop, sped off again to make sure every-thing was ok for us to proceed, as soon as he accelerated the drum major raised his mace pole pointing to the right, this usually indicated that we were going to turn right. But why were we turning right here? What the hell was going on? We seemed to pick up pace as we passed through a side street - then everyone started laughing. Now we all understood what the conversation between the band captain and the drum major had been, we might not be able to get to Londonderry, but we were going to have some fun messing with the motor bike cop! We were about play a bit of hide and seek and the cop, whether he liked it or not was "it". We continued on our new route, the lead tip, kept us on the tap by clicking his drumsticks, then the drum major raised his mace pole to in-dicate a halt. We just stood there laughing until we heard the sound of the motor bike coming towards us again. He'd went so far ahead of us he completely missed that we had changed direction on him. He positioned himself in front of us, and spoke to the band captain as he drove past.

"Don't disappear again"

"It wasn't our fault Ian, the drum major's a comedian"

The peeler obviously thought his little warning had been heard and heeded! Wrong! We disappeared two more times and by the time we had disappeared the third time, the cop was now laughing about it as well, he didn't speed on ahead of us again though.

Now that we were closely being chaperoned, we had no choice but to proceed home the way he wanted us to, we rounded onto the Newtownards Road, heading toward St. Matthews chapel. We walked on down to head up the Avenue. A small crowd started to assemble as the sound of flutes and drums in the air enticed them out of their homes like the Pied Piper as we made our way back into the heart of the community. We arrived at the orange hall and played the national anthem and this is where the Apprentice Boys left us, but that wasn't the end of our parade for the day, we formed up yet again and headed for the band hall, each step was bringing me closer to the end of my very first parade. I didn't want it to end at all, I could have walked the rest of the day in my uniform and played on and on, I was even staying in step now! We finished the parade playing "the jock" as we rounded the corner towards the hall, facing the opposite direction from which we had left this morning and arriving in almost the same spot. The band captain's whistle rang out one last time and we came to a complete standstill. The drum major turned around and faced the rest of the band and raised his hand in salute. "Three in a hoop" said the band captain, the bass drummer tapped the rim of the bass drum three time, we raised our flutes and began to play the National Anthem again.

"Band fall out!" was the final order from the drum major for the day and with a right turn we were dismissed and that was it, my first parade was over.

I stood there for a moment, just taking everything in, I took my hat off and wiped my forehead, The material of the hat felt wet in my hand, I looked at the hat and the royal blue plume attached to the hat badge on the right hand side, the feathers looked a little out of place and I cupped my hand and tried to make it look the way it had this morning when I put it on.

"Did you keep the cardboard cover for your plume?"

I turned around to see Chris one of the younger members of the band, but older than me, taking the plume out of his cap badge and placing it back in its white cardboard sleeve.

"Aye it's in my flute pouch in the hall"

"You may go and get it, you don't want your plume looking like crap tomorrow do you?"

Just like that I was painfully reminded that I wouldn't be walking with the band tomorrow. I'd be in Portrush, eating candy floss and pretending to be scared on the ghost train. I went into the hall and the place was packed with people, members of the band, their families, wives, brothers, sisters, everyone smiling and laughing. The pool table was in action, I could hear the familiar sound of the money dropping and the balls being released as whoever was up there playing got ready to set the game up and break. The makeshift bar was on double time as the queue to get a drink was pretty long. I found my pouch where I'd left it, took out my plume cover and cleaning tool for my flute. I separated the flute into two sections and cleaned it before returning it to the leather pouch and buttoning it closed. It was here now that the parade was over that I felt something I had never felt when I'd been in the band hall, here with everyone's friends and family around them, I actually felt like I was a spare part. I almost felt like I had turned up to a birthday party without an invite and only got staying because I knew some people who had. I started to make my way out of the hall.

"Are you not staying for a bit Glenn?" It was Alvin, he was sitting with his brothers and his Dad,

"Nah, I'm gonna head on mate"

"Ack come on stay for a bit, have a coke and stay for a bit of craic, it's your first parade sure."

"Alright, you've twisted my arm"

I took a seat at the table with Alvin and his family, his Dad shouted up to the guys in the bar,

"Two cokes for the wee lads here when you're ready"

And with that I was immersed in post parade conversation, there was music playing in the background and people hopped from conversation to conversation, from company to company. Suddenly it didn't matter that I wasn't related to anyone because I wore the maroon uniform and that meant I did belong here, my surname didn't do that for me but those colours did.

I knew I'd have to go home at some point, as I'm sure my Ma would want to hear all about my day, and then tell me that she was running a bath for me. I could almost hear her saying "There's no way in hell you're putting on your new Easter clothes without having a bath, I'm telling ye that now son"

So with the prospect of a warm bath and the anticipation of having TCP added to it, my Da swore by that stuff, I had no idea what it was really used for, my Da said it was like medicine for the bath, it was nice to know I was so dirty I made water sick! All I knew was that it smelled like it could cure a tramps B.O. I got up to head home.

Leaving the hall took longer than I'd expected, as I ended up shaking hands with nearly every member of the band, most of them had kind words for me.

"Well done kid"

"Good job today"

"Great to see you walking with the band"

"See you at practice" with those words ringing in my ears, I closed the hall door behind me and headed for home. Usually on my walk home from the hall I would play my flute, not today though, not because I didn't want to, this walk home was different, for a start I was in uniform, and everyone I knew from the area had seen me at some point today walking with the band, there was no need to prove anything, I had achieved something I had set out to do, and as I walked home, silently celebrating my personal achievement, I prepared myself for the grilling from my Ma, the prospect of the TCP bath and waking up tomorrow knowing I wouldn't be putting the uniform on to parade again. I arrived home, opened the hall door and went into the living room to be met by everyone. We weren't a family who showed affection much, definitely seems to be an East Belfast thing, don't show people how you feel. My Ma and Granny were beaming,

"There he is, my boy in the band, we're very proud of you son, and to celebrate we are going to get fish suppers from the Bethany"

Getting food from the Bethany was a real treat, it wasn't like we got food from the chippy all the time. I'm sure my brothers were loving it too, I know I was, I couldn't wait, my mouth was already salivating at the thought, fish and chips with lots of salt 'n' vinegar, pure bliss.

"Right Glenn, hurry up and get out of that uniform, I'll write out the list and you can go down to the Bethany for everyone" said my Ma, suddenly breaking my food thought bubble. I headed up the stairs to get changed, 'So we are having fish and chips to celebrate me walking with the band and I have to go and get it?' I thought to myself, I quickly reconciled it, I could be eating cold stew or worse, egg and onion sandwiches. I hung my uniform up with precision and decided that I could afford to put my shirt in the wash basket, seeing as I wouldn't be needing it tomorrow. I made space in my wardrobe to make sure no other clothes touched my uniform. I'd had this wardrobe for so long there was still a Magic Roundabout character sticker on the door and the brown wood circular handle had seen better days. It had a mirror above three drawers with a shelf where I usually kept my supply of Brut 33 and Hai Karate, but they had been taken off to be replaced with an ever-growing collection of flute band tapes. I had to rely on getting them from guys in school and from other members of the band, it wasn't like you could just walk into Grahams record shop and pick up the latest flute band releases! I originally had only a copy of the Blackskull tape because I had persuaded Fergie to lend me the tape, as long as he got it back the next day, I copied it using the high speed dubbing double tape deck on my stereo. I had played it that much I ended up getting a proper copy of it at Nutts Corner market. Bands had started recording their tunes to try and raise some funds and, in some cases, to show off their new style or new tunes. It was great because you got to hear all these new tunes and old tunes being played in new ways. I'd been told that they would be sold at parades or wee street stalls that would be set up at the field. A lot of bands had started to copy the Blackskull's style and their tape was one of the most popular doing the rounds with band members. I was just taking the tape out of its box to put it on whenever I heard the dulcet tones of my Ma.

"Glenn!! What the hell's keeping ye, come on, you won't want to get caught in a queue down there"

I had almost forgot about going to the Bethany, I put my blue puma tracksuit on and headed downstairs to receive the chippy instructions. There was no simple trip to the chippy, everyone had requirements and it was embarrassing walking into the place with a piece of paper and reading them out. Mum kicked the proceedings off.

"Now get me a fish, make sure you tell them to do it well done, I cant be having one of those soggy fish"

"Yeah make sure mine is well done too son, but not as well done as your mums, don't worry, ask for Marie, she knows exactly how I like it done, and if she's not on, ask for Sadie or Josie" were my Granny's requirements.

So now before I even got to ordering the food, I would have to do a roll call of the staff to make sure I got exactly what I was sent for.

"Now for your Da, he doesn't like a well done fish, but get him one anyway, he takes a sore stomach if it's not well done, in fact, don't get him a fish get him a pastie instead"

"A well done pastie Ma?"

"Yes, he likes his pastie well done"

I cast a glance over at my Dad sitting in the big chair at the window, he just rolled his eyes and went back to ignoring the oestrogen levels in the room. The instructions continued including the amounts of salt & vinegar and how the whole thing should be packaged.

"Ma, I don't think Eisenhower had this many order's for D-Day"

"Well you can have toast while you watch everyone else have fish if you want?"

Armed with the instructions and of course the money, I headed for the Bethany. I was trying my best to repeat what I had been told for fear of forgetting anything, but I knew something would go wrong and someone would end up with a fish not well done enough for them. Getting to the Bethany wouldn't take long, I just had to go across Martin street, and then down Belvoir street. I'd cross the road at the Skyline furniture place, go past the Belvoir Bar and I would be there. I looked up and saw the familiar red writing on the sign for the Bethany and a queue out the door! 'I'll be here all night at this rate' I thought, I took my place in the queue behind two aul lads whose coats had seen better days. I had to take a few steps back, one of them smelt like a stale wet carpet and there's only so often you can breathe that in without boking! Something must have changed in their situations while we stood there as they left the queue and I was able to get inside the chippy, and saw that there were only four people in front of me now.

"What can I get you love?"

I produced the list and the lady behind the counter sighed and awaited the endless list of instructions, when it got to the fish, she interrupted me.

"Is this for Isabel and Ida?"

"Aye"

"Marie, will you look after this it's for Isabel and Ida?"

"No worries love"

Their reputation had obviously gone before them, and ten minutes later I was walking back to the house with one of the biggest paper bags I have ever seen filled with food. I picked up the pace because I was sure the whole point of a well done fish was to eat it warm and not lukewarm. I entered the house, and was immediately, met with

"What kept you so long?"

"There was a queue Ma!"

"Oh aye there would be at this time of the night, we should have sent you down earlier"

"Now how could you have done that? I only got in a wee while ago sure?"

Sometimes my Ma just didn't make any sense, in fact all the adults I knew went through phases like this, where they just seemed to talk for the sake of talking. Although you couldn't point it out, you'd be on the end of smack around the ears or worse. Sometimes the worst crime a kid could commit against a parent was to contradict them or point our they had made a mistake, you learned to control the urge to do both. I handed the massive paper bag over for inspection, as my Ma and Granny went through it to make sure everything was as required.

"Did you ask for Sadie?"

"You mean Marie?"

"Aye that's what I said"

"No, you said Sadie"

"Well I meant Marie"

"Yes, I asked for Marie"

"Did you make sure she did mine less well done than your Ma?"

"Yes, I did"

"Right this one must be yours Ma, Tommy, here's your pastie! Right Glenn get the knives and forks out, and put a few mats at the table for you, Jim and Ryan, come on don't be just standing there with your arms the same length now!"

This was serious business now, place mats at the table, the next thing you know the good plates would be coming out!

"Tommy where did you put the tuppaware plates? I don't want to be getting the good plates out here just for this!"

Well there goes that idea then. Once the sorting office had got through its delivery, silence reigned as we devoured the food put in front of us.

"Now who's for a bit of dessert?"

What on earth was going on here? Chippy and a dessert. I

spoke too soon though as what would constitute dessert materialised.

"I made a few bowls of angel delight and they should be ready, and there's jelly as well"

Now that made things a bit different, jelly was always a welcome sight.

"What angel delight is it?

"I did strawberry and chocolate"

What a day this had turned out to be. Parade, chippy and dessert!

Mum and my Big Granny cleared up after everyone and filled the sink with hot water and fairy liquid, and between them they sorted the dishes out. I suddenly realised that there had been no mention yet of the dreaded TCP bath, so I figured now was a good time to make my escape and hope that I could make do with a quick shower in the morning.

"Right I'm gonna head to bed Ma, I'm wrecked after today, is that alright?"

"Aye keep the noise down and if you're gonna play those band tapes keep them low or put your headphones on alright?"

"Alright Ma"

"Say goodnight to your Granny before you go up."

"Night Granny"

"Night son"

I headed up the stairs to my room, result, no mention of the bath! This day had turned out to be an absolute cracker! I was only up the first flight of stairs, whenever I heard the living room door open, 'Here we go' I thought, seconds later my Ma's shouted up,

"Leave your clothes out for tomorrow and don't even think about wearing that tracksuit, you have your Easter clothes, put them on alright?"

"Alright, but can I wear my track suit top with them?"

"Yeah I'm sure we can let you do that, night son"

"Night Ma"

Yes! Take that TCP!! You're no match for me! I went into my room and just slumped on the bed, I was absolutely knackered, as I lay there looking out into the night through my skylight, I recalled some of the best parts of the day and laughed as I remembered the game of hide and seek with the cop on the motorbike. I went over to the wardrobe and grabbed my copy of the Blackskull tape, popped it in the tape deck, put on my headphones and drifted off to sleep accompanied by the sound of flutes and drums.

CHAPTER 8

The Easter Tuesday Incident

I awakened to find my Ma standing over me, shaking me.

"Come on you get up! We need to leave in the next half hour! Hurry up, you're holding everyone back. We need to be away before the parade, or we will never get there this side of Jesus coming back! And, you'll need to get in the shower seeing as you didn't get a bath last night!"

I don't remember falling asleep at all but waking up with the previous day's greatness fading and disappointment looming isn't the best way to start the day.

I rolled out of bed, stood up and stretched, I opened my skylight as had become the normal daily ritual, my Ma had got me into the way of doing this to make sure fresh air got into my room. I'd have to remember to close it when I left the house though, we wouldn't want the pigeons getting in! Mum's words, not mine! As if pigeons would be interested in the contents of my room. As I opened the skylight, pulling the handle attached to the wooden frame back toward me until it clicked, a rush of cold air entered my room, as did the familiar strains of flutes and drums in the distance. So, not only had I been rudely awakened I was now acutely aware that I really was going to miss the Easter Tuesday parade. I had held out some sort of hope that my Ma would relent and not force me to go on this family excursion, but sadly it wasn't to be. I made my way down the stairs and stumbled across the landing and into the bathroom. After a quick shower I was fully awake and ready to enjoy the wonders that awaited me in Portrush. A spray of deodorant, followed by brushing my teeth, I headed back to my room to adorn myself with my wonderful new Easter clothes, I didn't leave without grabbing my Puma tracksuit top, my favourite piece of clothing. I took my time going down the stairs, almost forcing my feet to act normally, until I heard my Da's voice.

"Right Glenn c'mon son!"

The last of the stairs were covered by a superman leap into the hall, I looked up to see my brothers plodding towards the car, obviously as excited as I was for the trip ahead. My Ma took a few minutes checking everything in the boot, making sure she hadn't forgotten anything, my Da got into the car, started it up and revved the engine as if to say, 'come on for crying out loud'. Mum ran back to check that the door was locked and then she made her way to the car, her door closed and we were off, heading towards Beechfield Street, turning right and heading towards the Avenue, looking to beat the bands out of the city and be on our way.

The drive up to Portrush was a disaster, both my Ma and Da smoke so they do, and inside the car resembled a chimney burning a bird's nest. I wondered how on earth my Da could actually see where he was going, in fact I wondered how we managed to drive past the fire station without the smoke bellowing around the car alerting them to my emergency situation and forcing them to sound the sirens and chase after us to put out the mobile bonfire that was so obviously destroying the inside of our brown Leyland Maxi. But alas they remained inside, playing cards and waiting for a real emergency! I absolutely hate the smell of smoke, no, scrap that, because hate doesn't actually do my feelings on this any justice, I would rather clean dog shit from my shoes than smell feg smoke. I bloody detest it, it just makes me nauseous. Ten minutes into the journey and I couldn't stand it any longer.

"Ma I'm putting the window down here ok? I'm choking back here for flip sake"

I wasn't trying to change the world here or even convince them to quit like, rolling the window down to allow the oxygen levels in the car to rise back levels safe enough for humans to me was an act of survival, but my Ma and Da they were having none of it.

"What the hell do you think you're doing Glenn?"

"I just told you what I was doing"

"Don't you get smart with me young man! Don't think I won't get your Da to stop this car so I can get out and give you a slap"

I was right behind her, all she had to do was turn around, but anyway, she continued on.

"Put the window back up we don't want to be catching our death from that cold breeze coming in!"

I sat there thinking 'What the hell?' Ironic or what? Reluctantly I put the window back up and retreated underneath my coat, it wouldn't protect me but to me it was at least some level of defence. As if travelling inside a mobile metal chimney wasn't bad enough, there was one other thing we had to put up with, their music choice in the car. I now knew how to spell 'divorce' due to the wonderful spelling lesson given to me by Tammy Wynette. Somewhere between a 'blanket on the ground' and 'standing by your man', I was ready for the hills! So far, this trip was already a runaway winner in the disappointment stakes! And the day was only getting started.

We drove on, somewhat hypnotised by country music, for what seemed like an age, I hadn't even looked out the window since being told to put the window up. I happened to glance outside and dream of fresh air when we passed a road sign that said Portrush was only five miles away, thank god this part of the day was nearly over. Soon Dad was pulling into a car park and I arrived at Portrush suffering from smoke inhalation, musical torture and smelling like an ashtray. As soon as my Da had parked the car, I opened the back door and started chasing the fresh air like it had gone extinct. This scene was replayed almost identically when our cousins arrived in their car as well. Surely to god someone should make it against the law to smoke in cars.

My Ma obviously didn't share my deep-rooted opinion on this, observing my desperate attempts to renew my oxygen supply she brought me back down to earth immediately.

"Ack for god's sake Glenn, stop getting on like an eejit and get over here and help us with the bags"

My pursuit of fresh air came to an abrupt end. No matter where we went there was an army of bags that went with us too, in some cases the same bag had been carrying the same stuff every year for every family trip! Every eventuality had to be covered, even if that meant doubling up on resources.

"Well you never know when you just might need two apple peelers!" my Ma would say and my Aunt and Uncle well they were just the same. They always brought way too much stuff, and all because you never know when you might need it. So, like slaves my cousins and I had to carry their folly, with the bags assigned we were ready, now all we had to do was find somewhere to set up camp for the day. We were like the Beverly hillbillies hawking all of our stuff around with us, and people knew we were just up in Portrush for the day. I walked along the street nodding to people who nodded back, obviously acknowledging their solidarity with me. I knew they were thinking "Ack god help that wee fella forced to come up here and be trailed around by his parents" one even took time to pity me and gave me words of encouragement.

"Don't worry kid, the sea air will do you good"

Using their kindness as inspiration I plodded on with my bag of tuppaware. I looked across the street and witnessed an all too familiar scene as another group of slaves, sorry, kids, traipsed behind their Masters, also having their Easter Tuesday changed to 'wreck a child's life day'.

We eventually found a suitable place to set up camp, on the beach, not too close to anyone but still close enough to the water and path back to the sea front and shops. The sun was shining and there were a few clouds in an otherwise clear blue sky, it was actually turning out to be a decent day after all. After the bags had been laid to rest and the customary amount of hoking in them to find what was actually needed over what wasn't needed, blankets were laid out on the sand and then it was time for us to be forced into having a good time.

"Right you lot, make use of the good weather and fresh air, away and play or something"

This was my Mums way of saying 'ok you have done what we brought you here for now clear off for an hour or two'

Getting the brush off when you didn't want to be somewhere was just harsh, but we were here now so we might as well make the best of the situation. We had a few things we had brought to keep us entertained, a football, which was standard, you never go anywhere without a football or a tennis ball, my cousins had brought some new game with them called 'swing-ball' which consisted of this pole that had a piece of string with a tennis ball already attached to it and rings that enabled to go up and down the pole and two people tried to hit the ball hard enough so the other person missed and you got it to your part of the pole to win, we had a fair few laughs with that and a fair few fights too. It was more exciting than tennis on the TV, my cousin Alan did his best John McEnroe impression when he lost a game, throwing his racquet to the sand with considerable force and anger. After we had tired of 'swingball' we reverted to standard games and started playing football on the sand, using a few rocks we had found lying about the beach area to make goalposts and marking out a penalty area with a stick that just happened to be lying nearby as well. We spent most of our time running after the ball every time a goal was scored, as there were obviously no real nets, once you scored the ball went on a coastal adventure of its own, landing on other people's towels, bashing into windbreakers or knocking over drinks and sandwiches.

After a few of these incidents we were told to play something that wouldn't annoy everyone else on the beach. So, we ended up building the obligatory sand castle and digging a moat around it and trying to fill it with water just for authenticity, this never worked as the sand just absorbed the water we had braved the icy cold waters of the sea to bring back in a bright red bucket. Each of us had taken it in turn to get as close to the water as we could without getting caught, all of us failing. Then someone had the bright idea that we should cover the bed of the moat with shells and rocks, what a futile task that turned out to be, we gave up after ten minutes and decided that we needed to do something else. I had noticed that my Mum was lying flat out on the beach so I suggested that we get as much sand as we could and then to cover as much of her legs with sand as we could. Not everyone thought this was a good idea, however it didn't stop them getting involved.

"This won't turn out well, Glenn"

They were right, it didn't turn out well, we got a good chase from my Ma all the way down the beach, a few of us fell over and got our good Easter clothes covered in sand. That was enough to bring the chase and having fun to an end,

"Look at the state of them clothes, do you think money grows on trees?"

"Right the lot of you get back down there it's about time you had some lunch"

Lunch time consisted of ham sandwiches that had been delicately seasoned with little bits of sand that got stuck in your teeth as we tried to eat like normal people on the beach. Even the cups for drinks had sand in them, the tuppaware bag had been left open and subjected to an influx of sand as we had played. My Ma had brought these yellow pack fake Mars bars with her, and normally I wouldn't have touched them through sheer embarrassment. But today, we'll we were far away from our own areas, I could get away with eating them. As we tucked into them, my Ma said.

"Now, didn't I tell you they tasted just like the real thing"

"Aye Ma you did" I said rolling my eyes,

"And don't they"

"Yes Ma, they do" there was no point arguing.

After we finished lunch, my cousin Alan and I decided we were going to go for a dander round the shops just to get away from things, we would need the permission of our parents and we also needed to tap them for some money as well. Having been successful in both instances, we headed off, and we were glad to get out of the way, mainly so we could say 'fuck' as much as we wanted without getting told off. We headed up the steps and away from the beach towards the shops on the sea front to commit the very grown up task of purchasing some Portrush Rock. There were loads of wee shops scattered around the town and they all sold rock. This unique delicacy was a long hard cylinder of pink sweetness that said Portrush in the centre of it, and when you bit a piece of it still had Portrush written all the way through it, not only was it delicious but it was magic as well. My Uncle Davy called them a 'dentist's nightmare', but they were pure bliss to us, who wanted to worry about the dentist?

Alan and I wanted to find the biggest, and cheapest rock we could with the money we had scrounged of our parents. We examined each shop's offering with an air of childhood expertise, tapping the rock to check its consistency and if it broke too easily then we had to move onto another choice. Some of the shop keepers weren't too keen on our testing methods and one of them told that if we tapped and broke another rock she was going to make us pay for them all, we told her 'she would have to catch us first' and sped of as fast as we could. We slowed down when we were sure there was no danger of having to pay for substandard produce. We came across a shop I hadn't noticed in Portrush before, it had loads of brightly coloured t-shirts and hats outside it with people's names and all sorts of pictures on them, the sign outside said that you could print your own t-shirt, now to me that sounded pretty cool.

"Right Alan, c'mon in here, I want to check this place out"

"The t-shirt place? Why do ya wanna go in there?"

"It looks pretty cool, and it says on one of those posters that they personalise stuff, so I was thinking of getting my bands name on the back of my track suit top"

"Your good Puma top? Your Ma will have a fit!"

"I don't care, sure I didn't want to come today anyway, so in a way she is making me do this"

"How do you figure that one out?"

"Simple logic! I didn't want to come here, right?"

"Right"

"So, I'm missing the bands because of her, right?"

"Right"

"So, if she hadn't brought me here and let me walk off to buy rock, I would never have found this place and had the idea of having the band's name put on the back of my track top in the first place"

Alan nodded as if my argument had swayed him, and we headed inside the shop.

"I still think she'll have a conniption"

I was past worrying about my Ma's reaction to the addition of

bands name to the back of my track suit top, I was now heading to the counter to get the low down on what this act of re-
bellion was going to cost me.

"Can I help you son" said one of the ladies behind the long
counter and peering over a reasonable sized pile of t-shirts.

At first I was taken aback at the smell of perfume wafting in
my direction, it was starting to catch in my throat, it wasn't
the same as being in the car with the smoke but the effect was
the same, I coughed and tried to answer her back.

"Yeah, I want to get the name of my band on the back of my
track suit top"

"I am sure we can sort that out for you, what are you looking to
get on the back then"

"Pride of the Raven Flute Band"

"Well that's 10p a letter.... The assistant then counted the rest
of the letters up on their fingers and then arrived mentally at
the total before revealing it loud and clear to me.... so that
will cost you £2.50"

"£2.50!! Are you geggin' or what?

"What" said the assistant.

"How much for POTRFB?"

"60p"

"Right, that's more like it now, here Alan can you lend us two
bob?, I only have a fifty pence spare here and I still want to buy
some rock"

"Aye, here ya go"

I handed the money over proudly and the assistant just looked at me with a look that said I should be doing something else.

"We will need your tracksuit top if we are gonna put the letters on for you"

"Oh aye, right enough"

I took off the track top and handed it over, the assistant took it over to a weird looking machine and put the track top down on it. She went to some small boxes nearby and found the letters she needed and placed them in the right order on the back of my top. Still concentrating on what she doing she shouted back to me.

"Are these alright going on here then?"

I couldn't see what she was seeing directly, I had to stand up on my tip toes and get as good of a glance of where she had placed the letters as my position allowed me, everything seemed to be good.

"Aye that looks ok to me from here"

And with that she pulled down the top part of the machine and suddenly my track top was being transformed from just a tracksuit top to an advertisement for Pride of the Raven Flute Band, although I would have to explain to people that's what POTR FB actually stood for. After a few minutes the assistant lifted the part of the machine that she had pressed down on my top and then lifted it off and carried it over to presented me with the fruits of her hard earned labour! To me it looked class.

"What do you think, will it do?" she asked

"Will it do?" I exclaimed, "It will more than do, its bloody great"

I pulled on the top and turned to try and look at it on my back, twisting and turning to get a glance at it.

"Well Alan, what do you think?" trying to show off my top as if some magical transformation had taken place.

"I think it looks like you now have letters on the back of your top"

"Haha very funny, I think it looks great"

"If you like it, then that's all that matters"

"Correct"

"Right c'mon, we will need to get back or they'll be sending a search party for us"

"Aye you're right there, but let's take a wee bit of time, we still need to buy some rock and I'm not sharing it with anyone"

We found a shop on our way back that was doing a wee deal, you got three for a pound, an absolute bargain, a delight for our pockets but a disaster for our teeth. We unwrapped the clear plastic from the rock and then tried to take a bite, this stuff lived up to its name, it was rock hard, we were gonna have to soften it up a bit before we were able to bite any a bit off. Then we would have one more thing to complete before we could fully enjoy the rock and that would be getting the paper picture of Portrush, located half way down and wrapped partially around the teeth rotting delicacy, off without leaving any on the rock, a task that not many have mastered but today we would have another chance to reign victorious in that quest. We failed miserably, both of us had white strips of paper left on the rock, at this point we didn't care, we had rock and we were happy. We headed back to where we had set up camp on the beach and arrived in time to see that they were beginning to pack things up. We ran over to see what had prompted this move.

"How come you're packing up" I asked.

"Don't you want to get back to see the bands"

A sneaky yet masterful move from my Ma. Turning the tables on me, they were leaving early because of me, making it my fault if others wanted to stay."

Luckily there wasn't much in the way of opposition to us leaving the beach early and heading for home. As much as we had had a good day, it was time to go.

We started to put things away and try and get them into the right bags, the ones they came in and not just the first one that came to hand, I noticed my Ma looking at me very strangely.

"Is there something wrong with your top Glenn? Did a bird shit on it or something?

"What are you taking about Ma?"

"On the back of it, there looks like there's white markings on it or something"

She had noticed the letters I had put on the back.

Alan looked at me as if to say, 'I told ye'.

I did the only thing I could, I lied.

"Nah ma, the sea air must have got to ya, you're seeing things"

"I don't think so, c'mere here till I see that"

I hesitated but my Ma was having none of it.

"Now!" She stated with a tone that suggested if I didn't show her, I would be feeling some serious regret.

'Balls', I thought to myself, there would be no getting out of this one now, so I slowly sauntered over to where she was awaiting my presence to inspect the top for seagull interference.

"What the hell is that on your top, POTRFB!" she said trying to turn the letters into a pronounceable word.

"It's the initials of the band Ma, it's short for Pride of the Raven Flute Band."

"What on earth possessed you to do that son? Have you no respect? Do you think I spent good money on that track suit for you to go and ruin it by putting the initials of your band on it, have you gone nuts?"

"No, I haven't Ma, I like it, I think it shows how committed I am to the band"

Committed? I'll be committing your body to the ground son if there's any more cheek out of you, give it here, I'll soon have it back to the way it was, Tommy have you seen this?"

I needed to do something quick she had already shifted to 'include your Da mode', this was spiralling out of control.

"You can't Ma, they said in the shop it would ruin the top if, if if..." I struggled to find the rest of the sentence and make it sound convincing and then it came to me "if you try to take the letters off so soon after they were pressed on"

"Oh, did they indeed? Isn't that convenient? Well maybe I will have to march you back round there and get them to tell me that to my face"

"Fine by me" I said as my confidence rose with every passing second "They'll tell ya the same thing, won't they Alan"

This was always a good tactic try and bring someone into the story who you know will back you up.

"Aye Auntie Isabel, that's what they said, true enough"

"Aye and it wouldn't be like you to stick up for your cousin would it?" with that Alan admitted defeat and did the only thing he could, say nothing and get on with packing up. But my Ma wasn't giving up, she was only getting started.

"Well tell me just how much did this loyalty cost ya then?"

"They were 60p Ma"

"60p for that! You were robbed, and just where did you get all the money?"

"I had some money left over from the rock and Alan lent me two bob to put to it so I could get it done"

I could see Alan looking up at me as if to say, 'you're on your own here Glenn, why are you involving me again'

Mum didn't miss the opportunity though turning to Alan, she hissed "Oh so, you're an accomplice?"

"A what?"

"You were in on it too?"

"No, I told him you'd take a fit, and I wasn't wrong"

"I thought you'd have had more sense than that Alan, letting him get that done"

"Me, what? It's your fault he got it done"

"Oh really? My fault? How do you work that one out?" Alan then proceeded to repeat what I had said earlier.

"Well if you hadn't brought him here and let him walk with the band, he would never have found the shop and got it done"

Silence descended and everyone was looking at us now; this had gone in a very bad direction!

"What did you just say to me?"

Then my Aunt Lillian, chimed in.

"I hope yer not back cheekin' your Auntie Isabel?"

"No mum, I'm just saying what Glenn said"

I looked at him and mouthed "TOUT"

In the blink of an eye it was all my fault again, this wasn't going to be a battle that I could win, so it was best to just give up now, besides I could do without the hassle.

"If you had just said to me you had got it done, I would have been fine with it"

I shot my Ma a look and said sarcastically.

"Yeah right, dead on, I'm sure you would have"

She seemed oblivious to this and just continued on with a lecture on how if I hadn't tried to hide it and just came out with it this would have all worked out better.

I just smiled and nodded at this stage, as I knew I wouldn't get a word in edge wise until my Ma had decided that enough was enough. Yep, it was time to just man up and take the verbal lashing that just keeps coming in wave after wave of parental advice drenched in 'back in my day' stories.

After eating the largest slice of humble pie, it was time to load the cars and head for home. The only commotion now was that what we had brought with us somehow, wouldn't fit back into the boot of the car. My Da was standing looking at the boot, one hand scratching his head, the other his chin, all the while being on the receiving end of questioning from my Ma.

"Why isn't it going back in? I mean we are coming home with less surely?"

My Dad looked exasperated.

"I have no idea Isabel; I'm trying my best here to pack it in but it's not going in"

"Well if it went in on the way down, it stands to reason that it's bound to go in now"

"Well, feel free to have a go yourself"

Dad was now nearing the end of his rope, my Ma seemed to pick up on this and softened her approach

"I'm only saying"

"Aye, so am I"

"Right, well, we can just put stuff in the back with the kids, I just want to get on our way"

Great not only will we have the billows of smoke to contend with on the return journey, we would now have our legroom further reduced by tuppaware, sand infested sandwiches and god knows what else. Dad put what he could in the boot, and we had to share our seat space with some plastic bags and a collection of purple tuppaware that had managed to befuddle everyone with its non-packability.

The drive home was nearly as bad as the drive up, compounded by the fact that the press on letter incident had meant a reasonably sour end to the day. As I looked out the window, I thought to myself, you know what? If I had to do that over again, you know, I wouldn't change a thing, I'd still get the letters put on the back of my track top.

"What time is it Ma?"

"What is it with you and the time this day?"

"Just checking to see if we might get back in time to watch the bands coming home"

"Seriously son! You're relentless"

"What do you mean, you're the one that mentioned that's why we were leaving, so we could get back and see the bands?" She obviously blanked out my response and continued with her own line of thought, and completely oblivious to the fact that she had indeed said that.

"You and this bloody band, you're obsessed"

"I don't know about obsessed Ma, It's just...." I paused, somewhat hesitantly.

"It's just what?"

"It's just that it means a lot to me, this isn't some passing fad, or in thing to do, the band's way more than that, I just can't explain it"

At this stage, I was expecting another lecture, however I was pleasantly surprised.

"I get it, you've found something that you connect with, and that's great, but don't forget about other things as well"

What was this? Some level of understanding from my Mum! Wonders will never cease.

"I won't forget about other things, it's just that I have worked so hard to get walking with the band, that's why I was frustrated, you've seen and heard the effort I have put in to this"

"Oh, we have all heard it, half of East Belfast has heard ya! and I know how much you have put into it, I've never seen you put this much effort into anything"

All that was needed now was for her to tell me if only I would put this much effort into my schoolwork, and right on cue she did. "If only you'd put as much effort into your schoolwork, you'd be doing ok"

There wasn't much I could say in response to that, I just looked out the window, spotting my face reflecting on the car window, I gave myself a wee smile, I was distracted from my feel-good moment by my Ma finally answering my question.

"It's just gone half past six son"

"Eh?"

"The time, its half six, so you never know you might get back in time to see the bands"

"I hope so, I want to hear how it went today"

"Well if you don't there's always the next practice to catch up with everyone"

The journey home was a little more hopeful and I was a little more at peace with my Ma and the world, my thoughts turned to the band, I wonder if anything funny had happened? Hopefully the band had played well. It would be strange standing on the footpath watching them march past. I didn't think that I would ever be doing that again, but here I was hoping to do exactly that. It was better than nothing I told myself. I really wanted to talk to my Mum and tell her that walking with the band whenever I could, took me away from the area and kept me away from trouble. She would know I wasn't getting involved in rioting and anything else when things kicked off in our area if I was with the band. It allowed me to do something productive and creative. who would have thought that I would be involved with music, let alone be half decent at it?

I didn't even realise that we had arrived home, maybe I had dozed off or something, the sharp cold air hit me as my mum opened the car door and the outside flooded inside.

"Glenn love give us a hand getting everything back into the house"

"Ok, mum"

I lifted as much of the purple tuppaware as I could and took it into the house. I walked into the kitchen to put the various pieces of purple plastic on the worktop, when that faint familiar sound I had heard many times before drifted in through the door, my ears attuned and ready to respond to the call.

"Mum, I think that's the bands on their way back, I'm gonna head round to the Avenue to watch them, is that ok?"

"Aye, go ahead, we will be round if we get all this stuff put away"

"Thanks Mum"

I headed past my Dad who was having an easier job getting the bags out of the car that he was putting them in as we left Portrush.

"It's alright Glenn, sure I'll just put all these away myself" he said as I walked passed him.

"That's good Dad, no one does that better than you"

I was running toward the Avenue as the sound of drums and flutes started to get louder, I didn't want to miss anything, I am pretty sure if I wasn't heading to watch the bands, my Dad would have been doing more than taking that kind of cheek from me. I actually didn't mean to be cheeky and lots of times that was the case, it just came out that way. I am sure I will pay for it later, but right now, I needed to get to the Avenue.

As I rounded the corner of my street and headed up Beechfield Street towards the Avenue, I spotted more people coming out of their houses to watch the parade, at the bottom of Westbourne Street, I spotted Brian, he saw me walking towards the Avenue and there was a look of confusion on his face.

"I'd have thought I'd see you walking past me tonight with the band?"

"Aye I know, I should have been, but I had to go and be part of a family day out in Portrush for dear sake"

You had to watch your language around Brian, partly because I wouldn't want it getting back to my Mum, but also because he was a Christian and he didn't like hearing things like that, he never said anything, but you knew it wasn't something he appreciated.

"All in a good cause then" he replied, "You need to make the most of your time with your family Glenn". Hearing what sounded like common sense about your family from someone not in your family seems to be easier to take than if it came from my Mum or Dad. I was completely disarmed and all I could say was, "I guess you're right".

"C'mon, I'll walk into the Avenue with you, is your band out today?"

"Aye Brian, this would have been my second parade, but I'll have plenty more opportunities to walk this year"

"Especially the twelfth"

"Oh yes, I can't wait for that"

Our brief chat led us to the Avenue, and the bands and lodges were walking up towards Bella's shop, headed by the banner-ette and colour party of the district and then the banner of the first lodge, members of the junior orange lodges were skip-ping along to the sound of the accordion band accompanying them. The tassels of the banner were flying in the cool evening breeze and the smiling faces of the lads and the seniors meant they'd obviously had a good day and the weather had held out. I'd heard that parading in the rain was a miserable experience, thank goodness I hadn't experienced that yet. I waved to a few people I knew in the lodge and asked "Where's the Raven?"

"About three bands back I think"

Great I wouldn't have to wait long on them arriving, I turned to Brian.

"You won't mind if I follow my band to the orange hall?"

I didn't want to just walk off and be ignorant or anything.

"Of course not, you do what you need to do"

Another two bands and their junior lodges passed by, and then they appeared. I had a strange feeling in my chest, pride rising as I watched them march towards me, the flutes and drums transcending the noise around me and all I could hear was my band, the Pride of the Raven, playing the march, Children's Love. I walked along with them, whistling the tune to make myself feel like I was part of it, and a few of the guys saw me and nodded in acknowledgement, Alvin waved then kept playing. The band walked along the Avenue towards the junction with the Albertbridge Road. They then passed through the district colour party that had formed a guard of honour on either side of the road, just a wee bit up from Mountpottinger Methodist Church, where I attended BB on a Tuesday night. They marched on through the colour party and turned right onto the Albertbridge round walking a short distance and coming to a stop just outside the front doors of the Ballymacarrett District Orange Hall. After the obligatory playing of the national anthem, the band broke up and members walked off the road, gathering in clumps on the footpath, talking to lodge members and other people gathered there. I made a bee line for Alvin, I wanted to get the story on how the day had went.

"You missed a good parade today", said Alvin, "The band played well and the weather was pretty good too"

"I'm sorry I missed it, couldn't be helped though"

"I know, if you could have been there, you would have"

"Here, wait till you see this"

"What?

I turned around to show Alvin the letters on the back of my track top.

"I got this done today, I may not have been there with you in person, but I was definitely there in spirit"

"That looks great, Glenn, nice one"

As I had been showing him the band captain had obviously saw the back of my track top as well, he came over.

"Missed you out today, but it looks like we weren't far from your thoughts"

"Definitely not, you like the back of my top?

"Love it kid"

As we were talking, another member of the band, Stevie, came over.

"And just where were you today eh?" he said in a tone I wasn't expecting.

"Umm, I couldn't make it today, everyone knew that"

"Oh really, well how come you're here now then?"

"We got back just before the bands arrived home"

"That was convenient, if you're in the band you walk with the band"

This took me a bit by surprise, and it was obvious to the band captain that I wasn't taking it too well, he stepped in on my behalf.

"Give it a rest Stevie ok, the wee lad couldn't make it, no need to give him a hard time about it"

"He should have been out with us"

"You're making the wee lad feel terrible here, he couldn't make it for god's sake, take a look at the back of his top" he motioned for me to turn around.

"He couldn't be here, but he wanted to be, look at that, if that doesn't show you, he's committed to the band, I don't know what else will, now give over"

Stevie ruffled my hair "Only raking ya kid"

And with that the issue was over and done with. The band formed up again and made the short walk back to the band hall. I walked alongside them promising to myself, that I would never miss another parade again.

CHAPTER 9

Trophies, Trophies, Trophies

T he marching season was now in full swing and I had a full calendar of events lined up. I was busier than a peeler at a riot. Once it's Thursday, it all takes off. Thursday night is practice then Friday night we are usually at a competition somewhere and the same on Saturday afternoons and Saturday night, and then there's the odd Sunday parade as well as Sunday night practice too. Most weekends the band can be out parading three or four times.

My main conflict was Saturday afternoons. They were when I went to watch Linfield play. For the last few years I'd been going to every match home and away without fail. Travelling to Windsor park or somewhere exotic like Larne or Portadown, to watch the mighty blues, and well, I just loved it. I'd meet up with my cousins and have a laugh, sing the songs and listen to the banter, and watch the game of course and most of the time, watch Linfield win. Losing was the worst, dark clouds descended like the pigeons when my granny throws out stale O'Hara's bread for them, and I enter Sunday in a state of mourning! My Ma never understood it, "It's only a game son" she would say, "Only a game Ma! Only a game! Did you ever hear what Bill Shankly said? 'Football isn't a matter of life and death, it's more important than that" What did she know about football anyway?

Losing any game was bad but losing to Glentoran was the worst, not just cause they were our biggest rivals, there was the stick I'd take from my mates on the street and the odd one at school, plus I would get raked at the band hall as most of them supported Glentoran. The worst was my classmate Bowersy, his brother Barney actually played for the Glens and if he'd a good game against the Blues, well he wouldn't be behind the door in letting you know about it.

My school had a big connection with Linfield though, Geordie Dunlop, the Linfield goalkeeper had gone there. After he got called up to the Northern Ireland squad by Billy Bingham, he gave his shirt to the school to frame. It was hung on the wall just outside the school office. The thought that I wouldn't be able to go and watch the Blues every week was a little disconcerting, but, you have to make decisions and choices in life and I had made mine. When the band was out on a Saturday afternoon, I would be out with them. If the band wasn't out, I would be at the match. I take my trusty Linfield diary to practice with me to fill in the dates of parades and competitions to keep a track of my schedule. Being a true supporter and a bandsman, requires commitment. I've watched how band members commit to everything the band does, and how my Uncle and the Linfield supporters take the time to arrange everything to get everyone to the games, so why should I be any different? I needed to be organised.

The amount of parades the band got invited to seemed to be endless. Every week places like Carrowdore, Portadown, Ballymena, Coleraine, Omagh, Kilkeel and Ballyclare beckoned us.

Invites were brought up at band meetings regularly. We accepted most of them, providing we had the numbers to go. This never seemed to be a problem, we had a good-sized band that even if some members couldn't make it, we would still be able to take part.

Attending the parades is great, you always meet new people, or run into someone you know but didn't know they were in a band. I really should clarify that these weren't parades with lodges like Easter and the twelfth, they were competitions, organised by local bands to raise money usually to help a band get new instruments or help towards a new uniform, sometimes the money collected was for charity. The competitions are very popular events and the locals come out in force to watch the bands. There are always wee stalls on the street selling flags and badges and basically anything you would associate with bands. I keep an eye out to see if they have any of the latest flute band tapes. I save money just in case, you never know when there might be a new one. Alongside the stalls there's always burger vans and chip vans, although what the difference is between them is beyond me. After the parade, no matter how long or short, you always are in need of a wee coke or a burger. If I'm flush with cash, I'll splash out on a cheeseburger with onions and red sauce! Travelling to competitions usually involves a bus journey, unless it's a local competition. There's a similar routine for competitions. Arrangements for travel are finalised a good week before the actual competition. We assemble at the hall, wait on the bus arriving and the odd member being late. If there's the potential for us to be back late, the band always get in touch with my Ma about the arrangements, just so she won't be worried. As long as Alvin is there, she knows I'll be alright and that the band always look out for us.

Bus journeys with the band are great craic, lots of laughs, re-telling old stories of the times we had been at this parade before and the usual talk about who else would be there, especially other melody flute bands.

When we arrive the driver usually leaves us as close to the starting point, we'd been given in the invite letter, this isn't always possible due to the number of bands turning up, getting a parking space can be difficult. Once we all get off the bus there isn't a lot of hanging around, you want to get formed up and get around the route.

Once we are given a space to start from, the band captain gives two short sharp blows of his whistle, like sheep being round up, we assemble in our usual rows. Once you get assigned to a row, that usually becomes your place for the season, I suspect that if I keep growing taller, I will end up in a row further back, but for now, I'm in the front row of flutes. Once we are in position the Drum major brings us to attention and we wait for the parade steward's permission to make our way around the route. Before we move off, the captain usually says something like this to us.

"Right lads, remember this is a competition, so I don't want any chattering in between tunes ok? There will be judges watching our every move, so let's not do anything stupid. Oh and no complaining about the tunes being called either! We want to win so, best marches will be called, let's do our best and bring some trophies home"

And with those words of wisdom ringing in our ears the Drum Major motions us to move off and we are on our way. The band captain calls out the starting tune. Two beats from the bass drum, two five beat rolls and we begin our quest for trophies.

I started to notice that at competitions there were longer than normal gaps between one tune being called and the next. We were at a competition in Carrowdore and my curiosity got the better of me, we weren't supposed to talk in the ranks, but

I whispered to Stevie "Why's it taking so long between tunes?"

"In case we run into a judge, we want to play our best tunes in front of the judges"

"How do we know who's a judge?"

"Clipboards"

"What?"

"Judges are on the footpath with clipboards"

The band captain had heard us talking "Right lads that's enough, there's usually a judge on up this street so let's be ready"

We returned to marching with purpose, arms swinging resolutely, arms with flutes by our sides. As we turned the corner just in front of us, there was one of these mysterious clip board holders. "Dinah's Delight!" declared the band captain.

One of my favourite marches. The judge made their way out into the centre of the road and motioned for the Drum Major to bring us to a halt. He then walked around the band, scribbling down notes and god knows what else about us as we played. We had just finished the first playing of the trio, when he motioned to the Drum Major that we were free to walk on. The Drum Major kept us marking time until we were ready to repeat the trio. This would give the judge another chance to hear the parts and hopefully help them make up their mind. We moved off and encountered another four judges who stopped us and performed the same routine. There are judges for all of the different categories of bands and styles so there was a good chance of bands getting mentioned in the placings.

I don't really know how they judged the bands or how they determine marks and everything. They would need be good at it as we only stop for a few minutes while they walk around making their notes, was that really enough for them to make a decision?

In Carrowdore we arrived at the end of the route and fell out, some of the older members went looking for a bar, Alvin and I went looking for something to eat, tonight we went for a burger as that was the van closest to us, there was a decent enough queue. That was usually a good sign if there are people waiting then the food is usually good. Once we had paid for our burgers we went to find somewhere to stand and watch the other bands arrive at the finishing point. We always wanted to see the melody bands to hear how well they were playing and trying to weigh up whether we potentially had the better of them that night. It didn't matter what we thought though, it was the judges with clipboards who decided that. At the end point of the parade was a trailer set up, with a table and a whole range of trophies on it. Whenever the last band came in, the judges added up the scores, and a member of the hosting band started tapping a microphone to see if it was on and thanked everyone for turning up and then got into what we were all waiting for, the results. There was always a good gathering of people for this, Alvin and I stood near the front, you know just in case there were any trophies to pick up. There were prizes for the whole range of bands and styles, first, second and third place in each category. Some of the categories were straight forward, like best blood and thunder, best accordion and best melody flute, then there were prizes for drum corps in each category of band, then there were prizes for best drum major, then other things like style and appearance, marching and discipline, best visiting band, most entertaining and the one everyone would want, best overall band. Best overall band would go to the band that had the most best place finishes in their categories. When it came to melody flute, I could feel myself getting nervous, where would we place? Would we place? We hadn't heard our bands name called for third or second place now we were waiting for the announcement of first place, did we win or where we just not good enough on this occasion? The sweat was on. The master of ceremonies, took a breath and spoke, "And the prize for first melody flute goes to..." he paused for what seemed like forever then declared "Pride of the Raven, East Belfast" Alvin and I looked at each other, then unashamedly let out the loudest "Yes, we won!" we made our way up through the crowd, half expecting them to part like the Red Sea and to break into a rendition of "How great thou art", to pick up what was one of the biggest prizes on display on the table. A large trophy with a gold quaver at the top of it. We shook the guys hand, accepted the trophy and headed back to where we had been standing, we were absolutely beaming and buoyed by the expectation that there might be more trophies to come. And that's exactly what happened, the results just kept coming and coming, "and best melody drum corps goes to.... Style and appearance goes to; melody bass drum goes to... senior drum major goes to... best overall band goes to.... Pride of the Raven East Belfast. We had cleaned up, winning every category we possibly could.

I'd never been a part of anything that had won trophies before and definitely not the number of trophies and shields that Alvin and I were carrying. With every trophy we picked up we looked to see who the previous winners were, and we kept seeing our name appear somewhere else on the trophy. I was impressed with the amount of organisation that went into these competitions; it must have been expensive too. These trophies weren't cheap by the looks of them, and to hand them out every year and then get them back for the big night twelve months later well, it just went to show that this was part of larger community. Tonight, we would just bring the trophies back with us on the bus and put them on display in the band hall. It was different when we won at a local parade, Alvin and I would leave our ranks, put our flutes in our inside jacket pocket and walk at the very front of the band, showing off the trophies we had won, the two of us sporting the biggest cheesers as we led our award winning band back through the streets to our band hall. There was nothing like winning and nothing like losing, picking up second place just wasn't the same, but it was a trophy nonetheless, and the more we won, the more I felt part of the band. When I had first walked into the hall and saw all the trophies, I never thought that I would be contributing to that, but here I was collecting trophies and adding to the heritage of the band.

Most of the time, depending on where the competition was, the band would came back late in the evening but we didn't come back crazy late, not intentionally anyway, the only person younger than Alvin and me was the cymbal player, but his Dad was always there, as was Alvin's, so it was a given that we wouldn't be out to all hours. However, there was this one time when we were out supporting a band in Antrim, and as usual the band had been in touch with my Ma just to let her know that there was a possibility, we would be late back. The competition had gone very well, the band had played great around the route and we had even won a few trophies which was always great, we had got on the bus to travel home and as usual the craic on the bus was great. We were driving along and looking out the window it was hard to tell where we were, it was pretty dark out, no one really cared, we had had a great parade and now we were on our way home. About fifteen minutes after we left, the bus came to a grinding halt. Everyone looked up to see what was going on, looking out the window to see if there was a Police checkpoint or something. There didn't seem to be a meat wagon or policemen anywhere, and there weren't any blue flashing lights.

"I wonder what's up here?" said Alvin,

"No idea" I replied

Rigby made his way down the bus towards the driver's seat and had a quick conversation and then the doors opened and he got off the bus, the driver appeared from his seat.

"Sorry lads, but it looks like we have broken down here, we are going to have a look at see if there's anything we can do, hold tight and we will let you know as soon as possible ok? Hopefully it's nothing major", he left the bus by the open doors, then they closed behind him.

At first, I thought it was maybe one of Rigby's practical jokes, I mean it wouldn't be like him to pull something like this. But after sitting for fifteen minutes and no update from the driver, it became clear this was no practical joke, the bus really had broken down. It was pitch black outside and everyone was sitting about talking and noticing that the temperature on the bus was rapidly starting to get colder.

"I wonder what's up with the bus" came a voice from the back quick as a flash Nigel said "It's broken down" which got more than a few laughs from the lads, but not from Stevie.

"No shit Sherlock, I mean I wonder what is actually wrong with the bus"

"It's not going anywhere, that's what's wrong with it"

"I know it's not going anywhere; I mean what exactly is wrong with it?"

"I think it needs repaired"

I'm sure Stevie regretted opening his mouth now after that little run of responses.

"Well you know what they say", said Terry, "Ask a silly question, get a silly answer"

Realising this was getting him nowhere Stevie gave up, he turned and looked out the window, everyone else was laughing. Then the doors popped open and the bus driver stood up on one of the steps and peered down the bus.

"Right lads, the bus is going nowhere, I'm going to have to and find somewhere that has a phone, we are gonna need a replacement bus to get ya home"

There were numerous groans around the bus.

"Listen lads it can't be helped, it's not like the driver did this on purpose you know" said the band captain.

With that statement the mood in the bus changed, there was an acceptance of our fate and now the focus was keeping warm and making the most of the situation we found ourselves in. I thought to myself "It's a good job this is a Saturday and not Sunday night" I could imagine my Ma going nuts at the thought of me being out this late with school waiting for me in the morning. Anyway, depending on how long it takes for the driver to find a phone and the replacement bus to arrive there's a good chance that she will be fast asleep by the time we get back, whatever time that turns out to be now. I needed a plan to get back into the house without waking her up. I figured that I'd just sneak in and sleep on the settee and she would be none the wiser. I mean there's no way I'd make it up the three flights of stairs without making a noise, and there was no way I was climbing the bannisters in the dark! We had been sitting for absolutely ages now and the mood was still ok, but everyone had had enough of the bus and wanted to get home.

"What time is it now anyway?" asked Alvin, looking at his watch Terry replied "Two o'clock"

"Where is this driver, is he inventing the phone or what?"

"His sun dial doesn't work in the dark"

"Where'd ya find that joke? In a Christmas cracker?

After five minutes of banter about clocks and the lost driver the doors on the bus opened again and it was the driver, even he wasn't immune from a raking.

"Well mate did you enjoy your holiday? Flight delayed from Spain?

"I've had another birthday waiting on you coming back"

"You'll need to stop at a garage so I can pick up some Grecian two thousand, my hairs went grey in here"

"Your hairs been grey from you were born, ya header"

The bus driver ignored the banter he obviously wanted to get moving as much as we did.

"Sorry about the wait lads, took ages to find somewhere with a phone and then get back to you here, but the good news is there is a bus on its way to pick us up, so hopefully we will be on our way soon enough"

"Good job mate, you didn't think to bring any sandwiches back with you or anything?

"I was too busy eating them myself, sorry"

Alvin and I were both absolutely wrecked but the excitement of being out so late did a good job motivating us to stay awake, but we also had another motivation. You didn't want to fall asleep when you were out with the band, because you'd more than likely end up with some new eyebrows, a pen moustache or something else you wouldn't be aware of until it was too late. Now, all we had to do was wait on the replacement bus arriving and we would be on our way. The replacement bus eventually arrived and left me outside my door around three thirty in the morning. As the bus pulled up at my house, I was surprised to see the lights on and then I saw someone in the front garden, my Ma and she didn't look happy. The band captain got off the bus with me, he was just about to open his mouth but my Ma was straight in.

"What on earth time do you call this?"

The band captain had obviously gone through this before, he let my Ma say her piece and then he explained what had happened.

"I'm really sorry, we didn't mean to be back this late, the bus broke down not long after we left the parade. The bus driver tried to fix it, but nothing seemed to work. He had to go and find a phone and then wait on a replacement bus, it not the norm for us, and we usually have had him back when we said we will, I'm really sorry" well, that seemed to do the trick, and my Ma's tone eased.

"Ok well thanks for taking care of him, hope you all get home safe" she turned to me and said, "Right you, get in and get your uniform off and get to bed".

I was so glad to get into my own bed, those bus seats had become pretty uncomfortable throughout the night, it was great to be able to stretch out and not feel like a squished bun. I don't remember falling asleep, but I woke up half expecting to still be on that bus with the band. What a night though, trophies, trouble and a ticking off. I couldn't wait to tell my mates what time I'd actually got in at, I imagined it would become one of those stories that would get told over and over, " Glenn tell us about the night you came home at three thirty on the morning" and I would recall the events and everyone would sit in awe.

One person who wouldn't sit in awe of the retelling would be my Ma, when I arrived down for breakfast I was quizzed again on the whole episode, she was obviously looking for gaps in the story, needless to say her efforts were futile as I told her the same story over and over, so thankfully she was pacified enough and I knew that going to Sunday night practice wasn't in jeopardy. The band captain asked if my Ma was alright about it all when I arrived for practice later on and that was that.

Competitions made up the vast majority of the parading the band did, and it was great to be out and about all over the place, but it was even better when you walked in your own area. All the local bands ran a competition, even we did, in the preparation leading up to our own competition we got an invite from the Gertrude Star for a new type of competition at our Sunday meeting.

"I'd just like to read out an invitation from the Gertrude Star" said the secretary.

"Didn't we do their competition already?"

"Aye I believe we did, wonder what's wrong? Someone didn't like that we won Melody at it then?"

"Well if you'd shut up and let me read the invitation, you'd know what the craic was"

"Oh aye, right no probs, continue…"

"I'm glad I have your permission. Right are we settled now? Ok good" he began to read the invitation.

"To the officers and members of Pride of the Raven flute band. The Gertrude Star are proud to invite you to our very first in-door competition, taking place in the Avenue One bar. Each band will play for 15 minutes in their chosen category, prizes will be awarded for all the usual categories.

There will be a door charge of £1 for band members and £3 for the public.

We do hope that you will be able to attend, we would be grateful if you could let us know ASAP if you intend to participate." There were some confused faces during the reading of the letter and that was expressed verbally almost as soon as the secretary had finished reading the letter out.

"Indoor?"

"Aye that's a new one"

"Is that upstairs in the Avenue One then?"

"No idea, it doesn't say"

"Would need to be though wouldn't it? you couldn't swing a cat downstairs never mind run a competition"

Having never been in the Avenue one bar I hadn't a clue, so I just had to take these guys word for it. All I knew was the bar had a reputation for being some kind of UDA hangout, and it was also where the Gertrude Star had their band practice, a friend of mine from primary school, Stewarty, had joined them and that's where he'd went to learn the flute. He had called to my house a few times to ask me for notes to tunes, as long as it was for kick tunes I didn't care, but marches? Well he'd have to find them some other way, I wasn't for sharing those.

"Do we have to stand up? Sit down for it?"

"Again, no idea, I read out what they sent, I didn't leave anything out"

"Alright don't get yer knickers in a twist like"

"Any proposals on this one then?" The question was just kind of thrown out there, as the secretary didn't seem sure what kind of response was going to come back. I don't think anyone knew what to make of it to be fair.

"Well I think we should do it, if we get more info about what they actually want, like are there time slots or something? I mean, we have kids in the band, we can't really have them hanging about the Avenue One until all hours like"

"Well that's true, we wouldn't want them to miss out either, right, we will need to get in touch with the Gertrude and find out more and if it's all good, we are up for going then?"

There was a general consensus that this was ok with everyone, the nodding of heads and affirmative grunts giving the secretary his cue to continue on with the meeting. As I went home from practice that night, I thought about this new indoor competition, who would judge it, and where would they judge? Usually on competition parades you didn't know where the judges would be, you had to be on your game the whole way around the route. This was different, very different, I wasn't sure I liked the idea and I don't know why. It wasn't like I was afraid that the band wouldn't perform well, but it would definitely sound different inside a bar instead of in the streets.

At the following weeks practice we all waited in anticipation for the details regarding this new type of contest. But before the excitement of all that transpired, at the start of the meeting there was an announcement made that Ian Parkhill had left the band. Parky was a great flute player, I was kind of shocked to hear this.

"Has he joined someone else?" I asked, the obvious question to those gathered. Initially there was a moment of silence, maybe no one knew? Maybe there was some other reason behind it? Then Terry responded "I have no idea. All I know is that he's left"

"Seems a bit strange thought doesn't it?"

"Yeah definitely, great wee fluter"

"Well someone will need to get his gear off him"

"I'll arrange that"

"His gear is bound to fit Glenn"

"Aye, right enough"

"Fancy getting rid of that jumper and getting a full uniform Glenn?"

"Of course," was my reply. While I was sad that Parky had left, the silver lining was that I'd get a full uniform now, not that I hated wearing the jumper, I was glad to be out walking with the band, but now I'd look the same as everyone else, decked out in the bands maroon and blue jacket.

"I'll get it dry cleaned for next practice and you can try it on Glenn"

"Great, thanks" I couldn't wait now.

Now that had been sorted it was time to move on and the next thing on the agenda at the meeting was the secretary giving an update on the indoor contest we had been invited to.

"Well lads I have been in touch with the Gertrude about this indoor contest of theirs, I let them know we had a few questions about how it's going to run, so here's what they told me. I'd appreciate it if you let me finish before you start asking any questions, ok?"

There were nods of agreement and with that sign of consent the secretary told us what he had been told.

"Bands will play upstairs, the dance floor area will be where bands are expected to perform, all bands are expected to stand, there will be time slots available and kids will be ok in the venue until 10pm, they hope to have the melody results announced by then as they want melody bands on first and blood and thunder afterwards"

"Well that doesn't sound too bad now, it'll be different, I'll give you that but should be good"

"Aye another opportunity to bring a few trophies back, who else is taking part, melody wise?"

"There's a few confirmed" said the secretary, "UVF, the Defenders, and us"

"That's it! Just the three bands"

"Hardly a competition then"

"All the better for us then"

"So, what are we going to play?"

"Well I believe that we should leave that up to Terry, he's the conductor, I am sure he will want to make sure we pick the best tunes and get us ready for it"

There were nods of agreement all round and then Terry spoke.

"I think this could be a great opportunity for us to try out the new tunes we have been learning over the last wee while, and for us to polish up on the parts for a few of our strong marches, we can go in with a strong solid programme then"

Alvin and I just looked at each other.

"New tunes"

"I know, happy days, can't wait to play them in public, we are going to blow people away"

The new tunes had been coming on well, one in particular, Queen of Battle, was quite difficult to play but we had been making steady progress with it. Alvin and I already had it memorised now that we weren't working against the list, we were learning whatever new tunes Terry was bringing to the band.

"Ok that's settled then, I'll let the Gert know we will be there and from next week we can start working on the programme Terry decides on, ok"

There was unanimous agreement in the room, and that was that. We were going to be taking part in our first indoor competition and we were going to be playing some new tunes. I couldn't wait, and I knew I'd have to practice hard and make sure there was no chance of any mistakes.

Terry had picked out seven great tunes for us to play, strong tunes with good parts that would give us the best possible chance of winning this indoor. Although, nothing was guaranteed, it all depended on the judge on the night. We played the programme over and over again, with Terry stopping us whenever there was something he wanted to work on or if he heard something that wasn't quite right.

On the night of the first practice for the indoor he said something that made everyone sit up and take notice.

"This won't be like the road lads, you won't be able to drop out if you don't know all of the tune, especially with us playing more parts in the tunes, if you drop out its going to be noticeable, at least on the road we can carry it, but you won't get away with that here"

There was nothing that escaped Terry's notice when it came to the flutes, he knew what he wanted to hear and where he wanted the band to go musically. Terry was introducing more counter parts to marches to develop the band's sound even further, he knew that we couldn't be just carrying anyone. Terry worked us hard in the run up to the indoor competition, to the point where he didn't have to say anything, we knew whether we had met his standard or not and by the time the night of the competition came around, we were as ready as we could be. Parky's uniform had been brought up to the hall, for me to try on, after having been dry cleaned. The jacket seemed to fit me perfectly, the trousers would need let down a little, my mum could handle doing that. I now had a full uniform now and I'd be wearing it at the indoor.

Arrangements were made to meet at the hall, and we would all walk down together and normally I would have gone along with that; I raised a point for myself as we talked about this.

"I live literally five minutes away from the Avenue One, so I don't see the point in me walking all the way up to the hall to walk all the way back down again"

"No worries kid, if you meet us down there, that will be good enough, just wait outside for us and we can all go in together"

"Not much chance of him getting in on his own to a bar like"

"Well he will be in a band uniform and I'm sure they will be aware of what's happening, and they might put two and two together and let him walk on in"

"Well if they do let you in Glenn, make sure you order drinks for everyone"

"No worries sure I'll write a list here"

"Just wait for us outside, if we leave the hall at seven it will only take ten to fifteen minutes maximum to arrive at the bar"

"Great I'll be there from about ten past then"

"Right, that's that sorted, everyone else meet here, ok?"

There was a general sound of agreement and that was the travel arrangements sorted for the indoor.

I fancied our chances of winning, after all we were a proper melody band, we tried to play as close the written music as possible. Terry could read music and a few others could too, but most of us just read ABC's, the rest, like phrasing etc we just picked up by ear from listening to Terry playing the tune for us. Some bands changed things about, left notes out or simplified harder phrases. Then there were a new breed of bands emerging that were trying different thing out, new drum settings, different arrangements. They played marches, but didn't play counterparts at all, they just played the straight melody of the tune, for me a proper melody band played parts, and tried to keep it as close to the music as possible.

On the actual night of the indoor competition, I didn't have to rush as much to get ready, given that I didn't have far to travel to get to the venue. I just got ready like I would have for any parade, making sure my shoes were shining, my hat was in good shape and my plume looked well. I had my flute in its pouch and I headed out through the door and on my way to the Avenue One.

It was a dry evening and would have been perfect for a parade.

I ran into my mate Dee near the bottom of my street, he was trying to pull wheelies on his bike and doing a pretty decent job, when he saw me, he pulled up alongside me.

"Bands out tonight?"

"No mate I'm just going to the shop and the only clean clothes I had was my band uniform"

"I was gonna ask if your Ma's washing machine was broke"

"It only broke after my Ma did your Ma's washing for her, them trunks of yours would break windows for god's sake"

We both started laughing, that was our sense of humour, take the piss and try to outdo each other.

"We are at the Avenue One tonight for an indoor competition"

"An indoor? Never heard of that before, so you walk around inside?"

It was a fair question. This whole indoor thing was new to everyone.

"Nah we stand in one place and play, then we get judged and they decide on a winner"

"Really, sounds a bit weird to me"

"I agree with ya mate, but it's another way for the Gert to raise money"

"Can anyone get in?"

I knew where Dee was going with this, he'd be looking to get inside the bar, so I had to shut this down straight away.

"You have to be in a band if you're a kid, or eighteen"

"Can I not just come on in with you?"

"Sure, you've no uniform on, no one will believe you're in a band, standing there in your ordinary clothes"

"I'd love to see it though"

"I'm sure you will be able to hear it if you're near the Avenue One, or better still, why don't you join a band? Then you won't have to stand outside or on the side of the street watching"

I was always on the lookout to ask friends and family to join the band, Dee's reply was swift though.

"I don't think I could join a band. I'd never make it"

"What do you mean, you can drum pretty well, you could give that a go?"

"Aye, I guess so, I dunno like"

"Well you're welcome to come to practice with me anytime you like"

"Thanks mate"

He followed me on his bike, and we arrived at the Avenue One bar at the Newtownards Road end of Templemore Avenue, it stood out from the rest of the buildings nearby, with its navy-blue doors and marble green pillars along the window. A sign advertising Harp lager lit up the area above one of the windows and cast a shadow on the bright red phone-box on the street. In front of one of the blue doors, that led to the upstairs bar, there were already some people hanging around waiting to go in, one of them was Ian Parkhill, "Parky" I wasn't sure whether to approach him or not, he turned around and saw me standing with Dee, he gave me a wee nod of the head.

"Alright Glenn, finally got a full uniform then?"

"Alright Parky, I have indeed, all thanks to you mate, I didn't expect to see you here tonight?"

"Oh aye, I thought I would check it out"

"Not much of a melody competition with only three bands on"

"Yeah, I know, but I hope you guys win"

"Me too mate, here what time is it Dee"

"Quarter past seven mate" came his reply after a quick glance at his watch.

"Wonder where everyone is? They should be here by now"

"Band running late?"

"Aye mate, they should be here by now or at least walking down, we are due to be on at half seven."

I looked in the direction of the Rupert Stanley and In the distance I could see the what looked like a maroon blob moving in the general direction of the Avenue One, as the blob got closer, I could see that it was members of my band, all just casually sauntering down the Avenue. I nudged Dee.

"Here they come now, they always like to leave it close to the wire, I'll catch ya later Dee"

"No worries mate, I'll catch you later"

Within a few minutes the maroon blob was standing in front of me, there were a few "Alright's" and then I found Alvin amongst the maroon mass.

"Alright mate was getting worried there. I've been standing

here for ages"

"We were waiting on the usual late comers"

We all went into the venue and headed up the stairs and into the bar area that had been set aside for the competition. As we walked through the door, I noticed that there was a good crowd of people gathered in the upstairs bar area, they were sitting scattered around the tables and booths. the booths being covered in the same colour material as the carpet on the floor, the area was surrounded by extra tables and bench like seating along the walls, they were trying to squeeze as many people as they could in. The bar itself was made of a dark wood and stretched along one side of the room. Directly in front of it was a reasonably sized square wooden floor area, a dance floor, this was obviously where the bands would be performing tonight. The place smelled a little like the band hall, that familiar odour of beer and smoke filled the air, the windows looking over Templemore Avenue were open slightly at the top, to let fresh air in I assumed.

We were going to be up playing first, I actually didn't mind that, it meant that we could set the standard so to speak and let everyone know what they were up against. We knew our programme and we had been playing it well in the run up, there was no reason for that to be any different on the night. It also meant that we could sit and listen to the other band's performances with our own performance behind us and judge for ourselves whether we thought we had done enough to beat the competition. Alvin and I would be sitting listening intently for every bum note, squeaky flute, any little mistake at all, but also to give credit where credit is due, if a band plays well, you have to acknowledge it even if it means not winning first place. We didn't feel bad about this in the slightest, as we knew the other bands would be sitting doing the exact same thing to us, they would be listening and picking our performance apart, and all for the same reason, they wanted to win. There is no point in just turning up to take part after all, that would make all the effort in practice and hard work mean absolutely nothing, you practice hard to be the best you can be and in a competition, well, you want to win don't you?

So now the time had come for us to put all that practice to the test. A member of the Gert popped up with a microphone near where the DJ was set up, after all us young ones had left there would be a disco on until late. Clearing his throat, the compere confidently addressed the crowd "Right, Ladies and Gents we are gonna make a start here, you're all very welcome to our first indoor competition and we are gonna start with the melody section. Can we ask that while the bands are playing, you give them all the very best of order? So, without further ado, put your hands together for the first band to perform tonight, the Pride of the Raven Flute Band".

There was some mild applause as we formed up on the dance floor area, pretty much like we did on parade but without the drum major yelling his commands. He was sitting having a pint at a table with other friends of the band, he was a spectator tonight. One thing we did do, even though we were indoors was mark time, the lead tip gave us the tap and we started marching on the spot, left right, left right, the sound of shoes and boots on the floor gave the impression that we actually were marching. Marching on the spot helped me feel comfortable, as this was somewhat unfamiliar territory for a marching band. Sure, we played indoors at practice all the time, but not like this, not under the scrutiny of so many people, at practice you could make mistakes and that was ok, here at this indoor competition, mistakes wouldn't be ok. The band captain called the first tune, there were two beats of the bass drum followed by a five beat drum roll, our flutes rose to playing position at the end of this first roll, it was quickly followed by a second five beat roll and we hit the intro to 'Imperial

Echoes' perfectly and it seemed like we were in the groove straight away, the parts seemed to sing as we played the trio, you know when something just gels, well that's what this sounded like to me. As we ended the tune, Alvin and I just looked at each other with a smug smile on our faces, we knew the band had played the march well, there was applause from the gathered crowd that faded into the atmosphere as the band captain called the next tune, Queen of Battle, one of the new tunes. We had listened carefully to other melody bands at parades, just to see if anyone else was playing this march. We hadn't heard anyone playing it, now that didn't mean that no one actually played it, it just meant it wasn't a common march being played at the time. Queen of Battle was a more technical piece, it had lots of quick phrases and if we didn't hit them clean without slurring it would sound messy. Now, with it not being a common tune we might just get away with the odd mistake here and there, but Terry was having none of that in the practices and he definitely wouldn't want to hear any tonight. Mistakes are easily made though, a sudden break in concentration and then you don't remember what you're supposed to play or just get lost in what is supposed to come next you can freeze. It had happened to me on numerous occasions, I was determined that it wouldn't happened to me during this performance. The part that I loved the most about Queen of Battle was the section that came after the trio and led into its repeat, there was a bass solo and then a tricky run of notes that built into a crescendo before the trio burst out into double forte. It had taken me a while to get that run and play it right and it brought me a real sense of satisfaction. But what was even more satisfying was hearing the band perform well and sometimes it sounded like just one flute playing, everyone playing together as one unit. This wasn't quite like that, but it was pretty close. We ended the tune strong and once again we were met with applause we kept marking time as it died down and before we had time to take in the crowds appreciation we were off again into the next tune, another new one, Vendetta, this had been even harder to learn than Queen of Battle. We had only played it perfectly a few times there were a few phrases that had caught us out but hopefully tonight that wouldn't be the case, the trio had a bit of a wobble, but we pulled it back and finished strongly again. Alvin and I looked at each other again, we knew that one hadn't been as good as the others, but there was nothing we could do about it now. We continued on with our set, and our last few tunes all came across strongly and the crowd showed their appreciation with some loud applause as we came to halt at the end of the last tune, our flutes dropping to our left-hand side. After a quick right turn we fell out and looked around for somewhere to sit and take in the bands that would follow us. The UVF band with my friend from school Junior playing in their ranks were up next their set was composed of marches done in a style very similar to the Blackskull, played at speed, well faster than the pace we played at and with different interpretations of certain sections, some of their tunes had parts in them, some of them didn't, on the whole they played a decent set, there had been couple of mistakes here and there, a couple of misplaced drum beats. Junior came and spoke to me afterward

"Well what did you think?" He asked.

"You played well, couple of wee moments with the drums that didn't sound right, but apart from that, I think you sounded well"

"Cheers mate, you were pretty solid, I'm not always sold on your style of play, but those second and third tunes were top class"

"Thanks Junior, we put a lot of hard work into them"

"Right I'm gonna sit with the rest of the band here, and get a good listen to the Defenders, I'd say they're your competition tonight"

"We'll see" I said "We'll see"

"Catch ya later mate"

"Will do"

And with that he headed off to a few tables to the right of us where the rest of his band were sitting.

We didn't have to wait too long for the Defenders to appear and take up their place on the floor to perform. They didn't mark time like the UVF band and us. They stood still and played. They played tunes that were well known as Defenders numbers, The New Colonial was a great march and they even hit the top A solidly, no screeches or anything. They were playing well; this was going to be a close one. They finished their set and the man from the Gert who had started the evening off came on the microphone again and said they would have the results for melody in twenty minutes, there would be the presentation of the trophies and then the blood and thunder section would start.

Twenty minutes wasn't long to wait for results, there would be prizes in three areas, bass drum, drum corps and melody flute. The bands gathered as one and we eagerly awaited the results. They wouldn't take long to read out given the number of bands, the guy with the microphone appeared again, this was it, the moment of truth.

"We will start with the prize for bass drum, in third place, Ulster Volunteer Flute, in second place, Ballymacarrett Defenders, and first place goes to Pride of the Raven"

There was some applause and Alvin went up to get the trophy for best bass drum, he held it aloft as he returned to our table. This was a great start, hopefully it would be followed by two more.

"And now, Best Drum Corp, in third place, Ulster Volunteer Flute"

This looked like it was going to be the same result as bass drum, our lead tip would usually go up to collect the drum Corp trophies, I looked over at Bobby, he was expressionless, he had been through this a thousand times and never took anything for granted.

"In second place…." The compere paused for a few seconds, the tension built a little… "Pride of the Raven…" I looked over at Bobby again, a little bit shocked to say the least, he just shrugged his shoulders and got up to go and get the trophy, I looked and saw the Defenders drummers patting each other on the back they knew they had won this one.

"And in first place, Ballymacarrett Defenders" there were cheers and shouts as this was announced.

"I can't believe they won" I said to Alvin, "I mean they were no-where near as good as our drums"

"I know, but that's what the judge has decided"

"Well there's still best melody flute to come, fingers crossed"

The noise settled down as the compere prepared to reveal who had won melody flute.

"And so onto Melody flute… in third place, Ulster Volunteer Flute" so far so good I thought to myself, "in second place….

Pride of ....."I didn't even wait for him to finish, there was no need we had come second.

"Ack no bloody way" I said maybe a little too loudly. A few heads turned in my direction.

"Right Glenn, you may go and pick the trophy up"

I walked up to pick up the trophy I didn't like losing but losing to the Defenders, that was always hard to take.

"You win some you lose some kid" said Terry when I returned to the table.

"I really didn't think we had lost this one, and losing to them"

"Take it on the chin big man, they played well"

From behind me came the result I didn't want to hear, first place melody flute went to the Defenders, you'd have thought they had won the World Cup the way they were getting on, jumping and shouting and carrying on.

With the results out there wasn't much point in sticking around too long afterward as we were sitting at our table one of the members of the Defenders come over, his curly hair and moustache already causing me offence, with the first place trophy in his hand, he pushed it towards my face.

"Take a look at that kid, that's all you can do, look at it"

Why a grown man felt the need to goad a twelve-year-old is beyond me, the wry smile on his face and annoying laughter, my response was off my tongue before I had even thought it through

"Nah mate you keep looking at it, sure we have hundreds of those"

This obviously didn't go down too well.

"What did you say?" There was an aggressive menace in his tone, my response had obviously aggravated him.

"You heard me well enough mate" I didn't even look at him, my heart racing a little as adrenaline pumped through me.

He moved towards me, he was angry now "I didn't hear you, say it again"

Terry came to my rescue "Right mate, wise up, he's a kid for god's sake, he's gutted not to have won you'd probably feel the same, congratulations, and enjoy your win, you played well tonight"

That seemed to calm things down, he laughed and put the trophy up in the air and walked off.

"That was a bit mad" I said.

"You did wind him up though"

"How, by stating the truth? We do have hundreds of them though, I wasn't making it up"

"I know, but you knew saying that would wind him up"

"Well I just don't like losing"

Everyone laughed and I got my hair ruffled by a few of the older members at the table "You're Raven through and through kid".

Hearing that meant the world to me. I walked home proud, even though we had come second, it wasn't always about winning, being loyal would always win out over everything.

CHAPTER 10

1st July

It's the last day of my first year at secondary school, and my class 1NJ are going through the end of year activities with aplomb. Having sat through the obligatory 'you have all done really well" speech from our form teacher informed us that next year we won't become 2NJ but rather we would be becoming 2JN. It turns out that this wasn't just a fancy rearrangement of initials but a complete change of form teacher. I'm not sure I blame him for getting rid of us, we have been a bit of a nightmare, but we actually liked big Norman Johnston, he was hard but fair, he took us for maths and some science, we never raked about in his class, his efficiency with a cane was known even at other schools. So, after that bombshell he lead us round to the assembly hall for the last time to take part in the end of year school awards, which really turned out to be our whole year group sitting listening to all the first form teachers announcing each classes best boy and achievements like best behaved class, which 1NJ was never in the running for. The most important category was saved to last, the winners of the junior five aside competition, again, not 1NJ, but we didn't care. We had come second in the all school tournament beating fourth and fifth year sides on our way to getting runners up medals. This was then followed by the achievements of the first-year football team. All this build up served as a starter before the main course, the Headmasters end of year address. I have to say that this was the biggest load of shite that I've ever had to sit through. It wasn't that Mr Weston was a bad headmaster, this was the last day of school and we had heard enough of his voice throughout the year. I was never as glad to hear a school bell in my life, we only had dinner to go to before we went to the final event of the day and then we would be free from school for a whole eight weeks. As the bell was ringing my class and I were filing out of the assembly hall and heading up to the dinner hall, all trying to work out what the last activity could be.

"I wonder what fun they have planned for the end of the day? It's hardly been a barrel of laughs so far" I said.

"I know, what the hell was Weston on about?" replied Junior.

Bowersy was next to join in "No idea, watching paint dry would have been better"

"They should have let us have our own awards, you know, at least that would have been fun!"

"Yeah we could have done it like one of those award shows on TV 'And now we have the award for the best caning in a classroom setting, let's have a look at the nominees, Mr Black for the shortest yet sharpest caning action in a geography class, Mr Hewitt for his role in Alex the Bat...." Now Bowersy wanted in on the act.

"Oh wait wait, I've got one, I've got one," pretending to clear his throat he began, "Mr Scott for his striking slapstick role in Being a Jehovah's Witness"

But the best one was definitely left until last.

"And now," said Junior in his poshest presenter voice "the final nominee in this category, Mr Drury for his unforgettable role in the ground breaking black and white picture, a dog taking a shit in Clarawood estate" we were killing ourselves laughing at the last one, we weren't laughing at the time though. Mr Drury was our art teacher, and a few months back, he decided that we would all benefit immensely from doing some photography. He split us off into groups and my group just happened to be my friends and we were given the liberty of leaving the classroom and taking photographs of things that were of interest to us. Now that kind of liberty was just crying out to be taken advantage of and of course we duly obliged. We thought it would be a great idea to take pictures of us doing blue moons, of bus stops, a patch of grass, an overflowing bin and the one shot that would land us in trouble, a dog taking a shit! We had such a laugh taking the pictures, we didn't think about the fact that Drury was actually going to develop these pictures and our artistic direction would land us in trouble. We returned to the class, handed over the camera and Mr Drury went into the dark room. Art was our last class of the day, and was always a doddle, but not today. Mr Drury came out of the dark room and just shouted, "Millar, Walker, Moore, Bowers, Rice, stay behind after class!"

We were well and truly busted!! The double period of art just seemed to drag on forever. Then we heard the sound we normally would have been hoping for, the bell. The rest of the class filed out, looking back at the five of us knowing we were about to get caned. We waited at our group desk and Mr Drury went on a tirade about abusing his trust and wasting expensive school resources and did we know how lucky we were to get these opportunities, blah blah blah. We were all thinking the same thing, hurry up and cane us so we can get out of here.

We weren't worried about getting caned, Drury wasn't known as the best caner in school, in fact if you were getting caned by anyone, you'd have probably chosen Drury to do it every time. His technique was shit, it didn't hurt, it had more of a sting and even that didn't last very long. It was nothing like our form teacher, his technique was flawless and inflicted serious pain. We stood there awaiting our fate without any sense of concern or fear, this would all be over in a minute and we would rake the shit out of Drury's caning disability on the way home. I stepped forward when I was told to, being first to get caned meant I could make faces at the rest of them and try and make them laugh, a technique we had all used whenever more than one of us got caned at the same time. I held out my left hand and waited…whack! The tape tipped bamboo cane came down across my palm, I felt the sting, but I didn't wince. I put my hand down and expected Mr Drury to move on, not today though.

"Who told you to put your hand down son?" he said with a sense of venom we hadn't heard from him before. I shot a worried glance down the line; this was unexpected territory. Drury continued on with this new persona.

"You'll keep your hand up until I tell you to put it down, understand?"

I didn't respond, but he did. He unleashed a further nine strikes and I was now bearing a left hand with large red welt marks on it. The slight pause in striking led me to put the hand down, I started to raise it again, wary of the threat he made to not put it down until he said I could, Drury broke the awkward silence and simply said.

"Other hand"

With that statement you could just smell the shit passing down the line, he was making an example out of us, there was no way out. I took another ten strikes to my right hand, I was crying, not sobbing but tears were rolling down my face. No one looked around, we all just stood there. I heard the same phrase and same amount of strikes another four times as each of us received our punishment. When it was over Drury just said one word "Out!"

We bent over to pick up our school bags, and that turned out to be the most difficult thing we had done all day. You try lifting book laden bags with hands that had just been beaten to a pulp and you'll understand what I mean. Just getting the bag up and then trying to sling them over our shoulders caused us all to grimace and grit our teeth. We walked home in silence that day and no one had mentioned anything about that day until now, now when it was a distant memory, now when school was over for the summer, we could finally make a joke of it!

"...and the award for best caning in a classroom setting goes to... Mr Drury, a dog taking a shit in Clarawood Estate", we could laugh about it now and we spent dinner time recounting the events of that day and what seemed like a thousand other memories we'd made this year.

We went back to our form room only to be told to line up again and be marched back to the assembly hall. In the hall there was a massive screen up on the stage, the final activity was going to be a movie! So there we are in the assembly hall, all blacked out, windows covered with dark and somewhat musty curtains, there was no outside light getting in at all, it almost could been a set up for the teachers to perform a hit on our whole year group and take us all out in one fell swoop, no one could see and no one would know! One of the teachers rolled out a massive projector and once it was set up announced that our whole year group would be watching a Bruce Lee movie! Now, I don't know what idiot decided that the best thing to show a group of around a hundred twelve-year-old boys was a Kung Fu movie! We are impressionable young males after all, we may just think that we can re-enact everything we are about to see, but hey teachers know what they are doing right? Needless to say, after the movie was finished and we had finally been dismissed for the summer holidays, there were a hundred new Bruce Lee kung fu masters on the way home, there were flying kicks and one-inch punches and Bruce Lee stances breaking out all over the place.

One of these new experts was Penman, he'd been picked on all year by just about everyone. He must have saw this as a perfect opportunity to get back at a few people, while everyone was toy fighting and making Bruce Lee crows and opening their shirts and pretending to lick the blood of their fingers, he launched a few punches and kicks towards 'Rossy' that were neither toy nor fake. First, he caught him square in the stomach with a front kick, knocking the wind out of him, and followed it up with a straight punch to the face. It was almost surreal, like watching a scene from the movie. No sooner had Penman finished his scene, reality must have kicked in, he paused just as he was about throw another punch, he dropped his punching arm, reached for his bag that was lying a few inches away from his feet, grabbed it and sped off so fast all that was missing from the scene was a RoadRunner 'Meep Meep'. Penman's end of year starring role was now over. He now had eight weeks to prepare himself for the sequel.

'Rossy' picked himself up, grabbed his bag and dandered off as if nothing had happened. Anyone who'd seen it though was stunned, no one had ever seen him retaliate, this had obviously been building up and here on the final day of school, he unleashed his inner Bruce Lee! So that was it, the end of the school year and we all headed home having completed the first year of a new adventure, secondary school, but for me it meant that there were a whole host of other things to look forward to.

Walking home and my mind was filled with the potential of

the next few weeks. Fergie and Junior were feeling exactly the same they were looking forward to the parades with their own bands. From Easter right up until now, I had been all over the country with the band, taking part in competitions, picking up trophies and generally being, in my opinion, the best band around. Now we were in the run up to the best part of the season, three events one-month, pure band heaven. The first of July, the trip to Scotland and the twelfth of July! I couldn't wait, it was going to be beezer!

With school having finished on a Friday it meant I only had the weekend to wait for one of the biggest parades of the year. The first of July! I'd heard my Ma and neighbours calling it the mini twelfth, but some of the older guys in the band said that calling it the mini twelfth was wrong, what the parade really was about was commemorating the Battle of the Somme, and remembering all the soldiers from Northern Ireland who had fought and died during that bloody battle of the First World War.

There was plenty to be getting on with before all that though, collecting for the bonfire had been in full swing for weeks now. The wood we have collected so far was being secretly stored in the backyards of a couple of empty houses. These were houses on Madrid Street that no one was living in obviously, they were due to get renovated and their yards were located up the entry at the top of my street. Collecting for the bonfire was great and especially as it got closer to the eleventh because that meant the chance to stay out all night now! We had to stay out all night because you had to guard your wood in case we got raided. Raiding was what happened when another area that was collecting found out where another area stored their wood, they would come late at night with a squad from their area and steal your wood. We had raided the Pitt Park bonfire last year and we fully expected to get raided this year. It wasn't necessarily done with malice it was more of a competitive thing. People would talk about the biggest bonfires for days afterwards, so everyone wanted to be the biggest. The last thing you needed a few days away from the 11th, was getting raided. When we went out collecting, we were like a wee army, scouring the streets for wood. We would be in empty houses, building sites, absolutely anywhere we could get ourselves into. We had this steel trolley thing that we had 'acquired'. We borrowed it permanently after someone quite carelessly left it outside the Liverpool club in Templemore Avenue after a delivery. Their loss was our gain, we used the trolley to help us with transporting the bigger pieces of wood we found to our hidden storage den. It was a bit of hindrance as well though, cause it's a bit hard to hide a trolley with loads of wood on it, and the noise that it made trundling along the streets was crazy, it sounded like a Grand Prix for shopping trolleys.

It's amazing what you can lift when you put your mind to it, I remember we were out collecting and came across this building site, they were always a good place to find wood of some sort, and in this one we hit the jackpot. We had found a few things, I heard this massive gulder from wee Dee.

"Here, c'mere 'til ya see what I've found!"

We excitedly followed the sound of his voice scurrying through an entrance to a shell of a house with a hole for a door and bare concrete floor complete with holes in the wall for plugs and light switches and stuff. We went through the dusty grey living room that someday in the not too distant future would become someone's pride and joy, complete with good carpet that you wouldn't be allowed to walk across with your shoes on, a picture of the family above the fireplace and of course some poor kid's embarrassing school photo! This led us into what most likely was the kitchen space area with its half-built cupboards and spaces for yet to be purchased appliances and then on out to the back yard where a bounty of treasure awaited us, now destined to be used on the eleventh. There in front of us was the biggest pile of old wooden doors, there must have been about fifty of them, just sitting there begging to become part of our summer wood collection, and who were we to disappoint these stranded pieces of forgotten room entry. Their days of fulfilling their purpose in a house were well and truly over. They were ours now.

We didn't even stop to think about how we would get them all out of there, we just started piling them up on our backs, and got on with it. I carried at least four of these things on my back, trailing then along the ground and moving as fast as I could, we were like a pile of hermit crabs moving house all carrying doors and moving as fast as we could.

We didn't all leave the place at once though; we just couldn't take the chance. After a quick scout about the place we found another gap that we could get out of the site with the doors. Two of us would go at a time and take them to where we stored the wood and then make it back for the others to make their trip, we couldn't risk anyone spotting us, we didn't want anyone else getting a hold of them. We seemed to go back and forward for ages, but eventually we got all of the doors and after we had put the last one up over the wall and piled them up properly in the yard, Alan suggested one of us ask our Ma's for something to drink like a big lemonade bottle full of Ribena or something, moving doors is thirsty work after all. Somebody had to stay with the wood and Alan was adamant he was staying as getting the drinks was his idea, so Dee and me went to our houses to see if we could score a bottle of juice. Dee and I both bombed out on the juice but we did manage to get a couple of bottles of water, my Ma made me promise to bring the empty bottle back as she needed it to make sure the lemonade man gave her money off her bill. We all had done this, when you take empty lemonade bottles back to the shop you can get 10p for them, it was great if you found a few that someone had carelessly left behind on the street, we would pick them up and then head straight round to Billy's or down to Gallagher's shop for a 10p mix up. A bag full of black jacks, mojo's and Chelsea whoppers, or if you'd got twenty pence you got one of those big snooker ball gobstopper things, they were massive and lasted for ages. If you were brave, you threw caution to the wind and got these things called fireballs, they just burned the gob right of ye, we used to challenge each other to see who could keep theirs in the longest, I won a few times, but only because Dee wasn't there, he was the king of the fireballs, he was like a circus act, a fire eater! One time he put three in at once, which was unheard of and he didn't even flinch!

Anyway with our bottles of water in hand, we climbed up on to the yard wall, straddling it like we were the builders on one of those black and white New York pictures, you know the ones where they're eating their lunch on half built skyscraper and not a care in the world, hundreds of feet up in the air. We basked in the glory of our treasure trove of doors and how we would show of when the rest of the gang came around later. Of course, we would have to embellish the finding of the doors story a little, just to make it even more of an achievement, a wee bit of bravado never hurt anyone. We ended the day feeling proud of ourselves, we had had a great day out collecting and we definitely deserved a good night's rest. Tomorrow was Sunday, and we would get a lie in if we were lucky before doing it all again. I was one day away from one of the biggest parades in the marching calendar and I couldn't help but be excited. Everyone from around the area would be out watching the bands, that's what you did, and if you were lucky you got to wear some of your July clothes, but not the stuff for the twelfth of course, no one's Ma would allow that!

Sunday as it turned out was pretty uneventful, the chances of two big wood find days in a row were slim, but we still looked and managed to find a wardrobe, a chest of drawers and a few sleepers. I knew I was headed for an early night, even though the parade was on Monday night, I had so much to do, well, I say that, but I would spend a good bit of tomorrow practicing and making sure my shoes were clean, my Ma would make sure my uniform was looking good, ironing my shirt and pressing my trousers, and then I would be able to remove the jacket from its suit bag. It took pride of place in my wardrobe, nothing else was allowed to even touch it, everything else was pushed to one side and my uniform had a whole side of the wardrobe to itself, my hat was housed in a box I had found outside crazy prices, and my royal blue plume was safely in its cardboard sleeve. My flute would get a little olive oil treatment, just to make sure it sounded sweet, I'd check all the keys and pads to make sure there was nothing wrong, nothing sticking or out of place, and even if there was anything to sort, I knew that Terry would be there to help out. But for now, as the sun began to set on another day, we sat on the top of the backyard wall, guardians of the wood, that in ten days' time, would re-enact the event that welcomed King William III to these shores hundreds of years ago. Even though the date we lit the bonfires was different to when it really happened it was a real connection with our past, and here we were keeping that piece of history alive. It was very rare that we had a conversation about this stuff, but in the moment, wee Dee said.

"Here, I was just thinking"

"Fuck, things must be bad if you're thinking" said Alan

"Aye you're funny 'n' all" he snapped back and continued "But seriously like, if the bonfires on the eleventh are about King William landing in Belfast and the 12th is about the Battle of the Boyne, what's the first of July all about then?"

There was a moments silence as if in respect for the question, but more like "I'm not sure if what I know is actually right"

I shared what I thought I knew about the situation. "Well I don't know everything about this, but I do know that the first of July is about the Battle of the Boyne too as well as something else"

"How the hell can the first be about the twelfth!" said Dee sounding slightly confused.

"It's not about the twelfth" I replied, and this just seemed to rile him even more.

"Then why did you just say it was?" Shaking his head and making an exaggerated breath.

"What I said was that the first was about the Battle of the Boyne"

"Aye the twelfth"

"The Battle of the Boyne didn't happen on the twelfth of July mate" Dee looked at me like I'd told him I'd kissed his sister.

"What the hell are you talking about, of course it did"

"It didn't mate, there was a battle on the twelfth of July but at a place called Aughrim"

"That place from the Sash?" said Dee, following it up with a sung rendition of the line, 'it was worn in Derry, Aughrim...'

"Yeah that's the one, so the twelfth celebrates the victory over King James as a whole"

"So, the first is about the Boyne then?"

"Well yes and no"

"What?" There was a look of perplexity and confusion on Dee's face, so I continued trying to explain.

"Well the first of July is the actual date the Battle of the Boyne took place on, but the parade we have on the first is all about the Battle of the Somme in the First World War"

"And when did that take place, the twelfth?" He said this with such seriousness I couldn't help but laugh.

"No, no, it actually did take place on the first of July"

"Well thank god for that, I was beginning to think I was going nuts here, why don't they tell you this stuff in school?" Dee was in P7, that wonderful transition year, between primary and secondary school.

"They do mate, just not in primary school, I learned about this stuff in history this year" but even this explanation didn't seem enough to Dee.

"Well they should teach this in the youth club, or the lodges should do something, I wouldn't mind knowing more about it like"

Alan, not one to be left out of anything, piped up.

"You know what this means?"

"What?" I said.

"It means you actually do seem to have a brain! Get you learning stuff in school and teaching us about history, teacher's pet!"

We started laughing and almost fell off the wall.

"Right..." I said, "I think we have guarded this enough for to-night, and besides its the twelfth tomorrow"

Dee started "No it's not it's the..." A moment of realisation took place, "Haha you're funny, almost got me there". We dropped down off the yard wall and headed down the entry towards my street, Dee and Alan turned right heading home to Madrid Street, I turned left to go to my house.

"See ya tomorrow" I said turning back on them

"Aye, see ya then"

I walked the short distance to my house laughing about the conversation my friends and I just had, then my thoughts turned to the day ahead of me, the first of July. I wondered if I would think about what that day was really all about, would I be able to? Given that I would be playing my flute and trying to make sure I didn't make any mistakes. Did anyone walking think about why they actually did it? Or where they like Dee and Alan and not really have a clue what it was all about? Then I heard the familiar voice of my Ma.

"Hey dreamer, are you coming in or are you gonna stand out there all night?"

"Coming now Ma" I hadn't event realised that I had stopped at the hall door. I walked inside and my Ma asked me to close the big door behind me "And make sure you put the snib on son" she said as she walked into the living room.

"Ok Ma" I said, and I pushed the round button on the door lock up to the appropriate position and pushed the lock lever to both sides to make sure it was definitely locked. I knew that my Ma would ask me if I had performed this little ritual as soon as I walked into the living room, and regardless of whatever I said she would go and check anyway.

"Did you put the snib on son?"

"I did indeed Ma"

"I'll just go and check anyway"

As she left to check the truth of my words and ultimately the position of the snib, I turned to my Da who was reading the late edition of the Belfast Telegraph, "I don't know why she's asks me to do it, when she never believes me anyway"

Dad barely looked up and said, "Don't ask me, I'm just a lodger" and he returned to reading the paper.

After inspecting the snib and ensuring it was appropriately secure, Mum came back into the room and asked, "Do you want anything before going to bed son?"

"No thanks, I'm just gonna head on up here, big day tomorrow"

"No problem son, and here, don't be playing any of that band music ok?"

"Ok Mum"

"And leave your flute alone as well, you will get plenty of time with it tomorrow"

I shrugged my shoulders and said "I'm too tired to play anyway, night Mum"

"Goodnight son"

I went upstairs, stopping at the bathroom for the nightly ritual of brushing my teeth and a quick wash before bed. I switched my light off and climbed into bed, lying flat out with my hands behind my head and looking up at my skylight, staring at the dark sky beyond the glass, faintly lit by the silvery moonlight that danced across the pane like a banner in the wind or a note in the air. It was around this time last year I was heading off to Canada, a lot had happened since then, maybe more than I could acknowledge but, at this point in time I knew history wouldn't be repeating itself and nothing was getting in the way of me fulfilling a dream, walking the first of July with the Pride of the Raven.

Sleep came quickly, as did the morning and before I knew it my eyes were staring at a very different proposition as I looked out the skylight, daylight, such as it was, greeted me like an old friend and welcomed me to destiny. There was already some hustle and bustle on the floors below me and I knew mum was up, god knows what she was doing making all that noise, I'd find out soon enough though.

I arrived downstairs still half-awake to the smell of toast coming from the kitchen, sometimes there was no better aroma, well maybe after some butter had been lathered on the toast, or even the point the bread starts to burn. My stomach rumbled, loud enough to be heard.

"Someone's hungry?"

"Yup I'm Lee Marvin Ma"

"Here's me thinking you were called Glenn"

"Ha ha ha, very funny Ma"

Mum seemed pleased with herself at that, "Do you want jam, on your toast?"

"Oh aye, of course I do"

"Black currant or lemon curd?" She enquired.

It was a bit early for lemon curd, so I opted for the more traditional black currant and salivated as I watched it being spread on my toast by the expert knife skills of my mum. She had a way of making sure every part of the toasts surface was evenly covered in jam, Hartley's jam no less, no yellow pack cheap shit here thank god. She sliced my toast into big triangles, and I retreated to the sofa with my toast on a small plate, as I took my seat mums voice rang out again.

"Cup of tea son?"

"Yes please" there is something special about a really good cup of tea in the morning, that is just so satisfying. Although why is it when you're in a hurry to get somewhere the tea tastes amazing, yet too hot to down and you don't want to throw it out? It wasn't that kind of morning today though, it tasted great and I had the time to savour it.

"What's your plans for today then?" Mum asked as she came into the living room from the kitchen.

"Probably gonna head out collectin' with the lads for a while, then put some practice in before getting ready and heading up to the band hall"

"Don't be wearing any of your good clothes out collectin', wear something old ok?"

"Aye no worries Ma"

"I'm tellin' you now son, if I find you out liftin' wood with new clothes on, you won't see the twelfth of July, do you hear me?

"Yes Ma"

I got washed and put on some old clothes, knowing fine rightly my Ma would check them before I left the house, I headed up the street and straight for where we stored our wood, I walked down the entry to see Colin and Darren standing there.

"Alright lads"

Alright Glenn, where'd all the doors come from then?"

"We found them the other day, took us ages getting them back here like"

"They'll make a good base for the boney when we start building it"

"We aren't there yet, still time for a raid or two"

"Well we will just have to make sure there's some of us out every night now"

We climbed up upon to the wall and surveyed the stash, "We should probably start making a hut if we are going to be staying out" Colin said, we will need to use some of the doors for that and we can get that aul sofa out as well"

"We need a ladder or something down into the yard, just to make it easier getting in and out"

"We could just stack some wood like steps?"

We heard some footsteps behind us and turned to find Dee and Alan arriving along with the Bennetts and a few of the girls from the area. We all had a hand in building the hut and a few hours later we were all very happy with what we had done. Having forgot to put my watch on, I started to get worried about the time, I mean, it was great building the hut n' all, but I had other things to be doing as well.

"What's the time Darren?"

"You late for your beauty sleep?" He replied sarcastically.

"Yeah you need that more than me mate, no I just need to keep an eye on the time, want to make sure I'm all set for the parade tonight."

"You looking forward to it then?"

"Oh god aye, it's one of the biggest parades of the year, I can't wait"

"Well we'll all be there somewhere along the route cheering you on"

The parade route was all over East Belfast, hopefully I'd get to see Fergie and Junior later on as well, and of course all of my family would be watching too. They'd be on the Albertbridge Road near the orange hall when the parade started, that's where we always stood year after year without fail. On the return they'd be outside the Rupert Stanley on Templemore Avenue. I would most likely run into neighbours and friends from all over, it was going to be quite the night.

"It's just coming up to half four mate"

"Right, I may go here, I'll need to get something to eat and get changed before I head up to the band hall"

And with that I dropped down from the backyard wall into the entry, looking back up at everyone,

"Right, I will see you all later"

"See ya"

"Alright mate, see ya later on"

I headed down the entry towards the street and to my house to begin getting ready for the parade.

After spending some time practicing, it was time to get something to eat before getting washed and ready. I could smell food being cooked and dandered into the kitchen to find my Ma making home-made chips.

"I thought I'd make you some chips son, before the long walk, that ok?"

"Aye Ma, that's more than ok, although…"

"Although what?"

"Well…"

"Well? Come on spit it out…" she turned around from her careful control of the battered orange chip pan that looked like it was old enough to have made chips for Moses.

"You better not be turning your nose up at my chips or you'll be getting skelped".

"Can you do them a little less crispy than you usually do them?

"And what exactly is wrong with crispy chips, eh?"

"Nothing at all Ma, I just like them a little softer"

The truth is my Ma fried them to beyond crispy, in fact they' were so crispy you could probably use them as tent pegs, but she liked them that way which meant we all had to like them that way.

"I'll take yours out five minutes earlier then, but if they're not cooked properly don't come running to me with a sore stom-ach"

Such motherly affection was on display here, I could hardly contain myself.

"Ok Ma, on my own head be it"

"Set yourself a place at the table and I'll bring this in for you"

"Ok Ma" lifting a placemat, a knife and a fork I set a place for myself and sat down to eat.

My Ma had some chicken on and there were peas on the go too! I loved peas, especially with mashed potato. I loved mixing them up together and then pouring some gravy over them, I'd have to wait until next Sunday for that particular culinary de-light though. I cleared my plate in no time, the chips were just right for me, I picked up my plate and took it into the kitchen.

"You want me to wash these Ma?"

"No no, you go and get ready, I'll sort this out"

"Thanks Ma, that was lovely"

She gave a bit of a smile, at the food compliment but almost in a way to suggest that the quality of her provision was never ever really in doubt.

I made my way upstairs to my room, I bounded up the stairs two at a time, I had lots to do, so I needed to get a move on.

I took my band uniform out of the wardrobe and stood under my skylight window, and gave the jacket and trousers a good look over to make sure there weren't any major issues, Mum had got the uniform dry cleaned for me so it was very much ready for the road. I hung that part of my uniform on the still open wardrobe door, I lifted out another hanger that had my white shirt and blue clip on tie attached to the shirt chest pocket. Mum had obviously ironed it, and all was good so far. My hat was stored up in the upper compartment of the wardrobe and the plume was in a cardboard sleeve beside it. I took my lint brush to the hat and removed any fluff that had dared attach itself to it. Everything was good and now my shoes would need looked at. At the bottom of my wardrobe were my black Dr Marten shoes, they had been polished a wee while ago so I would need to give them a fresh polish, so I got my polish box from its plastic bag also located at the bottom of my wardrobe and proceeded to give them a good polish, after a rub down with my musty yellow cloth, they were gleaming, I could see my face in them, that was always the ultimate test of a good polish. I looked at them from all angles, just to make sure there were no dull spots, and when I was sufficiently proud of my work, I placed the newly gleaming shoes beside my bed.

Now I just had to get washed, then I could think about putting some of my uniform on. I never put it all on at once, I found the quicker I put it all on, the warmer I seemed to get, and then I'd end up with the sweat running like a cheap pair of tights, and there's no way I'm arriving at the band hall for this parade like a sweaty betty. After getting washed I put on a pair of black socks, my marching socks. I had found that some socks while nice to wear, didn't actually agree with long walks in Dr Marten shoes, I had three pairs of thicker black socks that seemed to do the trick and made longer walks all the more comfortable.

As I pulled them on and lifted my trousers to put them on, I thought about the times I had seen the bands before joining the Raven. It had never crossed my mind that there was so much that went into getting ready for a parade and making sure you were fit to march. When something isn't right when you're marching it just puts you right off your game, you try to overcome it but it's just not the same.

My shirt was next to go on and then I would put my shoes on, and after that I would wash my hands again before thinking about putting my tie and jacket on, I never risked the chance of some stray shoe polish finding its way on to either. I took a quick glance at the time; things were progressing nicely, and I was almost ready for the road. I went over to my discarded jeans to do the ritual check for money, so I would know how much I needed to ask my Ma for before I left. I had the grand sum of four pounds and fifty-three pence in my pocket, I'd ask my Ma for a fiver, having nearly a tenner should do me for the night. I grabbed my flute case and put my plume in my inside jacket pocket, and lifted my hat, and with one last look in the mirror it was time to go. I headed downstairs and popped my head in the living room.

"Right Ma that's me away now"

"Alright son, c'mere 'til I see you"

This was where she checked if I met her requirements to be seen in public, and the dreaded face wipe with a hanky if all wasn't as expected. Luckily, I met her approval and I was able to proceed into the wide world.

"Have a good night son, and we will shout on you later, we will be in our usual spots, your Granny will be there as well"

"Happy days, I will see you all later on then" I turned to leave, and my Ma spoke again.

"Have you enough money for tonight son?" she enquired.

"Aye I've a few pound here Ma"

She walked over to fireplace and lifted her purse; she took out a fiver and handed it to me.

"Here, take that with you as well, just in case you need to get something to eat"

"Thanks Ma, are you sure now, I know we aren't made of money"

"Of course I'm sure, now away on or you'll be late"

"Alright, thanks again" and with that I left the living room all smiles. That was a result, I didn't even have to ask for anything I thought and then as I walked out through my front door, I was met with bright sunshine accompanied by a mellow breeze, perfect weather for marching. This was shaping up to be quite the night. Walking up towards Madrid Street I held my head up high, proud to be wearing my band uniform and proud to be honouring the heroes who fought in the Battle of the Somme, this very day almost seventy years ago. This was almost like reaching back into history itself to shake the hand of the brave and say thank you. A lot of the band said they looked forward to the first even more than the twelfth of July, I had wondered why? Maybe it was easier to connect with something that had happened seventy years ago than something that happened nearly three hundred years ago?

As I made my way on to the Avenue, there was a buzz about the place, families were starting to gather at their favourite parade spots, others fixing the bunting outside the front of their houses. There were a few food stalls on the streets, and the guy with a shopping trolley with all sorts of red, white and blue souvenirs inside it, he seemed to appear everywhere. I approached the crossing at the junction on the Albertbridge Road and hit the button for the pedestrian crossing, I heard the faint sound of drums in the air as I made my way across the road, some bands were already making their way to the starting point of the parade. It wouldn't be long before the Avenue was filled music and colour. I headed on up the second avenue, taking a familiar route to the band hall. As it came into sight, I could see the maroon uniforms in the ever-decreasing distance, and judging by the number of them, we would have a full band out tonight.

The hall was packed, even more than usual, friends and family, wives and girlfriends, kids and grandkids, they were all there, wanting to be a part of this special night. I couldn't see Alvin downstairs, so I headed upstairs to the pool table, most of the younger members of the band were hanging out there. Alvin and his two brothers, Mark and Colin, big Chris, Geordie, Smoky and wee Stephen, the cymbal player, were all there.

"Alright lads, quite the crowd in tonight"

"Aye it's always like this on the first" said Chris as he leaned down to take a shot on the pool table.

"And we have a full band out, twenty-four flutes and eight drums, there'll be some sound from us tonight!"

"Too right, god help whoever we are walking behind"

We had only played a couple of frames when we heard the familiar blast of the band captains whistle.

"Right lads get yourselves together, let's get formed up and on our way"

We started to get ourselves ready for the road, putting our jackets on, giving everything a once over before we headed out.

"Has anyone seen my hat?" said Smoky

"Where did you leave it?"

"I thought I left it on the seat big Chris is on"

"I didn't see it" said Chris

"Maybe I left it downstairs" Smoky left the room and went downstairs to look for it. Big Chris stood up and looked at the chair he'd sat down on.

"Here lads, he did leave it on this chair" Chris picked up the hat that he had obviously sat on, it looked ridiculous now, the coat hangers inside that gave it its shape where bent and twisted in some parts and completely flat in others. We were all killing ourselves laughing.

"How did you not know you were sitting on a hat?" asked Mark through his laughter

"I don't know, I just sat down"

"You may try and fix it before he comes back up"

"I've never done that before, Rigby did mine"

"Right enough he did mine as well, we may have a go though, he can't parade with his hat like that, someone keep an eye on the stairs for him while we try to fix this"

I went outside to 'keep dick' while Chris and Mark tried to fix the hat, the band captain spotted me at the top of the stairs,

"Right Glenn, come on, time to form up, tell the rest of them to get down here now"

"Ok" I said and headed back into the room where operation hat fix was in full swing. I flung the door open and everyone just looked at the door and stopped dead, I walked into every-one's relief.

"I thought that was him coming back" said Chris

"No just me, the band captain wants us all downstairs now, so we may get going"

"What are we going to do with the hat?"

"Leave it back on the chair and say nothing"

"We can't do that!"

"Of course, we can" Chris put the hat back on the chair "There, it's back on the chair, come on let's go"

We all filed out of the pool room and headed downstairs to form up with the rest of the band, as we were near the bottom of the stairs Smoky appeared and was looking to go back upstairs.

"Any luck finding your hat?" asked Chris, a few of us couldn't help but snigger, but continued on our way.

"Not yet, I'm gonna take one last look upstairs"

We formed up with the rest of the band outside the hall, anxiously awaiting Smoky's return with his hat. As we stood in our ranks, the band captain was losing patience.

"What the hell is keeping Smoky?"

Chris couldn't help himself, "He really needs to shape up", those of us in the know started laughing.

The band captain wasn't laughing though, he was heading back to the hall to investigate when Smoky came out absolutely raging.

"Look at the state of my hat! Which one of you fuckers decided this would be funny?" He held the wonky hat up for all to see, the only sympathetic support he got was from the band captain, most of us were laughing but were brought back to earth pretty quickly as the band captain shared his thoughts with us.

"So, you think it's funny to mess with someone's hat on tonight of all nights, when we want to look our best, when tonight is all about respect, somebody does this! Well, that somebody better own up"

There was silence for what seemed like forever, Rigby took the hat from Smoky and started to reshape it for him.

"I'm still waiting" the band captain wasn't letting this drop.

Finally Chris spoke up, "I did it, but it wasn't on purpose, I sat on it, it was an accident, we were trying to fix it, then we were told we had to form up, so we just left it upstairs"

"Why didn't you just own up?"

"I actually didn't realise I'd sat on it, sorry Smoky, I should have said"

"That's ok"

Rigby handed the hat back to him, "That's the best I can do for now, it doesn't look too bad"

"Thanks, appreciate you trying"

"Ok now that we are finally ready, let's look like we are a band here ok. Drum Major, over to you"

We were called to attention and the band captain called 'The Slopes' as our first tune and we were on our way to the Avenue. As we turned onto the second avenue, the place was just heaving with bands, lodge members and people on the footpaths, the energy was electric. We hadn't long to wait after we arrived at our designated spot until we were forming up again for the walk around East Belfast. Wheeling left on to the Albertbridge Road, the crowds seemed to grow even bigger, I kept an eye out for my family and spotted them just up a wee bit from the Orange hall on the right-hand side of the road. My Ma and my Big Granny trying to take photos while waving for my attention. I waved in acknowledgment and got back to playing quickly.

The crowds stretched out as far as the eye could see, and as we walked past the Short Strand towards the Ravenhill Road, we were closely watched by the police, if there was anywhere trouble might flare up tonight it would be here. We passed without incident and continued on our way.

The first marching test of the night was about to arrive, marching up My Lady's Road. It wasn't a long road, it was just very steep, and by the time we reached the top, I was a little short of breath, having to manage my breath to play properly and make my way up the hill was no small feat.

As we reached the top I turned to Stevie "Thank god that's over"

"Oh aye, all downhill from here" he laughed.

We meandered through some side streets heading for the Cregagh Road and then towards the Castlereagh Road, turning into Clara Street, in front of us I could see that the parade had stopped, and drums being set down, it looked like this was time for a break.

The members of the lodge started handing some drinks out, as we took a well-earned rest from the walk, it didn't last long though and we were soon on our way again, heading along the Beersbridge Road towards Bloomfield Avenue. This was a familiar area for me, as I would have walked home from school that way sometimes and then it dawned on me, we would be walking up Bloomfield Avenue, it was even steeper than My Lady's Road! So much for all downhill from here. I was never as glad to get to the top of that Road, the band captain had called Gladiators Farewell, one of the longest marches we played, one tune took us the whole way up the hill.

The crowds watching hadn't thinned out at all, it seemed like the whole of East Belfast was out watching the parade. We passed through some more side streets and then we were almost on the Belmont Road when the parade stopped again. This break was longer than the first one, Alvin and I had time to go to a nearby shop and get a drink. The band had been playing well and the parade had been great so far.

"Wait 'til we hit the Newton" Alvin said as we were heading back with our drink to the rest of the band.

"Why?"

"You'll see" was all he said.

We were playing Scamp and the Jig as we walked down the Belmont Road, we hadn't finished the tune, when the band captain blew his whistle and brought it to an early end.

"What's that all about?" I asked Stevie "We weren't playing badly"

"The war memorial is just up here on the right, we won't play anything walking past it, the drum major will say 'Eye's right' as we get closer to it, so we all turn towards the memorial, it's a mark of respect"

We walked on the tap for about a minute or so and just like Stevie said the Drum Major gave the command and we all looked towards the memorial. The lead tip tapped his sticks together instead of hitting the drum to keep us in step. I felt a swell of emotion, it just came out of nowhere, as we walked past paying our respect to the fallen. Men I never knew, who had given their lives for my freedom. I don't know why but I took my hat off and placed it on my chest as I walked past in my own silent, reverent appreciation.

As we passed the memorial the Drum Major gave the 'eye's front' command, we faced forward and the lead tip was on the tap once again. I put my hat back on, no one had asked why, instinct and honour need no explanation.

We were in the final stretch now, we just had to walk down the Arches, downhill for a change and then turn on to the Newtownards Road. The crowd on the 'Newton' was spectacular, it was so packed with people that in some places you couldn't see the footpath or the road and the atmosphere was like nothing I had ever encountered before. We walked past the Conn Club playing 'My Old Man' and the crowd erupted in song, it was like magic in the air and the hairs on the back of my neck stood up. As we finished the tune there was almighty roar and the crowd wanted more.

"C'mon let's hear ya" I heard from the footpath, "Give us another"

The band captain duly obliged and called 'The Sash' and as soon as we started playing I don't think there was anyone not singing along, the noise was deafening, the mood was jubilant and I had the widest smile on my face, I looked across to Alvin, he was lost in the moment too, now I knew what he had meant earlier. The walk to Templemore Avenue was filled with celebration and then I saw the crowd there, heaving and bouncing to the music performed for them by the band in front of us, the footpath couldn't hold the crowd and the space for us to march on the road narrowed as we turned onto the Avenue, the place I had first skipped along to the sound of the bands all those years ago skipped along to the sound I was now making for them. Then I saw my family on the side of the road amongst the crowd. My Mum's face was beaming, and my Granny had the biggest smile I had seen for some time. I waved as we walked past them, Brian was there, as well as Dee, Alan, Darren and Colin. To my left I heard another familiar voice calling me, my friend Stirling, his sister Julie and their Mum were standing outside their house waving as well. I might never become famous, but this felt pretty close. This was a night I would never forget.

When we arrived back at the band hall there was quite the crowd there waiting to welcome us home, we marked time outside the hall, and played tune after tune and the family and friends of the band joined in with us. I didn't want this night to end. It was dark though and there were some tired feet on the road. The playing of the National Anthem brought proceedings to an end, but the night was still young and the Raven family would party together for a few hours yet. One of the big three events was now over, next stop Scotland!

CHAPTER 11 – PART 1

The Trip to Scotland

Preparations for the trip to Scotland had been well under way with the leaders of the band. Alvin, me and the other younger members of the band were pretty much oblivious to any of this, we just turned up and went along with everything. We had absolutely no clue what had went into it at all. It's not like we could have anyway, can you imagine us phoning up the ferry company and trying to book places for a flute band?

My Ma had agreed that I could stay with Alvin at his house the night before and then travel up to get the boat with him, his Da and his brothers. I had already packed my essentials for the trip, my flute, drumsticks and drum pad and my favourite band tapes, and of course my uniform. My Ma had bought me one of those suit bags to put my uniform in and had put my name on it! I didn't know how I felt about that that, I mean having clothes with your name on them seemed a bit child-ish, I'd be thirteen next year for crying out loud. I had spoken to some of the guys in the band about it and they said it was a good thing, given that there would be loads of bands travel-ling over for the Scottish parade, knowing what was yours was a good move, so maybe my Ma did have a clue about life and things after all?

After having sorted the essentials, I had the clothes I'd need picked out. Among them was my new prized possession, a Rangers top! I had managed to get my hands on one after a lot of gurning and mentioning that all my friends had one, my Ma finally gave in! One of the guys in the band got it for me and I was all biz about taking it to Scotland with me. Where better to wear a Rangers top than in Scotland?

I had enough socks and pants to last me two weeks never mind three days, which made me wonder, did my Ma think I was going to suddenly start shitting myself? Did she forget that I was a seasoned world traveller? I had been to Canada on my own after all and had no need for this amount of underwear for eight weeks.

At least she hadn't packed any weird coloured socks that would really have finished me off. I had seven pairs of white socks with union jacks on them, there would be no foot-based fashion disasters. Along with my DM shoes, boot polish kit and two pairs of trainers, I had everything I needed for three days in Scotland. We were heading away early on the Friday morning ferry, with the parade taking place on the Saturday and then we would be on the last ferry home on the Sunday night. A short trip but it was sure to be eventful.

We still had band practice the night before we left, then three nights away from home. This would be great craic, and everything was going to be bands, bands, bands. Alvin and I were absolutely buzzing after practice on the Thursday night.

"You're still coming to mine, aren't you?"

"Aye mate, I've my bag an everything with me"

"Drumsticks?"

"Mate come on, of course I have them with me"

"Great I've been working on a new setting for Lass of Bonna-cord"

"I look forward to hearing that"

Our excitement was interrupted by the secretary who had been trying to get us to be quiet for a few minutes, finally there was just enough mumbling to resemble quietness and he spoke.

"Right lads, can I have your attention here?"

"Do we have to?" came a voice from near the front door of the hall.

"Well if you want to go to Scotland, it would be a good idea for you to shut up and listen to the arrangements", that seemed to do the trick. He had our undivided attention from that point on.

"Right if there aren't any more silly questions, here's what's happening tomorrow ok?" There was complete silence. He continued, "I'll take your silence as a yes. We will be meeting here at 7:30am sharp". There were a few groans around the room, oblivious to these the Secretary continued.

"The bus is booked and will take us to the ferry. The lodge we are walking with have arranged a bus to meet us over there and then it will take us on to Motherwell and we will get sorted with digs once we arrive. Now, don't be going crazy on the drink lads, as we have a long day ahead of us on the Saturday. I'll see you all in the morning".

Alvin and I were chatting like crazy all the way to his house, we were going to be doing some different tunes at a club on the Friday and Saturday nights, and we had been working with Bobby, on some new drum settings and different ways of playing things.

When we got to Alvin's house his Mum had supper made and told us not to be up all night talking as seven o'clock would come early in the morning, Alvin's brother Mark, said.

"Ma surely if it came earlier wouldn't that make it six o'clock?"

We thought it was funny, but he got a clip round the ear for it. We went to bed talking about what the trip would be like and about the tunes we hoped the band captain would call.

"Do you think he'll call Queen of Battle?"

"I hope so, sure we played it at that indoor competition"

"Aye right enough, I forgot about that"

"We've been practicing it long enough"

"Well we both have it ticked off, so it won't be any bother to us"

"True enough mate, I think it's a wonder march"

"Aye, I like it too, but for me it's hard to beat Dinah's Delight"

"What is it with you and that march?"

"It's one of those tunes mate, I just love it"

At this point Alvin's Da popped his head in through the door "Right boys time for sleep, you'll have plenty of time on the boat tomorrow to talk about all this stuff ok?"

"Ok Mr Nelson"

"Ok Da"

He turned off the lights and we put our heads down trying to stem our excitement by going to sleep.

Mrs Nelson had been right, seven o'clock did come early. When we eventually got up, Alvin's Dad had said it was like trying to wake the dead! It was now about six thirty and there was an almighty scramble to use the bathroom. After the flurry of activity, we all made sure we had everything we need and we were on the road, heading for the hall. Alvin and I were chittering away about everything and anything, but mostly about what it was going to be like playing in Scotland and if we would hear any new tunes or maybe pick up some new band tapes.

We arrived at the hall a wee bit before seven and there was a good crowd outside already. Opposite the band hall, parked up on the kerb there was a flexi-bus waiting for us. We'd used these a lot travelling up and down the country to competitions and other parades. I took a look at the size of the bus and then the amount of people waiting at the band hall and it suddenly dawned on me that there wasn't going to be enough room for us and all of our gear and just where was it going when we got onto the boat? I didn't much feel like carrying my bag, my uniform bag and my pack lunch bag around with me for the whole boat trip.

It turned out that one of the band members was going across

in a van and that would carry everything that we needed, so that sorted out where the drums and uniforms were going. The drive to the ferry didn't take long at all about forty minutes or so. The bus left us at the ferry terminal and the van with our gear went to join the other cars waiting to board the ferry.

We made our way through to the waiting area, the officers of the band sorted out the ticketing arrangements and soon we were walking up the gangway on to the ferry. Once we were on board the older guys took up residence in the bar, they let us leave our other stuff with them. We sat around a bit with them and there were all sorts of joking going on but the thing that had me in stitches was Rigby and Adrian putting a five pound note on a piece of thread! They were sitting in the foyer area just outside the bar near a set of stairs and went about their mischief! They waited until there wasn't that many people walking about and put the fiver on the floor, then they waited for a victim to take the bait! It wasn't long before they had their first catch of the day.

A wee boy was sitting with his Da and his Da asked him to get the fiver on the floor, the wee boy looked around to make sure no one else was making their way towards it and then just as he was about to pick it up, Rigby pulled the thread so it just escaped his grasp.

Alvin and I were in stitches as the wee boy chased the fiver until it rose up into the air as if by magic and back into Rigby's hand, the wee boy ran back to his Da completely unaware of what had actually happened. His Da knew though and he was laughing trying to explain but the wee lad still didn't get it. Like true professionals they moved to another part of the boat where people were gathered and waited for their next victim, they must have fooled about ten people who all saw the funny side, thank god! Satisfied with their efforts, they retreated to the bar area. Alvin told me that they pull this trick every time the band goes to Scotland and they hadn't lost a fiver yet!

The older members were now firmly established in the bar, sharing stories of previous trips to Scotland. It always amazed me how they remembered so much, given that a lot of the stories started with "Do you remember that time we were drunk" Alvin and I had heard enough though, our curiosity got the better of us and we set about exploring the boat. Having meandered our way through the sea of people and long corridors, we ended up at the back of the boat. Northern Ireland had all but disappeared into the distance. As we stood there watching the water break, it dawned on me that this was the first time I had actually been on a boat, well unless you count the short crossing in my Dads car at Portaferry!

We had ages to wait before we got to Stranraer, the boat didn't feel like it was travelling at a speed that would take four hours to make the crossing. Scotland wasn't that far way after all, on a clear day you can see it from the coast, four hours on a plane and I could have been halfway to Canada! The boat started to sway in a way that our stomachs didn't like very much, so we retreated back to where the rest of the band was, not because we might have a been a little scared of the boats movements, no, we wanted to hear more funny stories and see what everyone else was up to. We arrived back at the bar, the sound of loud laughter led us to our party, and they sounded like they were in great form.

"Alright boys, what did you get up to then? Did you pull any of the girls from the accordion band?"

We said nothing, being slightly embarrassed we just sat down and tried to divert the conversation.

"So, what's been happening down here? Lose that fiver yet Rigby?"

"No, we haven't done that again, but you should have been here ten minutes ago"

We had obviously missed out on something funny, "Why, what happened?"

"Well we were all just sitting here, telling stories as you do, and Frankie decides he's hungry, so he orders a burger from the bar"

"Right" I said, looking a little lost.

"So, he's eating away at it and decides he needs to go to the loo, he leaves the burger down and heads off, rookie mistake, you know you never leave food unattended! So, we got a couple of beer mats and made them the same shape of the burger and put the meat in a hanky, Frankie comes back and we're all just chatting, acting normal, Frankie eats the rest of the burger! It takes him a few seconds to work out what's going on, you should have seen the look on his face, and then starts spitting cardboard from his mouth, we were all killing ourselves"

"And you still won't tell me where the rest of my burger is"

I loved the way we all got on together, always looking for an opportunity to have a laugh or play a joke, it was all good clean fun. About an hour later we heard the announcement that the ferry would be docking in Stranraer very soon.

"Right lads, gather your stuff and make sure we stay together when we get off the boat, don't be going too far ok? There'll be a bus waiting for us, we've a fair journey ahead of us still, so, we will stop somewhere for something to eat if we have time."

"Are we allowed drink on the bus?"

"I have no idea, but I am sure we will find out soon enough"

"Is there a toilet on the bus?"

"I haven't seen the bus, so I don't know if there's a toilet on it, I didn't take my mystic meg pills this morning, so you're just gonna have to wait and find out like the rest of us"

"There better be a toilet, or we will be having to make a piss stop every half an hour"

"Speak for yourself bladder boy"

"Are there windows on the bus?"

"Hopefully, because you'll be going through one of them! Now has anyone any more pressing queries?" This last phrase was said with a don't mess with me tone, we got the picture.

"No no, carry on Sir" said Rigby, everyone threw him a look "What?" he said with a cheeky smile.

It seemed to take the ferry forever to come to a final standstill, we headed down a set of narrow steel stairs towards the foot passenger exit and then on to the terminal. We finally disembarked and followed the band Secretary as he seemed to know where we needed to go.

"Right lads the bus is this way"

"How does he know that? Sure he hasn't even seen the bus" I said to Alvin.

"Don't start him for god's sake, the mood he's in he'll get the bus to drive off without us"

"I'd like to see him try"

"Well I'm not taking any chances"

We were walking around the side of the terminal building in search of the bus following the man with the plan, "Just round here" he said, and we turned a corner to be met by a collection of bins. The secretary was standing scratching his head "I'm near sure they said this was where the buses would be"

"Yeah, looks like it, do we have to make our own from what we find in the bins"

"And now on Blue Peter we are going to show you how to build your own bus, make sure you have plenty of double-sided sticky tape"

We were all killing ourselves laughing, but the secretary he wasn't laughing at all. One of the guys piped up from the back.

"Mr Secretary!"

"Hold on a minute I'm trying to work out where the bus is"

"Did they say anything about our name being on the bus?"

"Yeah there'll be a card in the window, how did you know that?"

"Well there's a bus behind us with Pride of the Raven on a card in the window, I saw it five minutes ago"

"Then why the hell didn't you say something!"

"You seemed to know where you were going, so I just followed you"

We turned around and right enough there was a bus with a card with our name on it and two guys standing at the door.

"Right this way lads, said the Secretary"

"Are you sure this time?"

"Maybe there's another Pride of the Raven"

"Right enough of the shit, we have a long enough journey ahead of us, I'd like us to get there sometime today, let's get a move on"

We dandered over to the bus, to be met by two men, "Pride of the Raven?" said one of the men in a thick Scottish accent.

"We might be, who's asking?"

"Good to see you again Billy, haven't lost your sense of humour then?"

"I wish he would Billy and do us all a favour"

There was laughter all round as people moved up and shook Scottish Billy's hand.

"Good to see you all again, and some new faces as well I see, right c'mon, let's get you on board"

We had to wait on the van arriving so we could get our uniforms and take them on the bus with us. We filed down the bus and began taking up seats and hanging our uniforms off the edge of the overhead storage rails and settled down into our seats for the journey ahead. Then from the back we heard "Here, there is a toilet on this thing after all!

"That will suit you then won't it, because you certainly talk some shite" there was laughter all round, this was going to be one hell of a bus trip.

We had been travelling for about twenty minutes when a magazine landed on Alvin's lap. A dirty mag was being passed about, and now it had ended up with Alvin and me, having never really seen one we took our time with it, just for education purposes of course. We obviously were taking too long with it when one of the guys shouted.

"Here look at these two, they're reading the articles, picking up some tips for the girl's, here are we?

The bus broke out in laughter for what seemed like the thousandth time today. I took an absolute 'reddner' and didn't know what to say. I decided that silence was the best option here, that would save me from any smart-ass comments. Everyone was laughing and rubbing us on the head as if we had somehow come of age. We got rid of the mag quickly passing it on to someone else, but I just couldn't help myself. I couldn't just pass it on and say nothing.

"Here you better take this; you'll probably find some good advice in there"

"Really kid? What makes you think that?"

"Well, there's a whole section in there on what to do if your dick doesn't work properly" there was a short moment of silence and then the laughing and raking started again.

"Ooh the wee lad got you there"

"Good on ya kid"

I was met with an unexpected reply "How do you know my dick doesn't work?"

"Your wife told me" I said, it was out of my mouth before I could even think about what I had actually said, there was another awkward silence and then more laughter.

The band captain ended the conversation and told me to go and listen to my band tapes.

After more than a few unscheduled "piss stops" due to the toilet not working, we eventually arrived in Motherwell. This would be our base for the next few days and we were put up in lodge members' homes. Alvin and I got to stay together for the trip and the couple who put us up were great. They made us something to eat and then we went about polishing our shoes and thinking about getting a rest for the parade the next day. Thinking about a rest was all we got, we'd forgot there was an event organised in a local club and we were the main attraction. We gathered up our flutes and got into a taxi with our hosts and met up with the rest of the guys at the club. We arrived to find a small crowd waiting outside, they weren't waiting on us like, we weren't famous or anything so Alvin and I wouldn't be giving out any autographs just yet. No one batted an eyelid as we walked past everyone and entered the club, it was like a lot of places back home, a bar, dance floor and some flags hanging up, we weren't on just yet so we had time to find seats and get a drink or two in beforehand. Once we got seated, I went to the bar to get a couple of cokes for us and then as I was heading back to our seats someone caught my eye. She was standing at the bar in a red frilly skirt and it was like someone had turned the sound down in the room, I sat down at the table still transfixed and put the two cokes down in the table, my eyes glued to where she was, I didn't even realise Alvin was talking to me, until he punched me on the arm.

"What are you gawking at then mate?" He said as I managed to finally take my eyes away from the beauty that was before me "The wee blonde standing at the bar there, she's a cracker" I said, discreetly trying to point her out.

"Go and speak to her then" he said.

"What?" I nearly choked on my drink "Mate, she'd probably laugh me out of the place, and I'll get raked and look like a complete eejit"

Alvin was having none of it though "Well you're not gonna find that out just sitting here staring at her"

I had to do something about it now, I couldn't just sit here and potentially risk the ridicule of my mate and if the rest of the band heard I'd chickened out, I'd get a serious raking. What had I to lose? I stood up, took a drink of coke like a gunslinger heading for a showdown and strode towards the bar. I looked back and Alvin gave me a thumbs up as if to say "Go on! Give it a go" I turned back and the bar now felt like it was a mile away. When I eventually I arrived, I just froze, I stood there at the bar area, not having a clue what way to look never mind what to say, suddenly this didn't seem like a great idea after all, what if the guys were watching me, why didn't I just keep my stupid mouth shut? My internal agony was silenced by a soft Scottish female voice.

"Alright" said the soft voice and I turned around to answer, she looked even better close up and she had spoken to me! Talk about saved by the blonde. Either she had smelled the lavish amount of Brut I had put on and couldn't resist or she was wondering who the hell is this just standing here behind me and not ordering a drink.

"Alright" I said back, and then nothing, I was really turning on the charm here like, this obviously didn't deter her as she continued the conversation.

"Ah, you're from Belfast?"

"Aye just over with the band for the parade"

"So, you carry a flute around every day then?"

I laughed nervously "Well if I could get away with it"

She just laughed.

"I'm Glenn by the way"

"I'm Alison, nice to meet you Glenn"

"Likewise"

Alison and I talked for what seemed like ages and then in mid flow she stopped me "So are you gonna buy me a drink or what?"

"Oh yeah, yeah, sure, of course" I stuttered, "What are you having?"

"What can you afford?" came the reply, witty and gorgeous, I thought.

"Well given we are probably both underage I reckon the most exotic thing I could buy you is Lilt"

She laughed and put her hand on my shoulder, and I thought, hello, what's going on here? I placed my hand on hers and they moved of my shoulder together, they dropped to our sides and we were holding hands, we just looked at each other, smiled and then continued talking away to each other. I never thought this would be the outcome of my John Wayne stroll, I was feeling good about having had the balls to walk over, when I was rudely interrupted.

"Right Romeo, hurry up, the bands on now" I turned to see that the band captain behind me, I turned back to Alison "Are you staying?"

"I'm not going anywhere" she said, I turned to head over to where the rest of the band was, Alison didn't let go of my hand, I halted in my tracks, she pulled me back towards her, leaned in and kissed me full on the lips. For those few seconds I was oblivious to what was going on around me, I opened my eyes, after instinctively closing them during the kiss, to see the biggest smile on Alison's face, I smiled back.

"I'll be back soon" she followed me and took up my seat at the table I had left so nervously to go and speak to her. I joined the rest of the band in the middle of the room, and for the next half hour the band got the party going even further.

The band played a mixture of marches and traditional tunes. Our audience seemed to enjoy everything we played, clapping after every tune and cheering us on. We played 'The Sash' and the place went nuts. Once we had finished 'The Sash', Alvin and I put our flutes back in their pouches and headed up to where the drummers where. Two drummers took off their drums and straps and gave them to Alvin and I, as we adjusted them to fit, the crowd started to cheer.

"Let's hear ya boys"

"Show them how it's done kids"

Alvin and I had been practicing with Bobby, the lead tip, putting different drum settings to some tunes we played, and we would be taking it in turns to be lead tip. Our band has a very traditional approach to things, and it works, it's our style. Things have been changing for other bands though, they were trying to do new things. They were changing the way traditional tunes sounded, changing arrangements, and changing the way they drummed, using different and longer intro's to tunes and also incorporating some pipe drum techniques. Well we were about to give the people of Motherwell our take on all this. I was lead tip for the first of tune, Bobby gave me a nod and I started to drum. The crowd loved it from start to finish, all those weeks practicing on beer mats and drum pads had paid off, we hit every beat, made no mistakes, it couldn't have gone any better. Time seemed to fly by as we went from tune to tune and before we knew it, we had finished. As we took the drums off at the end of our performance, people were coming up to us and paying us all sorts of compliments like "Well done lads", "Great to see the kids involved", and "You're giving the older guys a run for their money". Alvin and I were buzzing, and the senior members of the band told us we had done the band proud. If there was anyone you wanted compliments from it was them, they were who we looked up to. I was feeling on top of the world.

Alvin and I headed back to our table and there, was another smiling face waiting on us, I had almost forgot about Alison, being caught up in the moment of our performance. She stood up as we arrived at the table, "Well done you two, that was amazing"

"Thanks" said Alvin, "We worked hard to get it right"

"Well you did that alright"

Moving towards me, she wrapped her arms around my waist and brought me close to her, "And you?" she said, putting her head on my shoulder "A man of many talents."

"Well I don't know about the man part" I replied, she laughed close to my ear and kissed me on the cheek, she then looked me straight in the face in a way I have never been looked at before, her blue eyes mesmerised me, I pulled her in close and kissed her. My arms tightened around her waist as she moved hers around the back of my neck and for the second time tonight, I had the feeling of not wanting something to end. Alison and I spent some time outside just to get away from the crowd and be together, when we went back in, the night was drawing to close, it was late, and we had to parade the next day. The family we were staying with told us that a taxi was on its way to take us home, so we went to the front of the club to wait for it. Once we were outside, it was quite the scene, people recalling their night and laughing about something or other, some leaning up against the walls to keep themselves vertical, obviously having had a little too much drink. Alison was still with me, her hand firmly in mine.

"Have you a taxi to get home" I asked,

"I don't need one that's my house just across the street"

"No worries, just wanted to make sure you were getting home ok"

"Aww you're sweet" she cuddled up close to me.

"Will I see you tomorrow at all?" I asked

"Depends where ya are in the parade I guess, although if you're coming back here after I'll definitely see you then"

"Aye I think we will be here after the parade, so I guess I will see you at some point tomorrow, if you want to that is?"

Alison hit me a light tap on the arm "Of course I want to, ya eejit, who else is gonna buy me cans of lilt all night"

"Play your cards right and there might be a round of Iron Bru"

"You really know how to treat a girl" she said laughing.

Five minutes later our taxi arrived, and we said our goodbyes to everyone, I had a special goodbye for Alison. I kissed her goodnight "See you tomorrow" I got into the taxi and waved as she strode across the street and entered her house.

Alvin and I didn't shut up on the way back to the house, our wee performance had gone well, what a great day. The taxi pulled up at the house, we headed in and upstairs to go to bed.

"Goodnight you pair, you've an early start in the morning so we'll wake you up and have breakfast ready for you, is there anything you would like?"

"We're not fussy, we'll eat anything" said Alvin stopping at the top of the stairs.

"Except haggis" I chirped in.

Our host laughed "Ok then no haggis for breakfast"

After a quick wash we both got into our beds.

"They seem dead on don't they" said Alvin.

"Yeah they're really dead on"

I don't think we stayed awake long, we were both knackered from a busy but brilliant, day.

I woke up to the sound of a house hiving with activity, the smell of fried bacon in the air, which meant one thing, a fry for breakfast! Sitting up in the bed I realised that Alvin was already up and out of the room, throwing on a shirt and a pair of jeans, I got myself up and ventured outside the room to see what the score was for breakfast. I made my way downstairs and there was a lot of people in the house already, dressed in shirts and ties for the day ahead.

"Alright sleepy head" came a voice from the kitchen, Alvin was already sitting at the table whacking a fry into him, "I didn't want to disturb you, I know you need your beauty sleep, but you're gonna have to do something about the snoring!"

"I don't snore!"

"How would you know? You're asleep ya eejit"

"I just know, I don't snore"

"Sit down and I'll fix you some breakfast" said our host, "You want everything on your fry?"

"Yes please" I replied.

"Ooh yes please, get you posh lad, next thing you'll be drinking tea with your pinkie pointing to the ceiling" said Alvin mocking my obviously exquisite table manners.

"That's better than what you woke up with pointing to the

ceiling"

"Now now boys, there's a big day ahead of you, here ya go Glenn, get that down ya"

I was presented with a massive plate filled with sausages, fried eggs, bacon, black pudding, soda bread and potato bread, all that was needed now was some brown sauce.

"That will set you up for the day alright"

"It will indeed, thanks."

"Think nothing of it son, now when you get through here, you'll need to get ready as quick as you can, we need to get you over to the Masters house, Ok?"

"No worries"

"Dead on, will do"

Breakfast was just what we needed. We put our empty plates in the sink.

"Don't you be worrying about those, leave them there and get yourselves ready"

"Thanks again that was lovely"

"Don't mention it"

We headed up the stairs to get ready.

"Do you want to get washed first and I'll get my uniform ready?"

"Aye, sounds like a plan"

"I wonder if they have any shoe polish, mine could do with a wee spruce up"

"I'm sure they have. We can ask when we're ready sure"

"Right, see you in a bit"

About fifteen minutes later there was a shout up the stairs.

"Right you two, are ya nearly ready?"

"Coming now, just putting on our shoes"

"We're nearly ready to go here"

We bounded down the stairs like the house was on fire.

"Is there any shoe polish? We need to give the shoes a quick clean"

"There's no time" turning to her husband our host said "Love, where's that magic sponge thing for the shoes"

"I think it's under the sink, why?

"Give it to the two lads here, they need to give their shoes a quick sprucing"

We were handed this sponge shaped a bit like the bottom of an iron, we were looking at it weirdly as if to say, 'what the hell do we do with this?'

Seeing our puzzled look our hosts said "Just give it a rub over your shoes, they will shine up quick as a flash"

We did what we were told and rubbed our shoes with the sponge and right enough, the shoes started to shine up.

"Here, I'm getting one of these when I go home"

"Aye me too, that's brilliant"

It was a funny thing to get excited over, a sponge that magically shines your shoes, but hey, at least we didn't have to get the polish out and spend twenty minutes on our shoes.

"Aye I'll be keeping it in my room, my Ma doesn't need to see it, she'd call it cheating and talk about how they had to do it in the old days"

"Aye my Ma's the same, sure what they don't know won't hurt them"

We laughed and headed out the door with the crowd from inside the house, sticking close to our hosts. There were a few cars parked and some taxis waiting, they directed us where we needed to go, and we were on our way to the master's house. As we drove along, I tried to take in my surroundings. Once thing struck me, and that was how much Motherwell looked like Belfast, there were some roads we went down and I could have sworn I wasn't in Scotland at all, the houses, everything, all looked very similar. Another thing very similar was how easy it was to tell Protestant and Catholic areas apart, flags and colours marked them out as clear as day. I found myself thinking that's why the Scottish and Ulster bands are so close, they come from similar backgrounds and situations. As we arrived at the master's house, we could see that the majority of the band were already there, Alvin and I were the last to arrive. We got out of the car and walked straight into a barrage of stick.

"Well look who finally decided to show up, the day's nearly over lads"

"What's wrong boys couldn't turn up for a parade without getting your breakfast?"

"Well our hosts did make us a cracking fry this morning" I had stupidly replied and instantly regretted it.

"Ooh get these guys, we had corn flakes this morning, Scottish style"

"Scottish style?"

"Yeah, with Bells Whiskey!"

"No you did not" I glanced towards Alvin, raising my eyebrows, but the reply came back fast and sharp.

"Believe it kid, corn flakes and whiskey, breakfast of champions" puffing out his chest alongside this triumphant declaration.

"More like the breakfast of alcoholics"

"When in Rome..."

"What happens in Scotland, stays in Scotland"

The band captain stepped in at this point, he obviously needed things to proceed a little quicker than they were.

"Right if the Delia Smith fan club have quite finished, is there any chance you could get formed up and look like you're here to walk with the band rather than exchanging breakfast recipes?"

His ability to verbally coerce people was amazing, his tone had just enough venom in it to get you to do what he said without feeling like you were ever being got at personally.

We took our places in the ranks, forming up was synchronised, we all knew our positions and naturally gravitated towards them. Alvin and I, as usual, stood in the front row. I wouldn't always be in the front row though. I was starting to grow taller and at some point, I'd look out of place there. The dream was to get the back row, that's where the most respected members stood and the tallest, and if I kept growing the way my Ma said I was, well, that's exactly where I'd end up. We observed our now familiar actions to get ready for the parade, and as soon as we heard the Drum Majors command "By the left quick march" we were off and the next stage of Pride of the Ravens "UK tour" was underway.

As we walked along, I was surprised at how many people were out on the streets already, stopping to watch us and applauding when they realised the band was from Belfast. Back in Belfast when the bands are on the road early, the streets are mostly empty, the crowds only start gathering as it gets closer to the time for the parade to leave. A decent number of spectators walked alongside us to the main parade gathering point. It wasn't that far of a walk, in fact it only took us six tunes to get there, and when we did, the notion of being on tour started to wear off. Looking at where we were to start walking from there was one of the longest looking hill roads I had ever seen, it wasn't so much that it was steep, it just seemed to rise up for ages, if there's anything that will sap the energy from your legs its hills. And I wasn't wrong, once we were on the move again, it took us fifteen minutes to get up that incline, the band captain even called Left Incline, as some sort of sick joke, we all groaned when we heard him say it, was still funny though. If we had been following the band trends of the time, we would have been up that hill in no time, as most of the Scottish bands seem to walk at a pace that would put the Ghurkha's to shame! But not us, we didn't plod along by any means, we walked at what I would call a sensible pace, but that really added to the pain of this hill and by the time we reached the top we didn't have our shoulders pinned back in pride, we were crunching forward and taking deep breaths when we could. Playing, walking and breathing, are all very simple things, when you're not on a massive hill. We reached the top of the hill and the band captain didn't call a tune straight away, giving us a chance to get our breath back.

The crowds that lined the street were amazing, there didn't seem to be anywhere on the parade route that there wasn't a good crowd, and there were outbreaks of applause and cheers as we marched past, when they saw that we were from Belfast, they cheered even more when we played some Scottish jigs, "Road to the Isles, Hundred Pipers, Scamp and the Jig" all went down well, people were dancing and humming or singing along.

In the distance I could see the crowd starting to swell, which could only mean that we were about to arrive at 'the field' the final point of the parade. There would be lots of bandsmen and women watching, looking out for particular bands, hoping to check out some new tunes. A lot of bands would play their best tunes at these points, you want to enter the field playing strongly and leave a good impression. As we approached, I wondered what tunes the band captain would call, just then he called the Sash. There was a rise in the noise level around us as people joined in and sang along, a good move, picking a crowd favourite, by the time we finished we were about to cross the threshold into the field and entertain the large crowd gathered at its entrance, the band captain called 'Queen of Battle'. This was a tune we had learned for this season, a tricky march to play, with some intricate high register runs and the counter parts in the trio, were fantastic. Needless to say it had the desired effect, bandsmen and lodge members alike applauded as we walked past, I overheard some comments like, 'They're a class act' and 'Listen to that, pure class' there were nodding heads as we played, approving of what they heard, they knew what it took to sound good, the hours of practice week after week. 'Follow, follow' was next, another crowd favourite, we finished the tune and came to a stop and fell out.

We were surrounded by other band members, lodge members, banners laid on top of drums, people catching up, sharing stories and more than a few laughs with each other. That was something I had noticed from my first parade, the laughter, there was always lots and lots of laughter. I remembered that the minister of the church I'd went to Sunday school at saying that laughter was good for the soul, or words to that effect. If that was true, then there was plenty of goodness around a parade! As we were dismissed, the band members were hanging around, finding out what the plans were for the break before the return parade, where would they go? Who was staying at the field? Alvin and I were putting our flutes back into our leather pouches and talking about finding somewhere to get something to eat and checking out the stalls to see if there were any tapes we could buy, when out of the corner of my eye I spied a familiar pretty blonde, in a white and tartan uniform making her way towards us, Alison!

"I'll be back in a minute mate just going to say hello here" I said to Alvin as I started to walk towards Alison.

"Don't be all day now"

"I won't" I picked up the pace I was happy to see her, there was a smile on her face, so she obviously hadn't changed her mind since the club.

We embraced as met each other's outstretched arms "I was hoping I'd see you" she said in that mild Scottish accent, as she pressed in and kissed me.

"Me too" I said as we leaned back to take each other in, "You look great, love the uniform" She blushed at the compliment "Ack thanks, you're looking alright yourself" she kissed me again and then our hands seemed to naturally find each other and we started to walk over to where Alvin was waiting.

"I can't stay long" she said "Our lodge has put on a wee spread for us you ken, but I wanted to see you before we left"

She must have seen the disappointment on my face, she stopped and put her hands on my face "We'll have plenty of time together after the parade alright? We'll all be at the club again later sure"

That put the smile back on my face and continued hand in hand over to where Alvin was.

"You remember Alison from the other night"

"Aye, how's it going, good day so far?"

"Ack aye, been a great wee day so far, how'd you go your-selves?"

"Yeah it's been good, thon hill at the start though was a killer"

We all laughed "It will be easier on the way back" Alison said. "Right I may get on here or I'll miss the bus"

She gave me a peck on the cheek and headed off, she looked back and smiled, "Maybe I'll see you again before the parade heads off again" she waved and then she was gone.

"I thought she might have stuck around" said Alvin.

"Nah the lodge have put on a spread for them, I'll see her at the club tonight sure, right, let's find something to eat"

Just as we were about to head off, a familiar voice guldered at us, "Here, you two! Remember where the bands gear is and be back here for four ok?"

I had a quick glance at my watch it was just about to turn one o'clock, we had three hours to kill before having to get back.

"No problem Da" Alvin said looking back to where the loud voice had come from, "See you at four"

"Are you both ok for money?" We both acknowledged that we were, "Right, I'll see you later, behave, the pair of ye"

We walked off in the direction that we could smell food coming from, "Why do parents always say that, behave yourself? What do they think we're gonna get up to?"

"I've no idea, probably want us to make sure we don't embarrass them in anyway"

"Aye like they never embarrass us, do you remember the way my Ma got on, at the first? Rubbing my face with a hankie as we waited to move off, I was scundered!"

"Aye, you took some ribbing for that"

"I know, I'm surprised it hasn't come up here"

"Well that can be arranged"

"Umm no! C'mon I'm starving"

We moved on and started to check out the food vans and when we had found one where the line wasn't that long, we joined the queue and took in the sights around us.

"What are you gonna get?"

"Probably just a chip and a drink"

"Aye me too, save some money just in case we see something else"

We got to the top of the queue and the lady serving spoke to us in the thickest Scottish accent I'd ever heard, well I think she spoke to us, Alvin and I just looked each other "What did she say?"

"I've no idea"

We both started to laugh, when the same noise came at us again, and this time mixed with frustration was even harder to understand.

"Maybe she's asking you out mate"

"Maybe she's asking us both out"

She stood there looking at us like we'd two heads, hands on her hips and definitely not impressed.

A voice from behind us said "Maybe she's asking you both what you want and if you could hurry up as there's a queue of people waiting"

Thankful for the interpretation, the reprimand from the person in the queue led us to order two portions of chips and two tins of coke. When she spoke to us again, we assumed she was telling us the price, we just handed her two fivers and hoped we got some change back.

Walking away, chips in hand and coke can in the pocket, we both started laughing again.

"I really had no clue what she was saying"

"She might as well have been speaking French"

"Right let's find somewhere that doing tapes"

"Sounds like a plan, there's a few stalls over there to check out"

The salt and vinegar tasted so good on our chips, just the right amounts too, sometimes you get an excessive amount put on them and it spoils the whole thing, that wasn't a problem here. We found a bin for the paper and polystyrene wrapper that had so aptly clothed and held our food, and now we were a few feet away from the stalls in the field.

There was all sorts of stalls, some that did bags of sweets, rocks and drinks and things, others that did some souvenirs and had flags for sale, one stall had the biggest selection of pin badges I had ever seen, they had everything from army badges to different flags and ones of King Billy, this one stall had lots of football scarfs and plaques and signed pictures, we thought they might have been fake though as we had seen the same picture in the same frame with a signature on another stall as well. But then we found a stall that was doing flags and scarves but also had a good selection of tapes and we were in band tape heaven. There were all sorts of bands tapes available, ac-

300

cordion bands, even some pipe bands! It was the flute bands we were really interested in, but there was a tape there of the US army called 'Sousa's Greatest Marches', I picked it up to have a look.

"Here, Alvin, look at the marches on this one, The Thunderer, Liberty Bell, Semper Fidelis"

"I'll bet Semper Fidelis sounds nothing like the way the Skull play it"

"Well it's probably played right on this, especially if this Sousa guy actually composed it"

"I love the Skull, but some of the ways they've changed the marches, well it doesn't seem right to me, they should be as close to the music as possible"

"It's their style though isn't it."

"Yeah that's true, they do what they do well, I just like the way we play though"

"Are you gonna get that?"

"You know what, I think I will" I turned towards where the guy working the stall was standing "Here mate, how much is this one?" I just kind of blurted it out completely oblivious to the fact that the guy was haggling with someone else over a Netherton Road flute band tape. We had met some of the guys from that band at the club last night, sound guys. They seemed like a good band, played a little on the fast side for my liking, but hey each to their own.

After another fifteen minutes of browsing and giving and seeking opinions on some of the tapes and getting the guy to play some of them for us, we walked away with five tapes between us. As we were admiring our purchases and thinking about the new tunes or arrangements we might hear, lost in a wee world of our own.

Alvin broke concentration first "Here what time is it?"

"It's a quarter to four"

"We may get back to where the drums are"

"Aye, there's bound to be some sticks, we can rattle a few tunes out while we wait on everyone coming back"

We were never as happy as we were when we were playing on flutes and drums, we passed the time we had left knocking out tunes we loved and tunes we had heard from other bands, trying out new drumming styles and coming up with something different, we had a wee crowd around us at the field, listening to us playing their hearts out, almost oblivious to the fact that we were being watched. The rest of the band started to reappear, and we knew it was nearly time for the return leg home. We wrapped up our little showpiece and gathered ourselves, fixing our jackets and ties and hats to make sure they looked as good as they did at the start of the day.

There was the usual hustle and bustle of bands gathering and forming up and getting back into their parade slot, along with their lodges, it was no mean feat to coordinate this amount of people in one place and get things back up and running again. The return leg was even more jubilant than the morning, maybe fuelled by the renewal of friendships or maybe a couple of drinks, there was a real party atmosphere. The singing seemed louder, the cheers when we walked by even more enthusiastic and appreciative, it's hard to explain what I was feeling, a mixture of pride and feeling lucky to be a part of all this, I felt a shiver down my spine more than once on that return leg, I looked across to Alvin a number of times and could tell he was feeling the same way, big cheesy grins on our faces. The band must have been feeling it too, out of nowhere we started to sing "We are some of the boys" a song that had been sung on the buses going to competitions throughout the year, we sang it together, loud and proud, and when we got to the line "let the Pride of the Raven by" there was almost a tear in my eye, the emotion seemed to well up as suddenly as the song had broken out. I stopped dead in my tracks, taken by the moment, lost for a second in what I was experiencing. I was rudely awakened from it as the person marching in the rank behind me ploughed straight into me.

"Come on Glenn, what are you doing, get back into your rank" I heard from the voice behind me.

Saying nothing I skipped forward back to my place and in step, without even a thought, a far cry from Easter Monday, when my marching had been all over the place, now after a few months, I felt like I was made to parade.

We finished the parade at almost the same point we started and then it was time to head back to club we had played in the night before, the lodge had laid on food for us, and it was very welcome indeed, a long walk definitely got the appetite going and your thirst!

We would be spending the rest of the night here, as we were due to perform again, and then tomorrow it would be over, we would head for the ferry and home. The night was every bit as good as the day, the laughter, the jokes, the stories both old and new, the camaraderie with our Scottish brothers. The only sad note to all of this was going to be saying goodbye, to our hosts and for me, saying goodbye to Alison. I knew it wasn't a full-on boyfriend girlfriend thing, but still it had been nice. We enjoyed the time we had together that night, all sat around the tables with the band and the lodge, the kiss good-bye would linger long on my mind and lips with the promise of reuniting next year.

The ferry journey home was less exciting than the one that took us to Scotland. Tiredness, sore heads and a desire to be back among the familiar surroundings of own homes and families, saw to that. As I stood and watched Larne appear in the distance, the thought that the marching season was nowhere near over, and that there were two big events just a few days or so away, filled my mind. Who would have thought that joining a band would have led to all this?

CHAPTER 11 – PART 2

The Eleventh Night

Having returned on a bit of high from the bands trip to Scotland, the next big event was only a few days away, the eleventh, bonfire night. Madrid Street, Tower Street and Westbourne Street had all joined together this year to collect wood, for the 'boney'. We had been collecting for months and now we were so close to seeing the fruit of our labour. There were a group of us staying out every night now, making sure that our wood was safe, the Pitt Park boney had tried to raid us while I was in Scotland. Dee and Alan said they ran away like two men and a wee lad when they saw that some of the Da's in the area were guarding the house we kept our wood in. They reckoned that they wouldn't be back after that, they wouldn't take the risk now after that night.

The amount of time we spent searching for wood lessened as a result and only a small amount went out every day, just on the off chance that they might find a few items to add to collection. The best they had done while I was away was about 10 doors and a neighbour was getting rid of an old wardrobe and a chest of drawers. Alan and Dee had apparently gave it a good hoke just in case anything of value had been left behind, we had been given one a few weeks back and there were some photo's left in a drawer, the owner was glad we brought them back as they meant a lot to them.

We had started to think about where the bonfire was going to be located this year and how we were going to build it, we would have to talk to some of the neighbours once we had sorted this out, wherever we built it would mean an obstruction on the road for a day or two. We decided that we were going to place it where Tower Street and Madrid Street met, partly because that would mean we wouldn't have to transport the wood that far. The previous year they had decided to have it closer to Templemore Avenue and it took ages to get all the wood there, I had missed all that with my trip to Canada, I wouldn't be missing it this year though.

The night of the tenth was a big night for us, almost everyone who had been collecting would be staying out all night. We all had different roles, assigned by the older lads like Colin, Darren and Keith. Some of us were responsible for making sure there were drinks for everyone, others were responsible for getting some sandwiches and crisps, so we had something to eat through the night. We would take it in turns in different areas near the stash of wood to keep an eye out for any last minute raiders. We had worked out a system of noises to alert each other that someone was coming, we had it worked out in such a way that if another area did risk raiding us that we would give them impression that there was no-one guarding the wood and then when they tried to make their move we would appear as if out of nowhere and challenge them. We would rather have a quiet night though, share some stories, and hope for a game of spin the bottle going with some of the girls if they were up for it.

My Ma was always a little cautious about me being out late, I had experienced this a few times out with the band already when we travelled a good distance away for a parade, but she seemed to be even more uptight about me staying out all night with the bonfire.

"Don't you be getting into any trouble, the first sign of anything, come straight home" she had said to me. Like that was going to happen, we were all in this together, nobody would cry off and leave the group just because they were a little scared and definitely not because their Ma had asked them to! The amount of raking you would take if that had got out as your reason for not guarding the wood, would be ridiculous. Best not to risk it and just suck it up and look like you're ready to roll.

The older lads would be in the hut, for most of the night, just because they were the oldest and that placed them the closest to the wood, so if anyone did get past the rest of us then we would have the best people right where we needed them the most. They also would take the opportunity to use the hut to spend time with their girlfriends, if they had one. When you were seeing someone you would use the entries to hide away to kiss and stuff, but people were always walking down the entries, using them as shortcuts home or stopping off for a piss if they needed it, hardly the most romantic of places to take someone. Then again neither was a hut made out of old doors and sofa's people had wanted to get rid of, but it was better than nothing and a lot more private as well.

Dee, Alan and I were going to be heading to the roof of the Rupert Stanley building that was close to the youth club, that would give us a good view of the streets leading to the entries where our wood was stored. We would be able to keep an eye on the lower end of Tower Street, as well as see a good bit of Westbourne Street and the entries that joined to Tower Street. We wouldn't spend all night there, but we would be there for a good hour or two, trying to stay out of sight and alert at the same time. We would have to climb over the gates at the cut off part of Westbourne Street, and hope that we weren't seen, we could have went around to the public toilets in Templemore Avenue and got in that way, but the railings there were pretty high and there was a lot more barbed wire around them, so we would take the safest option available to us. We knew all the ways to get in there. There would be times when there was trouble in the area and the police were looking to grab anyone involved, this was where we would go to hide, there were lots of places to get well out of the way up on the roof and once you had disappeared into the grounds of the Rupert, the police generally wouldn't follow. They were sneaky and waited and waited to make you think they had gone away and had a few vantage points to catch you out when you thought the coast was clear to return. I hadn't been involved in too much of that, I was either at practice, out with the band or at the football, but you still had to know the places to go, just in case, you never know when the police will go rogue and decide they are scooping you for next to nothing. The embarrassment of being taken back to the house by the police was a shame none of us liked to wear. Not only would your Ma be affronted, but you were pretty much going to be on the end of hiding from your Da for getting involved, even if you hadn't been, "the peelers don't lift you for nothing" my Ma would say, but we knew that wasn't true, sometimes they didn't need an excuse to harass you. I remember a good few months back, a few of us were hanging around my door and the cops came flying up the street in a meat wagon, they jumped out of the back and headed towards us with their sub machine guns at the ready. We had seen this plenty of times, so we didn't bat an eyelid, when they told us to go home, I didn't move. One of the peelers must have thought I was trying to act the big lad with him because of this.

"I told you to get up and go home son" he said to me with the machine gun pointed right at me.

"I am home" I said.

"Don't you get smart with me kid, now get up and move"

"No, I don't need to"

He grabbed me by the arm and brought me to my feet, "Right, I'm taking you home to your Ma, what's your address?"

"My address is right here"

"You live on the footpath, aren't you the comedian"

From behind us my Ma's voice joined the conversation.

"Is there a problem here?"

"It's all under control, this wee upstart will be on his way soon enough, taking him to his house now"

"Oh, are you now? You may open the gate and bring him in"

The realisation that he had got this all wrong was written all over his face.

"I told you I lived here"

"Have you been harassing my son?

He really hadn't bargained for this and immediately changed his whole approach towards me.

"Stay out of trouble and do what your Mum says" he said as he walked off towards the police land rover.

"Why don't you go and find real troublemakers to deal with

instead of hassling innocent kids?" my Ma shouted after him, she wasn't for letting him off with this, but he ignored her and a minute later the Police were leaving the street.

I still got a clip around the ear when I got in through the door, "What were you thinking? Back cheeking a peeler in the street, you should know better"

I didn't protest, it wasn't worth it, and I like my ears not to be ringing in pain from back cheeking my Ma never mind a peeler.

We made our way into the Rupert Stanley through a newly discovered gap in the railings, someone had spent a bit of time making this possible, we were glad that we didn't have to climb over the gates as they always made a lot of noise no matter how quiet you tried to be, and we obviously didn't want any residents telling us to clear off or worse still calling the police. We headed to the power generator that was right behind the barrier to the youth club, we would use this and the wall opposite to make our way up on to the roof, and in couple of minutes the three of us had scaled the wall and were now on the roof. The roof had a number of raised rows on top that ran the length of the building these would be our hiding points should we need them, we went to the one that was closest to the lower part of Tower Street and got ourselves in a position where we could see the most of the area.

"What time is it Glenn?"

"What's wrong Dee is your Ma gonna call you in soon?"

"Aye right, just tell me the time for flip sake"

I glanced down at my watch, it was hard to see exactly, so I had to use the watch light.

"Ooh get you with the fancy watch with a light"

"Hardly fancy, it's quarter past ten"

"It will be getting a lot darker soon, so we may stay out of sight for now, one of us will check every ten minutes or so until then, ok?

"Ok"

"Spot on"

We were sitting with our back against the columns that separated the roof area with our knees up round our chests, there wasn't a lot of room to stretch out, so we made the best of it.

"Well Glenn, tell us about Scotland, what was it like?"

"It was a lot like here, so it was, just different accents"

"You're joking! People in Scotland speak with different accents, I didn't know that" said Dee sarcastically.

"You know what I mean though, a lot of the places we went to looked like here, the flags were out, the kerb stones were painted and there were areas you couldn't walk through"

"What about the parade though?"

"Oh, it was great, there was a crazy hill we had to walk up right at the start, but the crowds were great"

"Not better than here though?"

"It's close, they were out on the street from early on, it was a great experience though"

"Any girls take your interest?"

"I'm saying nothing"

They both started to rake me at this, pushing at me and nudging me on the shoulder "Come on you, spill the beans" and they kept on with their constant prodding.

"Alright, Alright, knock all that on the head and I'll tell you, but keep your voices down for flip sake, we don't want anyone clocking us up here"

They calmed down and lowered their voices. "Right come on, out with it" whispered Alan.

I told them about how I had met Alison at the bar and how we just seemed to click, all they were interested in was finding out if I kissed her or did anything else, the only details they got where that we had kissed and that we might try and meet up again next year if the band went back over.

We were laughing quietly when we became aware of voices that didn't seem that far away.

"Shush, come on let's check this out"

We popped our heads up to see who this could be, "Can you see anyone?" asked Alan as he crawled along to find a better view.

"I think they're coming from Susan Street direction"

"They aren't collecting this year, so why would they be out and about now? I said as I stretched my neck to see if I could get a glimpse of anything that might give us a clue to who the voices belonged to.

Alan came scurrying back on all fours "It's Pitt Park, they're gonna try and raid us again"

We needed to act quickly. "Right Dee, you're the fastest runner, head back to the wood, take the entry up behind my house and warn the rest of them"

Dee nodded and quick as a flash he was gone, he had dropped down the wall and was running with the news that Pitt Park had come to try and raid us. Alan and I would have to stay out of sight but track their movement, we would have to get down as well, only this time we wouldn't be heading for Westbourne Street we would be heading for the big blue gate in Tower Street, and we would follow from behind. Once the crew from Pitt Park had passed our hiding spot, we made our move as quickly and as quietly as we could, we dropped down of the roof and then took cover at the 'port-a-cabin' and then over the gate, we were over it in seconds, it made a bit of noise as we dropped to the street, we hid behind a parked car and then made our way towards the path that would lead us past the youth club and into my end of the street. We had no idea if Dee had made it back or not, and we were hiding behind a wall and peeking out to make sure we could advance further up the path. They had left someone at the top of the path we could see them when we peered around the walls edge.

"Shit we should have went by Westbourne, we're never getting up there with one of them standing there" I said.

Alan seemed pretty calm "We should just walk up anyway and act like we are heading somewhere else, then we can try and get to the entry near your house from there"

He had just come up with a good idea, a risky idea, but it was worth a shot.

"Ok, so we just head up the path here, don't even look at him or respond if he says anything"

We both nodded to each other, and headed out into the path, we were talking about nothing, and trying hard not to draw attention to ourselves, but the cat would be out of the bag as soon as this person saw us.

Just as we were about to turn the corner, this Pitt Park stranger turned and saw us, he instinctively moved away from us a little bit, we just kept our focus, and headed down Beechfield Street, we crossed to the opposite side of the street and didn't look behind us until we turned onto Westbourne Street and then we sprinted for the entry. We had pulled it off, or so we thought, when we got to the entry we could see through to my street and there were the potential raiders heading for the entry that would take them to our wood. We flew up the connecting entry, hoping that we hadn't been seen, we went left at the top, back out onto Westbourne and then into Madrid Street and hid at the corner of my street. We couldn't see anyone in my street, so we headed to the entry again, Alan jumped over the wall of Dee's Granny's house which was right at the entry, I stood up against Big Aggie's gable wall and we both peered down the entry, it was dark and quiet, too quiet. Alan and I just looked at each other, there was nothing else we could do, we would have to wait until there was some movement, and then all of a sudden there was roar from the entry. The Pitt Park crew had made their move, then we heard a familiar voice shouting in the entry, it was Darren.

"And just what the hell do you think you lot are doing!"

"Shit, they're here guarding the wood, run for it" said one of the shadowy raiders,

Alan and I emerged from our hiding place and started walking down towards the action.

"They're coming from everywhere, back the way we came, RUN!"

They started to sprint down the entry as the rest of our crew came out of the yard and over the wall, I headed back for my street as they would be spilling out at the bottom of the street. The sound of running feet filled the otherwise peaceful night and I was near the entry when the raiders came piling out, one of them nearly fell as they slipped and lost their footing. The wee lad that we had seen earlier ran out and spotted me making my way towards him "I knew he was one of them" he shouted as he sped away "I knew we should have followed them two".

The rest of our crew came running out of the entry and we all ran towards the youth club pathway, we came to a halt about halfway down, and retreated, we weren't about to get ambushed by blindly following the raiders. We grouped together at the lamp post nearby, all catching our breath.

"That was close" said Alan.

"We fairly scared them away"

"Well done wee Dee" everyone crowded round him, patting him on the back.

"Right" Colin said, "Lets head back, they may chance their arm again later, but hopefully that has scared them off.

"We will keep someone at the end of the entries throughout the night just in case" added Darren as we all walked up the street together. The noise had brought a few neighbours out and of course my Ma as well.

"What was that all about?" she quizzed as we passed by my house.

"Pitt Park came to try and raid us, we scared them off"

"Well scare them off quieter next time, I thought there was a riot starting"

We all laughed, "Scare them off quieter, what's she like" I muttered to Dee, there was no way I was letting her hear me say that, I wanted to be out all night.

The rest of the night passed without incident, Pitt Park didn't make another attempt and at about eight in the morning we headed home to get breakfast and change our clothes. Then we would have the task of starting to move the wood and get ready to build our bonfire.

We started by getting the wood that we had stored inside the empty house into the yard, so that it could be taken over the wall and to where we would set the bonfire up. This was going to be a tricky process as some 'smart alec' had decided to lift the floor boards in the room with access to the largest window that still opened, this was the only way some pieces were going to be able to leave the house, others would have to be carried down the stairs. All that was left in this room were the rafters and we would have to be very careful navigating our way across them, with the first things I helped lift out of this room this wasn't an issue. When we started to move items from other rooms through here to the window it became a bit of a problem. And I was the first to fall victim to it. Alan and I were lifting a couple of large planks from the front room, I was walking backwards into the room, I completely forgot about having to navigate my way over the rafters, and slipped through the gaps in the floor, with my balls taking the full impact. I was in absolute agony; thankful I hadn't actually fallen completely through the floor. Initially there was a gasp from everyone as I went down through the gap in the floor, then there was laughter as they realised where I was hurt. Darren was the only one to come and help me and ask me if I was ok. I braced myself for the raking that would inevitably follow today, I would just have to suck it up. To try and limit that I ended up going down into the yard and helping lift the wood out into the entry, although on my way out, I had to endure the start of it.

"Watch out for the gaps in the stairs Glenn"

"Are you sure you can make your way down? Do you need us to remove some more floorboards?"

I said nothing, responding would only make this last longer. I was sure someone else would make the same mistake and the focus would be off me.

Once we got into the swing of things and people stopped falling through the gaps in the floor, the entry was soon filled with doors, sleepers, pallets and all sorts of things made out of wood. There was a collection of bannister rails, all in different paint colours reflecting the houses they had come from, wardrobes and other items that at one point had adorned someone's bedroom and housed valuable items of clothing or jewellery. Now they were being lined up to be burned as part of this annual act of commemoration.

It was a team effort to get the wood out of the house and to the location for the bonfire, everyone had to play their part and if you were slacking the older members of the group would let you know and encourage you to get back to work. Dee and I had been talking, while lifting a load of pallets, about how some day we would be in charge and the younger lads would be doing what we told them. That's the way this works, new people take the lead and the tradition lives on.

Time was just flying by, we had been so busy that when my Ma called me in for dinner it was a surprise, I had lost all track of time. Dinner was gulped down so that I could get back out to the wood and get it ready for later on tonight. My Ma told me to slow down and eat properly, the wood wasn't going anywhere and would be there when I finished. When I arrived back out, the older lads had the base of the for the fire built, they had used two large wardrobes to form the centre piece of the boney with our largest sleeper in between, they then placed doors around the wardrobes, this would allow us to put pallets, planks and sleepers up against them and keep the shape we needed. It was starting to look like a wooden tepee and careful consideration was given to where wood was placed to make sure that it was well balanced, and it wouldn't collapse under its own weight. When it was finished there was still a lot of wood and other items left over, this would allow to keep the fire going for as long as possible. The top end of my street and the middle of Madrid street were now blocked off because of the newly built bonfire, you could drive round it if you went up on the footpath, once it was lit though anyone driving up these streets would have to find an alternative route.

Families and friends were starting to gather around the boney area now in anticipation of the big event, friends from other areas nearby arrived as well, especially if their area hadn't collected for a boney this year, everyone wanted to part of one and some of them would visit a number of boney's all across East Belfast. Some of the younger kids were getting restless, the boney wouldn't be lit until somewhere between half eleven and midnight, so some of the older lads built a smaller boney beside the larger one just for the kids and it wouldn't be long before this was lit.

We had been in charge of everything to do with the boney up until this point, we would be stepping aside, and an adult would take charge of the lighting the fire, this year it was Alan's Da who would have that responsibility. At about half seven, Alan's Da poured some petrol on the smaller boney and asked every to step back, he had what looked like a brush shaft with a towel wrapped around it, he set it on the ground and doused it with a little petrol and then lit it, the towel became a flame and Alan's Da then lifted the brush shaft and threw it at the base of the smaller boney. The flames appeared quickly as the petrol ignited and there was a cheer from the gathered crowd, the evening's festivities were well underway now. Colin's Ma had opened her front windows and there was music blaring out, providing even more of a party atmosphere for everyone. Some neighbours had brought seats and small table out with some food and drink on them for the kids and themselves of course, everyone pitched in with something.

My younger brothers were trying to convince me to go into the house and bring my flute out and play a few tunes for everyone gathered, I tried to give them the brush off, but they wouldn't let it go and then Dee and Alan joined in and I eventually gave in and went home to grab my flute.

When I arrived back at the small boney, I was getting requests left right and centre, so I just played a few of the crowd favourites like the Sash and the Lily, Shanghai, and No Surrender. Everyone was singing along, and the younger kids were dancing about as if the bands were on the road, some of them even had wee plastic flags out with them and were waving them about. A neighbour then arrived with a big bag full of chips from the chippy for everyone and now the food was the main attraction. It must have cost a small fortune for all those chips, and no-one had asked them to do it, it was small things like this that made you proud of where you lived.

The small boney was starting to die out and that was the parents cue to get the younger kids off to bed, some of them weren't too pleased about it, there was some crying as they were led away to their houses, other were already starting to fall asleep in the arms of their parents, it had been a long day for them and they would have another long day tomorrow.

This was something I'd have to think about as well, how late I would stay out, I have to be at the Maple Leaf club early in the morning to meet the band. I didn't want to miss out on anything tonight, but I didn't want to be wrecked for the twelfth either. As it came closer and closer to the time to light the main boney, Alan had was getting very excited, he was pestering his Da.

"C'mon Da, light it now, I can't wait anymore"

"You'll just have to wait a little longer, It's not time yet"

"We've loads of wood; c'mon it will burn right through to the morning anyway"

"I've said no, now leave it at that, it will be lit soon enough"

Alan dropped his head and started to rearrange some of the spare wood to take his mind of it, he had been out collecting every day and was just a little impatient waiting to see it all come together now. I knew how he felt, we had been in this together, we all had played our part and we were proud of the boney that now stood before us.

As it got closer to the time of setting the boney on fire our wee crew gathered together around it, taking one last look at it before it went up in flames.

"It's way bigger than last years" said Darren.

"It wouldn't be hard, last year's wasn't great" replied Dee.

Alan got a little defensive, "It was the best we could do, if we hadn't raided Pitt Park it would have been worse"

"We have done well this year, and who knows, maybe next year we can do even better again"

Alan's Da appeared again, it was time to set our boney on fire, "Right lads, if you could all step back a good bit, we will get the show on the road here". Having a new torch to light the bonfire with and a fresh supply of petrol, Alan's Da set the base of the boney on fire and the flames lit up the street, our shadows cast on the walls, our faces reflecting the yellow and orange glow. We watched as the flames seemed to crawl up towards the top of the boney, slowly engulfing everything we had collected into a fiery mass. The heat coming off the boney was immense and we had to stand back even further, we cheered as the flames caught hold of the large sleeper sticking out of the middle.

Alan was already thinking about what was coming next, "All we have to do now is wait until it falls and we can start putting the extra wood and stuff on it to keep it going throughout the night, I'm staying out as long as I can"

"I'll not be out that late, I've got to be away early in the morning"

"Are you looking forward to walking your first twelfth then?"

"I think I'm more excited about that than the boney"

"Thanks, why don't you just go in now then?"

"No, no that's not what I mean, we've done the bonfire for a few years now, this is the first twelfth I won't be watching from the footpath"

"Right let's put some of the other wood on, keep this thing going"

We all started to put more wood on the fire, trying to spread it out and being careful not to get too close, the last thing we would need is someone having to go to the hospital or something.

The night drifted on and the crowd started to thin, the twelfth was looming, for more than one of us.

"Right lads, that's me away in here, I'd love to stay out longer, but I'll never get to sleep if I do"

"See you tomorrow mate"

"Aye, see you in the Avenue"

I walked the short distance to my house, glancing back at the boney as I opened the gate. In a few hours I would be opening the gate again in my uniform and stepping into my place in history and joining the footsteps of my big Granda who had walked the twelfth for many years before with his lodge. Now the historic day awaited me, and destiny was only hours away.

CHAPTER 12

The Glorious 12th

I awoke with an absolute sense of fear and couldn't find a watch or a clock anywhere to check the time, I had been out later than usual the night before at the bonfire, I didn't get to bed until way after one. I was absolutely "cream crackered". Now I needed to find out what time it was, what if I had slept in and missed the biggest parade of the year, the twelfth! Every time piece was conspiring against me, my usually reliable video player, was blinking at 00:00 which means that the power had went off in the middle of the night or my Ma on her nightly rounds turning every plug in the house off, just because some guy on the tv says that when the broadcasts stop at the end of the night, well now this safety precaution was in danger of ruining my twelfth of July. I went down my two flights of stairs towards my parent's room, I never normally rapped their door, but this was a mission of urgency, so cautiously I tapped on their door and awaited a frosty response, my Ma must have been expecting me,

"You're ok Glenn it's only just gone half six, you don't need to be at the Maple Leaf Club until half seven, you've plenty of time to get ready".

Thank god for that, I really didn't want to be late so with the pressure off a little I walked into the bathroom still in a bit of a daze and got into the shower. As soon as I switched the water on, I wasn't quite so zombie like anymore, "holy shit" I shrieked as the freezing cold water tightened my chest, leaving me gasping for air, I fumbled to try and find the hot tap and sort the water temperature out. I was hopping from foot to foot, as if that was going to change the warmth of the water, I kept doing it though! After what seemed liked forever, I found the tap, regulated the temperature to non-arctic and all was well with the world again. I love getting a shower, it's definitely way better than a bath. Getting a bath reminded me of the old days when we lived in Euston Street and when we first moved to Tower street and having to get washed in a tin bath in the living room. I always remember, taking a 'reddner' in the bath because I always seemed to be put into it just before someone came to visit. Total embarrassment is an understatement, there's me sitting in the living room in a tin bath with my tips and trick there for all to see! I remember my Big Granda saying he didn't like the bath either as he didn't understand how "Sitting in your own dirt could get you clean", there was definitely logic in there somewhere, and I tried using his line a few times, but never to any success. "Your Granda was a grown man" my Ma would tell me, as if this very utterance alone would somehow convey to me the reason why I had to take a bath, what being a grown man has to do with disqualifying you from sitting in a tin bath in your own dirt, I have no idea.

After getting out of the shower and I got myself somewhere in the vicinity of dry. That was another thing I noticed about getting washed, no matter how many times you think you've covered everywhere with the towel, somewhere is always left out. I had no time for a more thorough drying routine, I needed to get my skates on. I made my way downstairs and into the kitchen to make myself a few rounds of toast, I always thought that was a weird phrase for a few pieces of square shaped bread if you ask me.

Mum had got my uniform dry cleaned again, it looked and smelt great. While I was making sure that I had everything I needed for the day, Mum had got everyone in the house up. She was fussing over everything, making sure my two brothers didn't get their new clothes dirty before they even left the house.

"If you even think about getting a mark on those new clothes I'll go through the pair of ye"

She was like a hawk watching, every move and every bite of breakfast, on a mission to make sure everyone looked their best today, she'd show everyone that 'She didn't raise no wee tramps'.

I imagined that this scene was the same for all the houses in our area. Getting a hearty breakfast, drying the dishes with a King William III tea towel before putting their new clothes on. Getting new clothes always seemed to come at the same time as a big parade, not that I worried about that now of course. The other thing that accompanied the parade ritual was taking photos with those dodgy disposable cameras. My two brothers were forced to indulge Mums photography skills for the sake of future family photo albums.

"Right come on you two, get a picture with your big brother before he heads off"

With a sigh of disgust, they said almost in unison "Do we have to Ma?"

My brother Jim took the time to clarify their response "You did that at Easter and the first, it's only the twelfth of July flip sake" He probably wished he had kept his mouth shut.

"Only the twelfth of July! Only the twelfth of July, Tommy do you hear these two? Who on earth reared you? Sometimes I don't know where I got the pair of you from! It's one of the biggest days of the year and the pair of ya are standing there gurning about getting your picture taken? Well, maybe you should just take those new clothes off and wear some of those aul things you gurn about wearing instead?"

I was amazed at how my Ma could throw these long sentences together without even a pause for breath and it wasn't over yet, she continued on.

"Your Da works hard to put clothes on yer back..." At this my brothers rolled their eyes and reluctantly admitted defeat, when the 'Your Da works hard' line gets thrown at you the only wise and sensible thing to do is shut up and get on with whatever it is that you've been asked to do. We headed to the front of the house to get our pictures taken and after Mum was happy with the results, I made my getaway.

"Right, I really need to be off here, I will see you all later on"

"We will be standing at our usual spot near the top of your Granny's Street, if we get there in time with the way these two fart apart", she said pointing at my brothers, "Your Granny will be raging if we don't get the same spot, come on get a move on, and make sure the dog is in the yard"

I knew from pre-band experience that all they were about to do was walk to my Granny's house and wait on her getting ready and then head to the designated gathering place at the top of Tower Street. This was Mum's way of making sure everyone was ready in time and that they stood a good chance of getting to the right spot on the road or else the twelfth "would be ruined" according to my Granny. Not that this really something to worry about as the same families gathered at the same place every year, like they owned that part of the footpath on this particular day and woe betide anyone who would stand in your traditional spot. If someone dared break this most sacred of annual social etiquette, they wouldn't be long knowing about it. But it was also a real community moment, there was a lot of banter and gossiping as they awaited the main event of the day, the bands and lodges passing by. They would be waving to everyone they knew, dancing and singing when they heard a band playing "The Sash" or "No Surrender". This year for our family would carry the extra honour of having someone walking with a band, there were plenty of uncles, cousins, and other acquaintances who walked with the lodges, I was the only family member in a band.

The Maple Leaf Club was a good twenty minute walk away from our house, and as I waved goodbye to my family I went over my Ma's directions to the Maple Leaf club in my head and took my first strides towards walking on the twelfth of July and taking my place in participating in one of our long standing community traditions.

I walked along Beechfield Street towards the Avenue and contemplated going across Martin Street and heading to Belvoir Street before hitting the Newtownards Road and on to Dee Street to get me to the club, but the sound of bands in the near distance put this idea right out of my head. Even at this time there were bands already marching, this could be a good chance to check some of them out, hopefully I'd see some of the bands visiting from Scotland and there was the prospect of seeing a band out parading in a new uniform. The first and the twelfth of July were usually the times that bands would debut a new uniform, we would be doing this very thing next year. I headed down the Avenue toward the traffic lights opposite Island Street, turning right onto the

Newtownards Road and I could see a band in a blue uniform approaching, 'That could be the Pride of Down' I thought to myself. I walked towards the approaching band, there were a few people standing on the side of road watching clapping the band as they passed by. I had seen this type of respect before at competitions as well for bands that had travelled long distances to take part. It was the Pride of Down and I gave my mate Fergie a wave. I picked up the pace, I didn't have time to just dander about listening to bands. I saw another couple of bands on my way to the Maple Leaf, the East Belfast Protestant Boys, and the Albertbridge accordion band. I'm not a fan of accordion bands, but I can appreciate the skill it takes to play those squeeze boxes.

I would see more bands soon enough as we would walk into the Avenue there would be thousands of people gathered and more bands than at any other parade in the country and quite possibly the world. The twelfth isn't unique to Northern Ireland there are plenty of places across the world that join in with the celebrations, mainly due to people having moved to other countries and carrying the tradition with them, even my native Canada hosts a twelfth of July parade in Toronto. My Ma says she doesn't like the parade there because they stop the parade frequently to let the traffic pass through, something that doesn't happen here in Northern Ireland. Once a parade starts here, you can't walk through it at all, you have to wait until there is a break or it completely passes by. I'd love to be able to walk in the Toronto parade, playing my flute back in Canada now what would be something else, whether they stopped the parade to let the traffic through or not.

I made my way up Dee Street, heading for Mersey Street and from there it would be just a short walk to the Maple Leaf club. It wasn't much to look at when I arrived outside it, I had heard my Big Granda and Big Granny talking about nights out here, one of the photos we had of my Granda, that we framed after he passed away, was of him on a night out at the club, he looked happy, his pipe in hand and a smile on his face. I could see it clearly in my mind as I walked in through the gate and headed for the front door, and for a moment, the fact that he wasn't here to see this day hit me. My Ma says you don't know what you've got 'til it's gone, I never understood that before, I did now though.

I walked in and immediately caught a glimpse of the guys at a table, they were in jovial mood, laughter in the air, drinks on the table, even at this hour of the morning. There were the usual greetings as I looked for Alvin. Rigby saw me looking around the room.

"Your wee partner in crime isn't here yet mate"

"Ah right, I'm sure he will be here soon enough"

"He will indeed kid, he won't be missing today, you excited for the big walk?"

"Oh aye, I can't wait"

"Wait 'til your feet are burning off ye, hope those aren't new shoes you're wearing?"

"They are. Will that make a difference?"

Rigby just started to laugh, "Frankie, look at this, new shoes for the twelfth"

Frankie started to laugh "Rookie mistake kid"

"What?" I said with surprise.

"You'll know what we are on about by the end of the day son"

"Now come on, let's enjoy the day, stop freaking the kid out"

I took my band jacket off, putting it over the back of a chair and sat down.

About ten minutes later, Alvin, his Dad and two brothers walked into and made a beeline for our tables.

We were chatting away about all sorts and before we knew it the band captain was telling everyone to drink up and head outside as we needed to get to the Masters house, from there we would head down to the Avenue, where my love affair with the Raven began. There was no one missing today, just like the first of July, every member was out, twenty-four flutes, eight side drummers, two cymbal players, a triangle and two bass drummers and of course the drum major.

As we formed ranks, I took up what had become my usual position, in the front row just to the right of Stevie McAleese, Alvin was just across from me. I had grown into marching with the band, and I wasn't getting called out for being out of step or out of rank. The drum major gave his command, the drums rolled us into the first tune and the day was finally underway. We arrived at the master's house and there was the obligatory breakfast available as well as more drink than an off license. We would be on our way again soon enough, lots of bands were on the move, picking up lodges, and making their way to the assembly point in the Avenue. All the streets would be filled up with bands and members of their lodges decked out in their sashes and collarettes, all ready to make their way into the city centre and join with the rest of the Belfast districts to make our way to the field in Edenderry.

As we walked into the Avenue, I couldn't help but notice the amount of people on the streets, everywhere seemed to be lit-

330

tered with families and friends all vying for position, getting their traditional spots for the parade.

As we made our way down the road, the mass of people got even bigger, there were bands and lodges everywhere, every part of the road and the footpath was teeming with people. It was a sight to behold. The police were on hand, as always, to make sure everything was done decently and in order, our good friend Ian on his motorbike was there too, we wouldn't be playing hide and seek today, that's for sure.

I felt like I had been up for ever already, my feet had already started to get a little sore, and we hadn't walked that far. We came to a halt and fell out in Paxton Street. Alvin and I headed straight for the Avenue, we wanted to watch other bands come in and maybe hear some new tunes of some of our favourites being played by other bands.

"Don't you two be going too far now, we will be getting ready to go again soon" shouted Alvin's dad as we bounced up the street

"We won't, we will come straight back" we shouted.

"Don't have me to come looking for the pair of ye"

With that we just headed straight for the Avenue and the sound of flutes and drums.

We hustled and pushed our way to the front of the road so we could see everything, the UVF band had just fell out and were filtering onto the footpath as another band wearing sky blue uniforms appeared at the top of the Avenue, as they came properly into view, I thought I recognised the band.

"Alvin, I think that's the Pride of the Myle"

"No way"

"Yep, I'm gonna get a bit closer to hear what they're playing"

The Pride of the Myle were a Scottish band, one of the new breed of bands, doing things their own way, creating their own style, changing things up, we had one of their tapes and knew their tunes inside and out.

We walked alongside them watching their drummers and listening to the flutes, they were a great band, in tune and immaculately turned out. They came to a halt about midway down the second avenue. And as the whistle of their band captain rang out, they marked time for a minute and then their lead tip, tapped them out and they came to a halt. There was a fair crowd following them and their lodge, they would be a popular band along the route today. Just as our hero worship was kicking in, we both felt a tap on our shoulders. We turned around and it was Colin, Alvin's brother.

"Right you two, come on, you need to get back and get formed up"

"Already?" We both said in unison.

"Aye, come on, hurry up"

We made our way through the crowd, skipping past banners, men and boys tying their shoelaces and lots of side and bass drums left on the side of the road marking the spot their owners would leave from not too many minutes away from now.

Colin was ahead of us and he met his Dad before we did.

"Well did you find them?"

"Aye they were up near the top of the Avenue, watching bands arrive"

He turned his attention to both of us.

"I thought I told you not to go too far?"

"We didn't really go that far, Mr Nelson" I said.

"Far enough that we had to send someone to find you"

With that there were no more arguments.

"Right come on, we are going to be forming up here, so let's stay close together, ok"

"Ok"

He was only looking out for us, the whole band did, we were always the first names mentioned when they were forming up, gathering together or getting ready for a break.

"Right, I found them" Mr Nelson announced to the rest of the band.

"Great let's get formed up here, and be ready for the off"

Everyone found their place and we stood at ease waiting for the command that would lead us to taking the first steps of the parade proper and out onto the avenue and on our way to the town.

"Band on the rolls…"

That was it, we were off, and the noise was immense, between the bands in front of us and starting up behind us, I could hardly hear myself think, it was off putting and glorious all at the same time, I found myself hearing other tunes and different beats and timing, and I had to concentrate hard to hear what we were playing and not get distracted. We headed onto the Avenue and crossed the Albertbridge Road junction, I had adjusted my ears and all I could hear was the sound of our flutes and drums, everything else became background noise. We passed Templemore Avenue baths and I spotted Alan and Dee, standing on opposite sides of the road with their families. I waved at them as they shouted my name out. This happened regularly as we walked down the Avenue, everyone from my area was out, I'd plenty of people to wave at. Paul and Denise from my street where there, as were the Bennetts, Brian, the piano player from Westbourne Street and his wife waved at me from the front of the other Rupert Stanley College building, and directly opposite them stood Stirling, his sister Julie and their Mum, Agnes.

"Seriously Glenn are you gonna play your flute today?" said Stevie sarcastically to my left, "If you wave any more, you'll give the Queen a run for her money"

"You're funny Stevie"

"I know, play a few more notes though will ye?"

"I'll try but if my public want waves, I shall have to oblige"

We reached the bottom of the Avenue turning left onto the Newtownards Road, the sea of people continued as far as the eye could see, it was like there wasn't a footpath anymore, all that was visible were throngs of people out enjoying the parade, flying flags and the odd person letting a band pole fly up into the air, a risky move given the amount of people about.

I could see Jordan's bakery just in the distance then a little further up the outline of Westbourne Presbyterian Church, that's where my family would be along with my Big Granny, her friend Sadie and her family as well. The Storey's wouldn't be too far away from them, so there would be a lot of familiar faces. We progressed up the road, I could now see my family, right at the front of the road, my youngest brother Ryan stumbled onto the road, only to be quickly dragged back off it by the scruff of the neck, I can imagine what my Granny was saying to him. They would be to my left as I passed them, I heard my Granny's voice rang out loud and clear.

"Here's our Glenn's band now Sadie, where's my camera?"

I knew I would have to break ranks now to be in the photo. I could see my Ma getting her camera out and starting to take pics as we arrived alongside them.

I turned around to the direction of the band captain.

"Just gonna get a pic with my family?" I got a nod of approval and I broke rank to spend a few moments with my family. After some hastily taken pics and few kind words from others around, I needed to get back to the band and get back on my way to the field.

I ran towards the band and caught up with them quickly and took my place again.

"Ack was your Mammy all happy to see her wee son" Stevie was taking the piss again.

"She was indeed, haven't seen you waving at too many people today,"

"Just wait 'til we are in the town mate"

"You gonna pretend you know a few people then?"

With that he just shook his head and got on with playing. I made sure I was in step and joined in the tune as well. That was the beauty of being a full blower, you could join in a tune at any point, you didn't really even need to think about what notes you had to play.

The crowd on the Newtownards Road started thinning out the closer we got to the Short Strand apart from a few windows open and a few heads popping out, it would be one of the few places with no spectators. We passed under the railway bridge at the Scirocco works, then crossed the Queen's bridge and headed down Ann Street, then Victoria Street, turning left at the Albert clock onto High Street before the first break of the day at Bridge Street. Our district, number six were leading the parade this year, so we wouldn't have long to wait here. I was glad of the break though, my feet were getting really sore, I had walked further than this on other parades and never got sore feet. Now my once very comfortable new Dr Martens shoes were not so comfortable anymore, no matter how cushioned and full of air the soles were supposed to be.

I sat down on the kerb and began to undo my shoelaces, when Rigby raced over.

"Don't be doing that kid, you'll make it worse"

"But my feet are really sore"

"I know but if you take your shoes off your feet might swell and then you will struggle even more"

"Aye right, dead on"

"I'm telling ye, you'll regret it if you do"

Something about his tone told me he wasn't kidding and maybe I should listen to him.

"Tie the laces reasonably tight, you're gonna just have to grin and bear it, new shoes on a twelve-mile walk, what were you thinking?"

"I was just thinking I would wear my new shoes"

"You really need to break new shoes in before you even think of doing the twelfth in them"

"Well at least after today they will be broken in"

"And your feet just might break with them, take every chance you get on breaks to get your feet up, and if you don't need to walk about, don't ok? Right come on we are on the move again here"

That was definitely strange advice to be given on a day that was all about walking, but I listened and did exactly what he said, and I made sure that as we formed up again to remind myself that I would walk when I had to and would rest when I needed to, and regardless of how sore it got, I just had to keep marching on.

The road before us seemed to stretch out into the distance with no hint an end in sight.

During a break in tunes I turned to Stevie.

"How much longer do we have to go? I feel like we have been walking forever"

Stevie laughed "What's up kid, not hack the pace?"

"It's not that, these new shoes are killing my feet, but we just seem to be walking and walking"

"We don't have that far to go now really, try not to think about it"

Try not to think about it! I had been thinking about walking the twelfth parade from I was around eight years old for crying out loud, I had thought about this day nearly every day since joining the band, and now I had someone, as well as my feet, telling me not to think about it!

My head sank a little as we walked past Barnet's Demesne, the crowd was massive and cheering us all on, but the road just seemed to keep on going and then we turned right and headed up Edenderry lane. I had heard about this, and I knew that the field was at the end of this lane, it was mostly uphill and would go on for at least another mile, it felt like another five miles by the time we got to the end and the Drum Major had us fall out. The drums and bass drum were stacked neatly together, and the lodge laid the banner nearby. We would be leaving from here in a number of hours, so we needed to stake our claim on a piece of the field for our gear. Some of the lodge would head to the service that was just starting in the background, there was someone praying over the PA system and calling the brethren together to fulfil their duty. At its core there is a religious foundation to the Orange Order and the twelfth, it was a celebration not just of King Williams victory at the Battle of the Boyne, it was a celebration of religious liberty, or at least that's what I was told.

"Right come on let's have a look around the field" said an excited Alvin, "God knows what we will find"

"Do you mind if we take a few minutes before we do, we have been walking for bloody ages after all, it would be nice to take the weight off our feet, don't you think?"

"Well... Yeah, probably, let's not wait too long though, the smell of chips and burgers is driving me nuts here, I'm starving"

I have to say I shared his thoughts there; I was pretty hungry myself after that walk. I managed about five minutes rest and then curiosity got the better of me.

"Right let's go and see what the field is all about"

Alvin didn't need any encouragement, he bounced up and we both headed in the direction of the stalls and the smell of burgers and chips guided us on our way.

We stopped at the first couple of chip vans and had a look at the prices first before making a decision.

"My Ma says you get what you pay for"

"Aye well she's obviously not on our budget and shopping for food on an individual basis, with the potential of needing to buy a new band tape as well as satisfy her hunger"

"Aye what would she know about band tapes anyway, she still thinks that Aghalee Heroes is a war film"

Laughing we went for the cheaper option and got tucked into our chips and burgers after applying salt and vinegar and a wee drizzle of red sauce.

"Right let's go and find some band tapes"

We traipsed around the field and the stalls selling flags, Proud to be a Prod tee shirt's, and this years must have accessory, the Ulster flag flat cap, loads of people were wearing them, and of course a growing collection of tapes. Some of these were vocal tapes, people actually singing songs, we weren't really interested in them, not because of what the songs were about or anything but just because it wasn't band music. We were looking through the tapes on offer and something dawned on me.

"Why haven't we done one?"

"No idea, but we should do one"

"Dead right, I'm bringing it up at the next meeting"

"Well you know I'll second that proposal"

The stall worker broke into our conversation "See anything you like kids?"

"Nah, we have most of these already"

"Really" he said with a hint of surprise

"Yeah we do our best to keep up to date"

"I see well if there's anything I can help you with, let me know"

"Thanks" we said almost in unison without looking up and off he went to deal with another customer.

Having drawn a blank looking for new tapes we needed something to do.

"Maybe there will be a set of sticks left with the drums, we can play a few tunes while we wait on the rest of the band turning up"

"Aye, I'm up for that"

As we headed back to our drums passing some older members of lodges lying on the ground, taking a well-earned rest before the six mile walk home again. We saw a few of our guys milling around taking in the sights and sounds, catching up with people they hadn't seen in a while, everyone seemed to be having a great day, there was a real sense of unity, regardless of who we were, whether we were in a lodge or a band, this was our big day.

As we dandered over to the drums, we noticed that there were a few drum straps there and we were in luck, there were sticks!

"I'll drum first ok?"

"Aye no worries, what do you want to play?"

"What about Midnight is a Place?"

"Happy days, that's a good one, what intro are you going for"

"I'll just make something up, but you'll know when to come in"

"Go for it"

We were running through our wee repertoire of tunes, some the band played, and some of them were our favourites that other bands played, we took turns between drumming and playing the flute, some other band members joined in, and before you knew it, the bass drum was being played and we were making a fair bit of noise and a wee crowd gathered around us, listening in. The excitement was building and this wee impromptu session seemed to have got us ready for the walk home. It provided a healthy distraction as my feet didn't feel quite so sore now, thank god, because before this field based spontaneous practice, I really wasn't in the mood for the return leg of the parade. But now, I felt a bit more invigorated and I could imagine us walking down the Newtownards Road and then up the Avenue on the way home, and it was going to be great, there would be a real party atmosphere. The crowds will have been waiting and looking forward to celebrating with us on our way home.

"Right lads save yourselves for the journey home" the band captain brought our little performance to an end.

"Don't want you youngsters having to use the taxi to make your way home"

Well with that comment we all started to smarten ourselves up, making sure our shirts were buttoned up, ties were straight, trousers pulled up and jackets buttoned. We were definitely up for the walk home now neither of us wanted to contemplate having to get in the taxi on the way back, that was for aul lads in the lodge, not us.

I started looking around and noticed that bands were going through a similar ritual to ours, some were adding a few little party extras to proceedings. Some lodge members were wearing funny hats or sunglasses, and one band had bought red white and blue wigs to replace their hats for the way home. This was going to be a lot of fun. The noise around us started to intensify as more and more band members and lodge members began re-entering the field, the hustle and bustle of the day was re-emerging and before we knew it the whole band and lodge were gathered together again. Some looked a little worse for wear, some still tired from the walk to the field and trying their best to appear as if they were really looking forward to the walk home. There were one or two that maybe had one too many beers and not enough food and a few more like that around the field, they were happy and that's all that matters.

It was all building up to the bands and lodges leaving the field and heading back home the way we came, before splitting off in the town again to go back to our respective districts and the final journey home and onto our band hall.

The return leg of the parade was a more stop, start affair than it had been this morning, things seemed to be progressing and then we would walk a few steps and stop again, as bands and lodges tried their best to join the parade in exactly the same spot they had earlier in the day. We didn't play too many tunes on the whole walk down the small lane, there wouldn't have been a lot of point. When we eventually exited the lane, we were able to spread out and fill the road, which was great from comfort point of view, but the band always sounded louder the closer we ranked together, as we spread out so did our sound. On the route home there seemed to be just as many people watching as there had been earlier, in some places there seemed to be even more. Coming off the Lisburn road and heading for Shaftesbury Square was absolutely heaving with people, all enjoying the sights and sounds of the bands. Every so often there was a roar and a swell of noise as the crowd began to sing along to a band playing a popular tune, it was building and building and I couldn't wait until we walked along here as well, hopefully the band captain would call a crowd pleasing tune.

"My aul man" shouted the band captain, after the drum rolls and a few notes, we were joined in full voice by the im-promptu street choir in their pavement stalls on either side of the road. The tune is a popular football chant, supporters of different teams have their own slight variations, but as we headed into the repeat and double forte, the noise rose like the sun in the morning, and the shivers ran down my spine as hundreds and hundreds of people sang to the sound of our band. There was nothing I could compare to it to, I struggled hard not to break into a smile, I looked around and we were all in the same boat, caught in a moment of connection between the music and the crowd.

"Follow , follow" was called next and the crowd continued to sing as we passed by, then we played 'the Sash' and you'd have thought King Billy himself had appeared, the noise was deafening and exhilarating, there were smiles and laughter everywhere I looked, flags flying, young kids pretending they were playing drums and throwing real and imaginary band poles in the air. The crowd started to recede a little as we progressed down great Victoria Street and headed for the city hall where the districts would split and head home to their respective areas. As we passed the war memorial at the city hall, the drum major gave the eyes right command to the band, the lead tip stopped the tap on the snare and clicked his sticks together instead as we paid our respects to the fallen heroes from our wee country during the two world wars, fresh poppy wreaths had been laid there during the morning parade and now the red glistened in the early evening sun as thousands walked past honouring the supreme sacrifice they had made for King and country, for some only forty years had passed, for others almost seventy, no matter how long though all were worthy of being acknowledged and remembered.

The next stop in the parade wasn't that far away as we approached the Albert clock, the parade came to a halt, a final fifteen minutes rest before heading across the bridge and on towards Templemore Avenue where this glorious day would end. For some the break was a welcomed friend, time to catch their breath and rest their tired feet one more time before the final push for home. Some wanted the parade to just keep going, eager to see East Belfast with its familiar places, familiar faces, family and friends lining the streets welcoming the tired parading masses home. Our lodge had some sandwiches and drinks in the car that had accompanied us all day as we walked, and we tucked into them happily making the kerb our park bench as we took on some energy and fluid to spur us on. In that moment I thought about my Big Granda, and how he would have loved to have seen this day, I imagined the smile breaking on his face as he caught a glimpse of me walking in the ranks of Pride of the Raven, my flute in hand, raising my free hand to wave to him as we walked on past, although I figured if he was there that a wave would never have been enough, I would have had to break ranks and hug the man that was my hero. I wondered if my Big Granny would be thinking the same and now, I couldn't wait to get to the Avenue and see my family waving and singing at the side of the road as we marched by. A piercing whistle blow broke through my thoughts and a tug on the arm from Alvin brought me to my feet and I headed to my place in the ranks for the final walk home.

A sharp cold breeze hit us as we walked across the bridge onward to the green just opposite the Short Strand, bending to the right and bringing us on to the Newtownards Road, where the good people of East Belfast would be lined up in their droves to welcome us home. The bunting and flags came into view as we rounded the corner past St. Martins church and now the reality hit home that today, the twelfth of July was drawing to a close, although there would be celebrations and parties carrying on into the wee small hours of the morning all over the country. We passed the chapel on our right and Bryson Street, which was sealed off by the police, pressing on towards Templemore Avenue, the top of my Grannies end of Tower Street was merely steps away now and I found my family right on the front of the road, spilling of the kerb onto the road.

"There he is, there's our Glenn" said my big Granny pulling and pointing, "Glenn, Glenn" I waved and acknowledged my family.

"Fan club still out in full strength today then Glenn?" said Stevie

"I wouldn't have it any other way mate"

"I don't blame you kid, best feeling in the world"

"You got that right"

As we rounded the Avenue playing familiar tunes, the crowds celebrated with us, we ended 'Shanghai' and the band captain called Dinah's Delight, I couldn't believe it, my favourite tune and as we were walking up the Avenue, my chest puffed as pride swelled up within me. What a way to end the day. We walked up the Avenue and I got the same feeling as I had when I had first encountered the band all those years ago.

We walked through the district guard of honour that had formed just outside the hospital a wee bit up from Mountpottinger Methodist church. They clapped as we passed through. We were minutes away from the parade coming to an end. The crowds were five or six deep along the footpath at the junction of the Avenue and the Albertbridge Road, it was a good place to watch any parade from. We rounded to the right, marching past the Orange Hall, we veered left and paused, marking time in Frank Street. We finished playing and came to a standstill. I heard a few people call my name from the side of the street, and I looked to see, Dee, Alan, Darren and Colin standing there, I nodded in acknowledgement, I'd get talking to them soon enough, there was the small matter of the national anthem to be played. Three clicks of the bass drum rim and we started to play God save the Queen, as we finished, I lowered the flute from my lips to my side for the last time that day, I breathed a deep breath just as the drum major gave the final command to fall out, after a quick right turn, we broke ranks and headed for the footpath and my friends, Alvin passed me with his Dad and two brothers as they headed to meet up with the rest of his family.

"See you at the next practice?"

"Of course, and we have a parade coming up again anyway"

"Cracking day mate"

"Cracking day"

I turned back towards my friends they were eager to find out all about the day.

"Well mate, what was it like?"

"I don't know what to say lads, all I know is, I wish every day could be the twelfth of July".

ABOUT THE AUTHOR

Glenn Millar

Glenn is a Canadian born, Belfast bred musician, community worker, podcaster and author. He has been involved with marching bands for over 35 years. He is committed to increasing understanding of marching band culture and traditions as well as facilitating creative collaborations across a wide range of art forms and genres.

AFTERWORD

I hope you have enjoyed this small insight into my early days within the marching band scene in Northern Ireland. Playing the flute and marching have been an integral part of my life for over 35 years and has generated some of the best experiences of my life.

The marching band community in Northern Ireland is massive and few outside it's ranks realise the scale. The community boasts some 620 bands spread throughout the province and is probably the largest voluntary community arts sector in Northern Ireland. The marching band scene comes in for a lot of criticism, and I wanted to provide a positive narrative from the perspective of being a band member, a side of the story that hasn't really been explored.

My hope with 'Made to Parade' is to shed some light on the inner workings of a band, how they are organised and what motivates members to stay involved and completely committed.
There is a saying that understanding is deeper than knowledge, it is my hope that this book will deepen your understanding of marching bands beyond what you may currently know.

I would like to thank everyone who has helped me or encouraged me with the writing of the book.

Alvin Nelson and the members of the Pride of the Raven for getting behind the project and supporting it so much.

Robert Grattan, thanks for the original artwork, taking my rough idea and turning it into a painted memory.

Kim Jackson and the members of Heel & Ankle Community Theatre Company, the work you guys have done inspired me to make this a reality.

Darren Ferguson and Beyond Skin for unwavering belief and support.

Terry, for teaching me how to play the flute and starting me on my musical journey.

My Mum and late Father for putting up with me learning to play, I didn't become the next James Galway, but I hope I have made you proud.

Glenn Millar

MADE TO PARADE